Beyond Weapons
A Guide to Holistic Self-Defense

Beyond Weapons

A Guide to Holistic Self-Defense

Clay Escobedo Olsen

Beyond Weapons
A Guide to Holistic Self-Defense
By Clay E. Olsen

DISCLAIMER AND/OR LEGAL NOTICES

ISBN-13: 978-1-952281-61-7 paperback
ISBN-13: 978-1-952281-62-4 large print paperback
ISBN-13: 978-1-952281-63-1 eBook

Table of Contents

For Mom, whose kindness and love are an inspiration to everyone she meets. She is the definition of a classy lady. This book wouldn't have been written without her. I am truly blessed to be spending time with her.

For my eldest sister Linda, who passed away from cancer complications as the final edits of this book were completed. Almost 13 years older than me, she was like a second mom in my childhood years. I miss you sis!

Acknowledgments

I've had long conversations with many people about self-defense. Troy Coe from Reality Defense in Arizona was a very approachable and interesting person whose conversations I enjoyed quite a bit. I talked with several individuals at Independence Training and C2 Tactical in Arizona, the Arizona Citizens Defense League, and Attorneys for Freedom. The writers Rory Miller, Adam Plantinga, Varg Freeborn, Nick Hughes, Laurence Gonzales, George J. Thompson, Marc MacYoung, and many others have markedly influenced my viewpoints here. I have not conversed with these writers, and they may disagree with what I have written here, but their insights have been essential to me over the last few years. I want to single out Varg Freeborn's concept of a "mission" as extremely valuable and a turning point in how I view self-defense. Gerd Gigerenzer inspires the risk management approach to self-defense. I thank him for all the work he has done for risk literacy. I also want to thank the people at the Bureau of Justice Statistics. They always responded to my emails promptly and politely, even though I was clearly an amateur.

Publishing a book requires expertise from many different people. I want to thank my reviewers, Mark Camilleri, Steven Olsen, Marc J. Victor, Dominic Schwebs, Mark Angle, Matteo Sesia and p-Value Consulting LLC, Red to Black Editing, Cathy Suter, Judy Weintraub, and Art Lizza. I am of course responsible for any errors.

Throughout this book, I recommend products or services that I use. I have purchased them with my own money and found them to be of good value. I do not have a financial interest in these products. I have not received any monetary consideration for these products, nor have

I received any products for free. Other products look promising, but I do not have direct experience with them. I mention them and ask the reader to investigate them more.

As the topic of self-defense has enormous breadth, there are limitations to the present study. In 2020, there was an increase in groups acting against individual citizens. This topic is not covered here. This book focuses primarily on personal self-defense strategies in which the attacker is an individual, not an organized group. In addition, the pandemic and government pandemic responses in 2020 and 2021 could make these years different than other years, so they were not included in my analysis.

Textual Conventions

Nonfiction to Fiction: Parts of the book will be labeled as "Story-time"—fictional stories I use to clarify ideas. These parts are spaced away from the main text under a "Storytime" heading. To make it easier to tell when the Storytime ends, I close it with a hash symbol "#."

Links: I use hyperlinks to help the reader review the source material. I link first to my website, from which these links will automatically redirect to the actual source links. I chose to do this in case the source URLs change after publication, which allows me to update the links without updating the book. In addition, I list the links in endnotes so that paperback readers with a computer at hand can quickly pull up the source without typing different long URLs.

CCF: I use the acronym CCF to stand for a few things: the Concealed Carry of a Firearm, Carrying a Concealed Firearm, or the Carrier of a Concealed Firearm. The context will make it clear which meaning is to be used. I took this approach because writing the words out often resulted in wordy and hard-to-read sentences. Other acronyms, like CCW, often refer to state-issued permits, and I wanted to limit any confusion.

Uncomfortable Truth: When my analysis is a bit surprising, and the conclusion overturns a bit of received wisdom, I'll call this an uncomfortable truth.

Ordinary Civilian: The term civilian is defined by Merriam-Webster as "one not on active duty in the armed services or not on a police or fire-fighting force."[1] I will sometimes use the term civilian. I will also use the term "ordinary civilian" to mean a civilian who is not a first responder, has never experienced violent crime, is not familiar with self-defense techniques, nor engages in criminal activity.

---

[1] https://clayeolsen.com/civ

Background

I lived for many years in Northern California while most of my family resided in Arizona. My father's health began to decline in 2010, and he passed away in 2012. After he passed, I felt like my mom needed an activity buddy, and in 2014, I made the decision to return home to live with her. In 2015, I sold my house, quit my job, and returned to the area where I grew up. Immediately after I moved in, we started to travel and see family my mom hadn't seen in quite a while due to my father's health.

As we traveled I realized if we ran into trouble (e.g., a robbery), I had no defensive skills to protect my mom. I couldn't ask my mom, at 83 years of age, to sprint 100 yards and climb a six-foot fence to escape a dangerous situation. Sadly, I had only been worried about myself up to this point in my life. In fact, a former girlfriend claimed the Drowning Pool song "Tear Away" was my theme song—the chorus being "I don't care about anyone else but me." Yikes!

I did what I thought anyone would do: I went out and got a concealed-carry permit and took a fourteen-hour course that focused on legal issues, simulations, and range qualifications. This course forced me to think about self-defense differently. After that, I continued taking other training courses. Some focused on physical defense, some on less-than-lethal defenses, and others on lethal defense. What I learned and how I applied it to my situation created a turning point in my understanding of the nuances of self-defense.

You may be asking yourself: What other qualifications does the author have to write such a book? Well, I've been shooting guns and handloading ammunition for over 40 years: *I know what guns can do and what they can't overcome.* I have watched friends descend into drugs and been unable to stop them; I lived in the aftermath of a friend's suicide; I've watched my father and uncles struggle to breathe after decades of smoking: *I understand the long-term consequences of short-term decisions.* I was with a girlfriend when her child was diagnosed with cancer; my mom and I were bedside at a hospice facility when my sister took her last breath due to cancer; and I saw my devoutly religious grandmother suffer with dementia for years: *I'm aware of the fragility of life and how life can be horribly unfair.* I've been victimized by crime, watched violence unfold, and been first on the scene to horrific accidents: *I have experience with stressful encounters.* I've worked on multi-million-dollar projects in development, testing, and customer escalations: *I understand the difference between the theoretical and the practical.* I've written technical papers to distill complex topics and trained hundreds of people on those topics: *I understand that if I can't explain a subject to a beginner, then I don't understand the subject.* I've worked closely with people from all over the world, young and old, with those raised in rural environments, and with those raised in urban ones: *I understand that solutions need to be multi-faceted if they are going be adopted and make a difference.* Importantly, I don't have my own private security team, nor do I live in a mansion sequestered away from society: *what is in this book is what I do to protect myself and my loved ones. If it fails, I fail.*

Additional details about this book are available at https://clayeolsen. com. If you find an error or a problem, or perhaps have a compliment (!), please report it there. Thank you!

Introduction

Imagine browsing books in the self-defense section of a bookstore and seeing a book titled: "Protecting Yourself from Family: The Concealed Carry of a Firearm for Family Reunions." Would you buy it? I suspect not. After all, if you considered a member of your greater family a threat, the best thing to do would be to avoid the reunion. Why risk your spouse and kids? Why be on your toes constantly wondering if a member of your greater family would turn violent? How could you enjoy yourself at such a reunion? Given the context of the threat faced, you would focus on different self-defense strategies instead of carrying a concealed firearm (CCF).

A few books down from that one, you see another one titled: "Firearms Training: What you need to know when an armed criminal attacks you in public!" Would you buy it? I know many people who would. It seems to tell you precisely what you need to know. First, however, if you dive into some violent crime statistics, you might discover a bothersome fact, or what I call an **uncomfortable truth**: If you were victimized in a violent crime and you were injured, the offender was likely someone you knew.

Now let's go back and look at those books again with that uncomfortable truth in mind. The first one, the family reunion book, is more accurate about the threat than the second book. After all, family reunions are typically filled with people you know and not all family members get along. For example, if your brother decides to bring your ex-wife and announce to the family that they are now dating; there may be some problems. However, these problems are not going to be solved by CCF.

The second book has the correct self-defense choice for the threat. If your threat is a stranger who is an armed criminal, you probably need a lethal self-defense strategy to survive. But as pointed out in the uncomfortable truth, that threat is very uncommon for injurious violent crimes. Therefore, we need a different book that accurately represents threats and provides the appropriate self-defense options against those threats.

This book aims to match the best self-defense strategies to the most likely violent crime threats an ordinary civilian may face. Unfortunately, critiques and promotions of self-defense strategies are often based on how the author feels about firearm rights and restrictions. I certainly have strong opinions on self-defense and my right to own firearms. I've had a concealed carry permit for several years, carried a concealed firearm many times, owned firearms since I was about ten years old, and started handloading my own ammunition when I was 12 years old. In this analysis, I assume everyone has access to firearms and can choose to use a firearm to defend themselves and their loved ones. However, I evaluate firearms for self-defense as I would any other self-defense method; I evaluate them in terms of benefits and harms. Sometimes the harms outweigh the benefits, and sometimes they do not.

Let me work through an example of the benefits and harms of self-defense methods: According to violent crime statistics, homes are a common location for violent crimes. As such, it makes sense to protect your home from unauthorized entry. However, your protections can also severely impede first responders. If you feel ill, press a medical emergency button, and then pass out, depending on your home security protections, you may die before first responders can defeat those protections and get to you. Is it more likely that you'll need help from first responders or more likely for your home to be involved in a violent crime incident? Often, the answer is "it depends." It depends on your health, where you live, the people you know, and what you do for a living.

These considerations are what I mean by holistic self-defense and going beyond weapons. Unfortunately, the relentless focus on weapons often blinds people to these other considerations. One reason for the emphasis on weapons is the perception of violent crime, mainly that a stranger who is an armed violent criminal is an ordinary civilian's primary violent crime threat. It is understandable why this is so. First, turn on the television and see the local news' lead story, which probably depicts a violent crime. Next, pick up any self-defense magazine, and you'll see advertisements with armed masked men in the bushes or scary shadows on the parking garage wall. Then, if you sign up and go to a self-defense class, you'll likely find that your instructor is a current or former law enforcement officer with plenty of stories to tell you about violent criminals. These violent crime incidents clearly happened, but are they typical for ordinary civilians?

The answer to this question takes us to the beginning of Part I, Perception, Analysis, and Evaluation. Here I will analyze why civilians have these perceptions. Then, I will go through violent crime statistics and find out what the circumstances of violent crime look like, what is rare, and what is more common. Once we understand these circumstances well, CCF will be evaluated as a self-defense method. In doing so, I will use a benefits and harms approach. This approach can be used to assess other self-defense methods for ordinary civilians, so it is covered in depth.

To get beyond weapons, I begin to describe holistic self-defense considerations in Part II, Strangers, Criminals, and Public Locations. Here I look at the circumstances from violent crime statistics and see if there are ways to reduce our chances of meeting a violent criminal. Based on my analysis, robbery represents the violent crime where ordinary civilians would most likely face a violent criminal. I cover several different ways to considerably reduce this risk. In addition, should you be a victim of robbery, I cover technology that can help law enforcement catch robbers and get your valuables back. Finally, I discuss physical defensive options, weapons, and training for those who want this additional protection.

In Part III, Strangers, Civilians, and Public Locations, I look at escalations that happen between ordinary civilians which can result in criminal charges. As an example, these individuals would be in an argument that escalates and spirals out of control. Here, I focus on our attitudes, behavior, and de-escalation techniques.

As I mentioned previously, injurious violent crime usually involves people you know. If someone you trust suddenly tries to victimize you,

you are at an incredible disadvantage. Part IV, The People You Know, discusses ways to prevent this situation from ever developing. Additionally, there are often tell-tale signs that someone will eventually cause trouble for you. I discuss these signs so you can proactively distance yourself from these individuals before any problem develops. Lastly, I discuss consent issues that happen between civilians. When there is a misunderstanding of consent, a crime has occurred, and I will cover techniques to ensure that doesn't happen.

Injurious violent crime circumstances reveal another shocker—your home is a common location where these crimes occur. In Part V, Home Defense, I will cover a substantial amount of ground, focusing on everything from common security problems to better solutions and advanced solutions. How to protect yourself from strangers as well as people who may know something about you and your defenses are also covered. I also go over how to protect your valuables, especially your firearms, in detail. Lastly, I spend some time going over a topic that isn't really discussed: how modern floorplans put your children at risk in the name of parent privacy.

In Part VI, Interactions with Law Enforcement, I will cover a topic that many self-defense classes do not handle very well. An ordinary civilian will interact more with law enforcement officers than they will with criminals. To put it bluntly, ordinary civilian interactions with law enforcement do not improve when you have a weapon. In fact, they can become deadly very quickly. I provide guidance on this challenging topic.

Lastly, in Part VII, Legal Implications, I discuss some things that could have legal ramifications in a self-defense case. Some of these things will be pretty obvious, and others will not. Nevertheless, you can help yourself prior to violence (easiest), and you can help yourself in the aftermath of violence (harder).

Part VIII, Conclusion, brings the book to a close. I try hard to avoid bias and conflicts of interest in my research. As such, this book uses a "follow the data where it leads us" model. I prepare readers to do their own research and draw their own conclusions. Appendix A and

Appendix B describe how to gather the same information I have. You will also be able to use these techniques to research years not covered in this study. Appendix C discusses the statistical approach I use. The Bibliography also provides references to quality crime research data you can review.

Everyone is afraid of falling victim to violent crime. Home invasions, armed robberies, and random shootings are the staples of the evening news. But these things don't happen as often as it seems. As a veteran New York homicide detective once noted, if you live in the United States, are relatively law-abiding (i.e., you're not a meth dealer or an enforcer for the mob), and are reasonably cautious about where you go, especially at night, your chances of being killed by a stranger are about on par with your odds of being struck by space debris.

—Adam Plantinga,
400 Things Cops Know: Street-Smart Lessons
from a Veteran Patrolman

PART I

Perception, Analysis, Evaluation

1. Perception

Perception often drives lifestyle changes. For example, after the 9/11 terrorist attacks, many Americans decided to drive rather than fly. However, for long distances, flying is much safer than driving. Some Americans who chose to drive rather than fly ended up being injured or killed in traffic accidents.[1] Of course, in the immediate aftermath of a violent incident, we should remain cautious, and in this particular case, cautious about air travel. However, once air travel normalcy resumed, we need to critically explore our perceptions and make sure they aren't leading us astray. For some Americans who chose to drive rather than fly months after the 9/11 attack, their perceptions did lead them astray.

Now, imagine if your local news showed a different airplane crashing into a different building every evening. Air travel would surely stop as people would be afraid to fly. However, think about the local news showing someone in the world being struck by lightning every evening. There are almost eight billion people in the world at the time of this writing. A different person, somewhere in the world, probably gets struck by lightning every day or so. How would this news story impact viewer's perception of lightning and the danger of storms?

---

[1] Gigerenzer (2002)

It would certainly get people talking more about lightning and weather. However, what may be lost on viewers is a probability distinction: there is a difference between the probability of lightning striking someone somewhere in the world versus lightning striking a specific individual in the world. The constant news exposure to lightning striking some individual in the world begins to erode this probability distinction, and a specific viewer of the news may conclude that *their* probability of being struck by lightning is now higher.

I will argue that this probability confusion exists with violent crime. This section explores how violent crime is portrayed in media, in self-defense classes, and how that portrayal influences the civilian perception of violent crime threats. This perception, or so I argue, is responsible for driving a lethal weapons-based approach to self-defense. It also has resulted in a dramatic rise in the concealed carry of firearms for self-defense.[2]

1.1 Violence in the News

Almost everyone has heard the line "if it bleeds, it leads" about the news. But it turns out, it is even worse than that. Matthew R. Kerbel, a former news insider and news writer, comments:[3]

> Once you get past the specifics, local news stories tend to be about the same assortment of things, and they're things that could happen at any time. So, while it may be interesting to a real news viewer to know which fire, murder, assault, shootout, or accident occurred on any given day, those details are irrelevant [...]. All that matters is that local news presents us with an endless assortment of fire, murder, assault, shootout, and accident stories, [...] [T]hey would be as suitable for air this week as they were three years ago, and as they would have been five or even ten years ago. The local news formula simply has not changed that much.

---

[2] https://clayeolsen.com/ncc
[3] Kerbel (2000)

Kerbel's analysis in his book is both disturbing at times and hilarious. You would be mistaken if you thought news programming was fundamentally different from daytime shows like Jerry Springer. It appears, at least to me, that Kerbel's analysis is just as relevant today as when he published his book in 2000. As the above quote indicates, he was confident that news programming hadn't changed so much that the same stories he looked at in the late 1990s could be run in the late 1980s. It is rare to have a formula for television be successful for almost 40 years. In fact, researchers refer to the crime story in the news as a "script." Gilliam and Iyengar comment:[4]

> As told by television news, the crime news script unfolds in three ordered segments. It usually begins with the anchorperson's terse announcement that a crime has occurred. The viewer is then transported to the scene of the crime for a first-hand look supported by accounts from bystanders, relatives of the victim, or other interested parties. Finally, the focus shifts to the identity and apprehension of the perpetrator and the related efforts of law enforcement officials.

Gilliam and Iyengar conduct experiments to determine the scripts' impacts on the viewer. They write: "In sum, the local news experiment demonstrates that exposure to the crime script significantly influences attitudes about both crime and race."[5]

Interestingly, television news has been around since the television was invented. Crime wasn't always the top concern. What changed? Stephen Mann comments:[6]

> In the United States in the 1970s, local "action news" formats, driven by enhanced live broadcast technologies and consultant recommendations designed to improve ratings, changed the nature of television news: a shift from public affairs journalism about politics, issues, and government

---

[4] Gilliam Jr and Iyengar (2000)
[5] Gilliam Jr and Iyengar (2000)
[6] https://clayeolsen.com/mann

toward an emphasis on profitable live, breaking news from the scene of the crime. The crime rate was falling, but most Americans didn't perceive it that way. From 1993 to 1996, the national murder rate dropped by 20%. During the same period, stories about murders on the ABC, NBC, and CBS network newscasts rose by 721%.

Local and national news reporting of violent crime came into prominence around 1994—about the time O.J. Simpson was always in the news and just a couple of years after the Los Angeles riots over Rodney King. Some researchers consider these to be triggering events. The result was an unprecedented rise in how Americans viewed violent crime.

The movie *Nightcrawler*[7] emphasizes many themes present in this new era of news programming. Using the latest technology, the main character can film violent incidents and their immediate aftermath before law enforcement arrives on the scene. Rather than assist victims, the main character films them and eventually moves to manipulating crime scenes and even causing violence and death to film it. Via a partnership with a news firm, this footage causes the ratings of the news firm to skyrocket. Although fictional, some of the themes in the film have empirical support, from promoting suburban crime[8] to the battle for ratings driving content. As Yanich comments:[9]

> Who among us can take the time to deconstruct a news story about a violent crime when we are bombarded by images of victims, suspects, and yellow crime scene tape? To understand that the reality that we are being shown is designed to hold us as consumers until the next commercial break and not to inform us as citizens? The danger is that we think that we are being informed when, in fact, we are only being sold.

We've seen how crime coverage increased, which wasn't in line with actual crime statistics. Does this impact viewers' perceptions of crime?

---

[7] https://clayeolsen.com/nc

[8] Yanich (2004)

[9] Yanich (2004)

Yes. Research has shown that local news programming about crime has caused an increase in fear of crime, independent of actual crime statistics. For example:[10]

> The frequency of both local and national news consumption is significantly related to fear of crime, independent of the influence of other predictors, including crime rates and victim experience.

This research leads us to an **uncomfortable truth**: If your knowledge of violent crime comes from news programming, you will likely perceive murder as being far more common than it is. In addition, you will probably assume that firearms are the most common weapons used in the commission of violent crimes.

1.2 Mass Shootings

Although mass shootings are a part of news reporting, I've chosen to deal with them in a separate section. One of the most common fears I've heard in self-defense classes is the "active shooter," or someone who is in the process of committing mass murder using firearms. A 2019 City University of New York dissertation by Jason R. Silva titled "A Media Distortion Analysis of Mass Shootings"[11] will further delve into media factors highlighted in the previous section. This dissertation "[…] provides the most comprehensive investigation into the media coverage of mass shootings to date."[12] As Silva notes: "Mass shootings unnerve the general public because they violently target large numbers of seemingly random victims in public locations […] This gives the perception that a mass shooting could happen to anyone, anywhere, anytime. As a result, the public is drawn to information surrounding mass shootings as it

---

[10] Chiricos, Padgett and Gertz (2000)
[11] Silva (2019)
[12] Silva (2019)

relates to their own lives."[13] This observation matches what I experienced while in self-defense classes and when talking to people interested in getting a concealed carry permit.

Like other violent crimes, mass shootings are subject to the selection bias of television news. For example, imagine there are ten violent crimes in a city of one million people. The local news only has the slots for two out of the ten to detail. Which two they select is the first type of bias. The second type of bias is that for those two violent crimes, there are a set of facts associated with them. Therefore, the news may only select specific facts from those cases to highlight. Assuming these biases are consistent, a frequent viewer of the news may develop the perception, due to the availability heuristic,[14] that these crimes reported (first bias) and the circumstances of these crimes (second bias) are common. Furthermore, since most civilians are not experienced with violent crime, no everyday experiences exist to counter this presentation. Silva continues, "Taken together, research suggests media coverage of mass shootings can impact public concern over victimization, skew perceptions of potential perpetrators, and contribute to the implementation of ineffective security measures."[15]

Silva's dissertation looks at 275 mass shootings from 1966 to 2016. I'll cover a few discussion highlights from the dissertation which contradict some mainstream perceptions of a mass shooter, particularly those of the weapons self-defense mindset.

- The top three locations are workplaces, open spaces, and schools. Schools were a little over 20 percent of the total.
- Handguns are used over 50 percent of the time. Rifles are used less than 10 percent.[16]

Workplaces and handguns are the most common circumstances of mass shootings. However, you may not have gathered that from media reports

---

[13] Silva (2019)

[14] https://clayeolsen.com/ah

[15] Silva (2019)

[16] Silva (2019)

due to the biases discussed. For example, media outlets who tend to promote firearm restrictions may focus on mass shooting events like schools, while media outlets that are against firearm restrictions, may focus on open spaces where the offender was brought down by an armed civilian.

In conclusion, how the news depicts mass shootings and violent crime, in general, has an impact on civilians and their perception of violent crime. In many cases, individuals recommending a weapons-based self-defense strategy have not compensated for the real distortion of media representation. As an example, if workplaces are the most common mass shooting location, it is very unlikely there will ever be an ordinary civilian workplace that allows an armed workforce. In addition, sporting events, concerts, nightclubs, and so forth are also unlikely to allow for armed civilian attendees. Hence, the debate, for example, over schools and arming teachers is focusing on a problem and a solution that is much smaller in proportion to other incidents of mass shootings.

1.3 The Engagement Bias

Today, many people go to Internet websites to get their news when they want rather than wait around for the television news to come on. Guess how websites typically make their money? Well, through advertising revenue, which is the same as television news. Websites use page views to determine advertising revenue and many features of a website are designed to increase page views via likes, comments, and shares. These features promote viewer engagement with the website and are referred to as engagement metrics. We should not discount the influence that engagement metrics have on content. To put it bluntly, it skews the content for websites in in a similar way it skews the content for television. However, in some ways it is different. For example:

- Websites may have users battling it out in the comment section. This keeps the commenters and others coming back to the website multiple times.

- A large number of likes in social media can lead to the story reaching more readers because it appears in more news feeds or in a "Trending" section on the site.
- Users sharing the story on other media sites will increase the exposure of the story and increase engagement.

Sadly, controversial rather than accurate stories tend to increase engagement metrics. This type of content skewing is what I call the Engagement Bias. This situation may sound familiar. It turns out that this same battle for revenue took place when newspapers were first implemented. Holiday describes it:[17]

> There are three distinct phases of the newspaper (which have been synonymous with "the news" for most of history). It begins with the Party Press, moves to the infamous Yellow Press, and ends finally with the stable period of the Modern Press (or press by subscription). These phases contain surprising parallels to where we are today with blogs—old mistakes made once more, manipulations made possible again for the first time in decades.

The Yellow Press, which required bold headlines and gossipy stories to sell papers, resembles modern news media focusing on advertising revenue.[18] Likewise, the advent of Internet blogs and news sites, again focusing on generating traffic to generate more revenue, resembles the Yellow Press. As Holiday points out, this style of reporting is subject to manipulation. For example, a widely inaccurate story can be initially reported to spike engagement metrics, then when engagement metrics decline, the story can be "updated" with more facts. It is anyone's guess whether the author simply chose to leave out those facts in the initial posting. In addition, engagement metrics themselves can be manipulated with bot farms (a large number of fake automated accounts that act together) that artificially increase the popularity of a story.

---

[17] Holiday (2012)

[18] https://clayeolsen.com/yp

Once again, subscription models come to the rescue. I subscribe to several journalists and data analysts on Substack.[19] Substack even has options for local news reporters.[20] They are my alternative news source. I reward sound methodology by paying for a subscription to the authors who implement that methodology. I look for the following:

- A commitment to the truth, simple when simple, complex when complex.
- Context, Context, Context.
- Clarity in writing. Obscure writing is not profound. Obscure writing is confusing.
- Willingness to admit limitations and bias, indicate speculations, and take ownership for mistakes.
- Fully disclose conflicts of interest.

Subscription models inherently offer a better model for content once you find a content provider with the appropriate commitments, especially when our primary news providers have failed in such extraordinary ways. Sadly, our traditional news media and advertisement-based Internet news sites are just the Yellow Press again. One should still be vigilant with subscription models as a content provider can fall into bad practices to increase subscribers and maintain subscribers.

1.4 Self-Defense Classes

Based upon listening to the various attendees in self-defense classes talk about why they are taking the class, here are the two primary reasons I've heard:

- Television/Internet News—As depicted in the news, violent crime directly influenced the attendee's reasoning for taking the training.

---

[19] https://clayeolsen.com/ss-1

[20] https://clayeolsen.com/ss-2

- A crime incident occurred in their life or a friend/relative's life that makes them seek out self-defense training—This incident could have been road rage or another brush with violent crime. It could also have been a property crime, something like a burglary, where the victim felt vulnerable afterward.

Most self-defense classes are based upon a curriculum developed for law enforcement officers and, in some cases, the military. This curriculum has an impact on how the audience perceives threats.

1.4.1 Threats to Law Enforcement

Current and former law enforcement officers as well as current and former military personnel typically conduct quality self-defense training. For example, the world-renown Gunsite Academy[21] (founded by Lt. Col. Jeff Cooper, a World War II and Korean War combat veteran) has profiles on all their instructors.[22] Their experience is incredible. It makes logical sense that their experiences define how they would prepare their curriculum, which leads us to a key question: who are the greatest threats to law enforcement officers? First, let's look at the Uniform Crime Reports (UCR) data, which keeps track of law enforcement officers killed. I'll focus on 2015-2018[23,24] for these statistics, representing offenders who feloniously killed a law enforcement officer:

- 88% had been previously arrested.
- 76% were on either parole or probation.
- 73% had been convicted as an adult of a crime.
- 61% had been previously arrested for a violent crime.
- 50% had been previously arrested for drug law violations.
- 39% had been previously arrested for weapons law violations.

---

[21] https://clayeolsen.com/gunsite
[22] https://clayeolsen.com/gunsite-instructors
[23] https://clayeolsen.com/ucr-leoka-2019
[24] A few changes were made in 2019, so I will only cover 2015-2018 for consistency.

- 26% had been previously arrested for resisting arrest.
- 12% had been previously arrested for an assault on a law enforcement officer.

These statistics indicate a law enforcement officer's primary threat is a criminal, with 61 percent being previously arrested for a *violent* crime and 76 percent having an active criminal justice status at the time of the incident. What about the criminal being armed? I've pulled the following statistics by year, focusing on offenders who used firearms to kill the law enforcement officer. The first number is the number of law enforcement officers killed by a firearm, and the second number is the total number of law enforcement officers killed:

2019:[25] 44/48 = 92%
2018:[26] 51/55 = 93%
2017:[27] 42/46 = 91%
2016:[28] 62/66 = 94%
2015:[29] 38/41 = 93%

An average of almost 93 percent of the killed officers were killed with a firearm. Handguns are the primary weapon, and the distance is usually close, but rifles do make an appearance, and sometimes shotguns.

Did the officer know their killer? Unfortunately, I do not have the data to say whether the officers killed knew the offender. However, there is some circumstantial evidence: most officer deaths occurred on vehicle patrol, and it doesn't seem likely they would know their killer. Also, considering these officers were on patrol likely indicates that the law enforcement officer was killed in a public location.

---

[25] https://clayeolsen.com/ucr-lefk-2019
[26] https://clayeolsen.com/ucr-lefk-2018
[27] https://clayeolsen.com/ucr-lefk-2017
[28] https://clayeolsen.com/ucr-lefk-2016
[29] https://clayeolsen.com/ucr-lefk-2015

Before becoming a law enforcement officer, a portion of police training is focused on handling weapons and the use of force. Former law enforcement officers who are self-defense trainers use their previous training to develop their civilian curriculum. I know because I've gone through simulations in a civilian self-defense class that was repurposed from law enforcement training. In addition, these self-defense trainers will use any dangerous experiences they had to further improve this curriculum. However, there is an assumption here, and it forms the basis of the following **uncomfortable truth**: There is an unstated assumption in self-defense training that the predominant violence threat to law enforcement officers is the same predominant violence threat ordinary civilians face.

1.4.2 The Assumed Audience

Whenever we take training initially developed for a specific audience, gaps could be missing when given to a different audience. These gaps are often critical in weapons-based self-defense classes based on law enforcement and military training curriculum. For example, if your curriculum is developed for an audience of law enforcement officers, there will not be a section on how to interact with law enforcement. However, interacting with law enforcement is critical for a civilian learning weapons-oriented self-defense. If fact, I'll be bolder with this **uncomfortable truth**: Ordinary civilians will interact with law enforcement more often than they will experience a violent crime. When you carry a weapon for self-defense, *misunderstandings* between you and law enforcement mean the primary threat to your well-being could very well be from a law enforcement officer rather than a criminal.

It is important not to misunderstand what I am trying to convey. Many civilians who are interested in self-defense are advocates for effective law enforcement and my intention is not to criticize this relationship. However, after receiving weapons-oriented self-defense classes based on law enforcement curriculum, these civilians do not compensate for the fact that they are now armed and how dangerous their interactions with law enforcement can now be. I will cover armed civilians and law enforcement interactions in detail in Part VI.

1.5 Conclusion

Many of us watch local news programming in the hopes of learning about our community and becoming better residents of it. For similar reasons, we watch the evening national news, learning about what is happening in our republic and worldwide. However, I asked myself many years ago: Have I ever changed or altered any aspect of my life based *on what I saw on television news*? The answer was that I had not. So, I turned off television news and have never returned. I ended up doing the same thing with popular Internet news sites. Sadly, you can't base practical decisions upon what you read on popular Internet news sites, nor can you do so on popular television news programs. Given that reality, you have to wonder why you pay attention to them.

It is clear, however, that many people do pay attention to them. The endless parade of violent crime, injured victims, and firearms takes a toll. A devout viewer of the news comes away believing their community is full of armed violent criminals targeting ordinary civilians. When they look elsewhere, such as the CDC's firearm violence page,[30] they may see violent crime rather than suicides as responsible for most firearm violence. Yet, had the media reflected reality, they may have been better prepared to face reality.

When these perceptions prompt a civilian to take a self-defense training class, they'll see confirmation of the "stranger danger" perspective due to the influence of the law enforcement training curriculum. When they go from being unarmed to armed, they do not learn how that changes their relationship with law enforcement. An armed civilian must take abundant precautions in all interactions with a law enforcement officer. Unfortunately, due to the curriculum, these precautions are not often discussed.

---

[30] https://clayeolsen.com/vpf-2

Does the civilian violent crime threat demand a weapons-based mindset? Are carrying weapons worth the increased risk in interactions with law enforcement? To answer these questions, we need to know what violent crime looks like in the real world. This topic is the subject of Section 2.

2. Analysis

This section will review data to get around the biases discussed in Section 1. However, each data gathering method has strengths and weaknesses. I'll go through this data and compare the different methodologies.

2.1 National Safety Council

Let's look at some "odds of dying from" data from the National Safety Council[31] (NSC). I've only listed the odds up until "Accidental gun discharge." There is more data available on the NSC web page. Note that these are *lifetime* odds.

Lifetime odds of death for selected causes, United States, 2020	
Cause of Death	Odds of Dying
Heart disease	1 in 6
Cancer	1 in 7
COVID-19	1 in 12
All preventable causes of death	1 in 21
Chronic lower respiratory disease	1 in 28
Opioid overdose	1 in 67
Suicide	1 in 93
Motor-vehicle crash	1 in 101
Fall	1 in 102
Gun assault	1 in 221

---

[31] https://clayeolsen.com/nsc

Cause of Death	Odds of Dying
Pedestrian incident	1 in 541
Motorcyclist	1 in 799
Drowning	1 in 1,024
Fire or smoke	1 in 1,450
Choking on food	1 in 2,745
Bicyclist	1 in 3,396
Sunstroke	1 in 6,368
Accidental gun discharge	1 in 7,998

We can see that heart disease and cancer are America's top killers. We can also see the drastic impact of choices on our odds of dying: heart disease (diet), opioids (lifestyle), and chronic lower respiratory disease (smoking). Perhaps the news should be spending much of their time on how to avoid these choices. This table leads us to an **uncomfortable truth**: The odds of dying from suicides, falls, and opioid overdoses, are far ahead of gun assaults. In terms of accidents, dying from an accidental gun discharge is rarer than having a fatal sunstroke.

However, there are some things that are easy to overlook with this data:

- We know COVID-19 targets the elderly and people with health problems, typically problems due to obesity. Therefore, the odds of dying are age dependent and health dependent. For everything the NSC lists, the risk could be very low for some groups and very high for other groups, and that is not highlighted.
- The NSC looks strictly at deaths and not victimization, meaning you could be victimized by an armed violent criminal but not killed.
- "Gun assault" probably includes criminals killing other criminals and justifiable homicides, something an ordinary civilian would not want to be factored into their risk assessment.

All told, the NSC gives us the first clue that firearm homicides may not be as typical as presented in the media.

2.2 Centers for Disease Control and Prevention

Let's look at another government source. The Centers for Disease Control and Prevention (CDC) has declared firearm violence a public health threat. They created a web page that talks about firearm violence prevention.[32] Unfortunately, the CDC seems to be simply adding up various firearm statistics and presenting them without context. About halfway through, you find out that over 50 percent of firearm violence is made up of suicides. It isn't clear what the group working on firearm violence prevention would be doing that a group working on suicide prevention would not be doing. In any case, I didn't find anything useful there to compare and contrast with media representations of violent crime.

2.3 Introduction to the Uniform Crime Reports and National Crime Victimization Survey

Two other government entities gather violent crime data: the Bureau of Justice Statistics (BJS) and the Federal Bureau of Investigation (FBI). The data they collect is publicly available and, besides what Americans pay in taxes to fund it, it doesn't cost anything.

These entities have created two very different primary resources: the Uniform Crime Reports (UCR) from the FBI, and the National Crime Victimization Survey (NCVS) from the BJS. The UCR collects "crimes reported to law enforcement," while the NCVS is a survey of crime victims that includes crimes not reported to law enforcement. When examined for self-defense insights, each resource has various strengths and weaknesses.

Before we jump into the data, it will be helpful to go over some basics of violent crime, and how it maps to these statistics. Please note that each US state has different laws around violent crime. For a complete understanding, you should discuss the matter with a competent criminal defense attorney who works in your state. In what follows, I

---

[32] https://clayeolsen.com/vpf-2

provide a general overview to clear up any initial misconceptions. This information is not legal advice.

For the UCR, violent crime consists of aggravated assault, robbery, rape, and murder/non-negligent homicide. For the NCVS, I use the violent crimes of aggravated assault, robbery, and rape/sexual assault.

Aggravated Assault

For most *civilians*, who are unfamiliar with violent crime terms and their meanings, the term "aggravated assault" would mean something like being attacked and severely injured. The word "assault" is the driver for this understanding as many people associate the word "assault" with physical brutality. Even government entities seem to use "assault" in different ways. As we just saw, the NSC uses "Gun Assault" to mean something like "intentional death of another by firearm."

However, what we need to understand is definition used by the statistics we will reference. To this point, here is the partial NCVS definition[33] of assault: "The threat, attempt, or intentional infliction of bodily injury." This definition is important as threats, attempts to inflict bodily injury, and actually inflicting bodily injury would all be collected *under the same category*. This statistical definition, when combined with a layman's understanding of the term "assault," results in numbers that can be easily misinterpreted.

Although the term "battery" is not used in these statistics, what many people think the term "assault" means is closer to what the term "battery" means. You've probably heard the phrase "assault and battery." Battery refers to physical brutality and does not include threats or attempts at brutality. In fact, some US states have separate criminal charges for battery. However, other states, like these statistics, simply use the category of assault to refer to both circumstances. To help clear this up, let's go through some examples.

---

[33] https://clayeolsen.com/ncvs-terms

Simple assault: Think of this as a verbal and threatening confrontation that puts the victim in fear of imminent injury. For example, you are in a minor car accident, and the person you hit gets out of their car and starts yelling that he will beat you up. This crime would statistically be classified as a simple assault.

Simple battery: The situation described in the simple assault may have escalated to a simple battery if the guy yelled, threatened, and tried to get you in a headlock. If you were able to get away without injury or with a minor injury, and nothing further happened, this situation would also be statistically classified as a simple assault. For example, here is the NCVS definition[34] of simple assault, which clearly includes simple battery: "An attack or attempted attack without a weapon that results in no injury, minor injury (e.g., bruises, black eyes, cuts, scratches, and swelling), or an undetermined injury requiring fewer than two days of hospitalization." Typically, simple assaults result in misdemeanor criminal charges.

Aggravated assault: An aggravated assault is like a simple assault except that a weapon constitutes the threat to the victim's well-being. For instance, you get into a minor car accident, and the driver of the car you hit gets out with a one-quart beer bottle. Again, he yells at you and threatens you, except this time he tells you he is going to hit that quart bottle over your head until it breaks. This would be statistically classified as an aggravated assault.

Aggravated battery: Logically, aggravated battery would occur when a weapon is used to injure the victim. So, in our previous example, the guy threatens you and then beats you over the head with the beer bottle until law enforcement pulls him off. This situation would be statistically classified as an aggravated assault. However, aggravated battery is more nuanced. It can also occur if the victim was severely injured, but the offender did not use a weapon. Using the simple battery example, where the offender tried to get you in a headlock, if the offender succeeded in

---

[34] https://clayeolsen.com/ncvs-terms

making you lose consciousness and then severely beat you, this would also be statistically classified as an aggravated assault. For example, here is the NCVS definition[35] of aggravated assault, which clearly includes aggravated battery: "An attack or attempted attack with a weapon, regardless of whether the victim is injured, or an attack without a weapon when serious injury results." Typically, aggravated assaults result in felony criminal charges.

I have spent a lot of time covering aggravated assault because it is by far the most common violent crime in the years studied. However, you can see how the category may be more misleading than informative to a civilian audience, primarily because *it doesn't distinguish between threatened brutality with a weapon, attempted brutality with a weapon, actualized brutality with a weapon, and serious injury without a weapon.* In short, the statistical term "aggravated assault" will group together all four of these situations. This issue mainly exists in the UCR data—although the NCVS shares a similar definition of aggravated assault, it gathers more data and gives you the tools to sort through some of these very different instances of aggravated assault.

Robbery

Robbery was the second most common violent crime. The UCR and NCVS definitions of robbery are similar, but I'll use the UCR definitions because they also define larceny-theft. The UCR definition of robbery is "the taking or attempting to take anything of value from the care, custody, or control of a person or persons by force or threat of force or violence and/or by putting the victim in fear."[36] Thus, in robbery just as in aggravated assault, the victim does not need to be injured. However, we should distinguish non-injurious robbery from larceny-theft. The UCR defines larceny-theft as: "as the unlawful taking, carrying, leading, or riding away of property from the possession or constructive possession of another. Examples are thefts of bicycles, thefts of motor

---

[35] https://clayeolsen.com/ncvs-terms

[36] https://clayeolsen.com/ucr-vc-2019-ro

vehicle parts and accessories, shoplifting, pocket-picking, or the stealing of any property or article that is not taken by force, violence, or fraud."[37] Larceny-theft can be criminally charged as a misdemeanor or felony, depending on various circumstances, such as the dollar amount of the theft. Typically, robbery results in felony criminal charges.

The only other wrinkle is that the UCR data includes robberies of commercial establishments, such as banks. This inclusion is acceptable for understanding violent crime in general. Still, as this book is about personal self-defense, I'll focus more on the NCVS data where the victim was a person, not a commercial establishment.

Rape

Rape was the third most common violent crime. Starting in 2013, the category of rape significantly changed in the UCR. The data now includes cases where someone was raped without physical force. As an example, if a man drugged a woman and had sex with her while she was unconscious, this situation would now be categorized as a rape. This change resulted in a dramatic jump in the number of rapes reported in the UCR, although it is still reported to law enforcement less than robbery. Typically, rape results in felony criminal charges.

The NCVS includes sexual assault in the same category as rape, while the UCR only includes rape. Sexual assault is a much broader category than rape. Therefore, to better compare the NCVS data and UCR data, I'll filter the NCVS data and only look at rape/sexual assault statistics where the victim was injured.[38]

Murder/Non-Negligent Homicide

Murder was the least common violent crime. From a self-defense perspective, I will attempt to understand the situations where a criminal

---

[37] https://clayeolsen.com/lt

[38] Note that in the NCVS, a completed rape is classified as injurious regardless of whether the victim was physically injured. See Appendix B.

targets a civilian and cases where two civilians interact. However, there are clearly cases where criminals are killing other criminals, and unfortunately, these cases are difficult to detect and filter out. For example, drug dealers killing other drug dealers over territory violations would be included in these statistics. As expected, murder and non-negligent homicide will result in felony criminal charges.

The NCVS surveys crime victims, and as such, there is no data on murder/non-negligent homicide. Therefore, we must use the UCR data exclusively.

2.4 Findings From 2015 to 2019

In what follows, I'll be doing a deep dive into violent crime statistics. I understand that this is not everyone's cup of tea. If you wish to skip over these technical details, please go to Section 2.8 for a complete summary.

Background

The UCR covers crimes reported to law enforcement and breaks those down into various categories, such as victim-offender relationship, location, etc. As an analogy, think of a large classroom holding hundreds of students. I can group these students into age ranges, sex, level of schooling, etc. After such groupings, I can ask questions like, "How many women are in the classroom? What was the average grade in the class?" and so forth. However: imagine that every US state has many classrooms like this one, and each of the teachers gathers classroom statistics a bit differently. To make things uniform, a federal agency decides to standardize these classroom statistics and provides these standards to the teachers of these various classrooms all over the country. The teachers are not mandated to send this information over, but they do so on a volunteer basis. Over the year, the reported standardized statistics for each classroom can be aggregated by the federal agency. This approach is similar to how the UCR gathers its data from law enforcement agencies around the country.

The NCVS uses a sample of the US population as a stand-in for the entire US population. Sampling is used when it would be cost prohibitive or logistically prohibitive to interrogate the population. This approach is similar to conducting a poll. For instance, I may want to know how many people prefer vanilla ice cream to chocolate ice cream in the city I reside. I do not have the time or money to ask everyone that lives in the city. Instead, I ask 1000 people, and they respond that 20 percent prefer vanilla and 80 percent prefer chocolate. The next day, I ask 1000 *different* people, and I get 30 percent who prefer vanilla, and 70 percent prefer chocolate. Each time I ask a different 1000 people, I get different percentages. This difference is called standard error. Statisticians calculate this formula and another formula called Confidence Interval (CI). You can think of a CI as a "margin of error," primarily stated as a 95 percent CI. Back to our example, I crunched the numbers and came up with the following: 80 percent (65 percent–95 percent) prefer chocolate to vanilla in my city. The CI (basically) means that if I were to conduct another survey, 95 percent of the time, the average survey results would show the city residents prefer chocolate ice cream over vanilla between 65 percent–95 percent.[39] When I present the percentage values for the NCVS, the values in parenthesis represent the 95% CI.

The difference between the UCR and NCVS is due to how they gather their data. Both approaches are helpful and both approaches have downsides. If you wish to reproduce my work for the UCR, refer to Appendix A. For the NCVS, things are a bit more complicated, and I cover that in Appendix B, and my statistical approach to the NCVS in Appendix C.

---

[39] However, thinking of the 95 percent CI as a "margin of error" can be misleading. In the previous example, 80 percent is the average or mean, and the 95 percent CI range is 65 percent–95 percent. It may be tempting to indicate that a future sample is just as likely to have an average of 65 percent as it is 75 percent. That is not correct. Future samples are much more likely to be closer to 80 percent than 70 percent because the future sample data would resemble a bell curve around the average of 80 percent. UCR percentages will not have a CI, while NCVS percentages will have an average and a 95 percent CI.

General Findings

Ninety-five percent of the arrests law enforcement makes do not involve violent crime. When violent crime does occur, aggravated assault and robbery represent 89 percent of the total in both the UCR and NCVS.

Aggravated Assault

UCR

- The offender was a male 73 percent of the time and 67 percent of the time the offender was 39 years old or younger. Additionally, 56 percent of the time, the location of the assault was a home, while 27 percent of the time, it was a public area. 28 percent of the time, it escalated from a property issue (vandalism, damage, etc.) Finally, firearms were *not* used as a weapon 75 percent of the time.
- When the victim did not identify the offender, the victim/offender relationship is listed as "relationship unknown." For this period, it is 22 percent. The offender was a confirmed stranger at 16 percent. For "relationship unknown," we can only guess whether the offender was someone the victim knew. Perhaps the offender was masked, or it was night and the offender's face couldn't be seen, or the victim simply didn't want to identify the offender for fear of retaliation. Based on the percentages, the victim knew the offender somewhere between 62 and 84 percent of the time.

NCVS

Aggravated Assault did not result in physical injury to the victim most of the time 67.69% (64.16% –71.21%). I break down the differences in circumstances depending on whether the victim was injured in Table 2.2.1. The row "Stranger" indicates the offender was a stranger to the victim. The row "W: [X]" represents the weapon the offender used. The rows for marital status represent the victim's marital status.

Table 2.2.1 Not Injured vs. Injured, Aggravated Assault, 2015-2019

Measure	Not Injured (%)	Injured (%)
Stranger	46.35 (41.36 – 51.33)	24.80 (18.77 – 30.83)
W: Firearm	38.23 (31.61 – 44.84)	13.40 (9.92 – 16.87)
W: Knife	27.70 (24.10 – 31.30)	20.55 (16.32 – 24.78)
W: Other	27.61 (23.96 – 31.26)	28.06 (20.13 – 35.99)
W: None	N/A	25.85 (17.02 – 34.69)
Police Called	55.89 (51.66 – 60.12)	62.79 (57.33 – 68.25)
Male Victim	60.90 (56.73 – 65.08)	43.68 (35.32 – 52.03)
Female Victim	38.94 (34.92 – 42.97)	56.14 (47.68 – 64.60)
Never Married	51.74 (46.88 – 56.59)	48.33 (41.96 – 54.71)
Married	28.45 (24.81 – 32.10)	23.49 (19.01 – 27.98)
Divorced	14.33 (11.65 – 17.01)	19.91 (13.70 – 26.12)

For aggravated assault, the location of incident works out as follows:[40]

Victim Not Injured

- At or Near Victim's Home: 32.3% (28.5%–36.1%)
- At or Near F/N/R Home: 7.4% (4.9%–9.8%)
- Public Areas: 28.3% (23.9%–32.7%)
- Apartment Complex Shared Area: 5.4% (3.8%–7%)
- Commercial Places: 9.5% (7%–11.9%)
- School: 4.6% (3.1%–6%)

Victim Injured

- At or Near Victim's Home: 41.8% (36.4%–47.2%)
- At or Near F/N/R Home: 5.9% (3.2%–8.6%)
- Public Areas: 13.9% (10.4%–17.5%)

---

[40] F/N/R is shorthand and stands for Friend's, Neighbor's, Relative's (home); Public areas are streets not directly adjacent to the victim's home, and parking lots, or parking garages. If the victim lived in an apartment complex, the parking lot or garage of the apartment complex is included in the category "Apartment Complex Shared Area" rather than "Public Area." See Appendix B.

- Apartment Complex Shared Area: 4.8% (1.6%–7.9%)
- Commercial Places: 6.4% (4%–8.8%)
- School: 12.9% (5%–20.9%)

Robbery

UCR

As a reminder, because the UCR includes commercial robberies in their statistics, I will primarily use the NCVS. However, there is a valuable statistic from the UCR. Robberies occurred at a Highway/Alley/Street/Sidewalk 25 percent of the time, a home 19 percent of the time, and a Parking Garage/Lot at 10 percent of the time, which were the three highest percentage locations making up 54 percent of the total. Almost all the rest of the locations are primarily stores which likely represent commercial robberies.

NCVS

Robbery did not result in physical injury to the victim the majority of the time 67.42 percent (63.06 percent–71.77 percent). This percentage is extremely similar to aggravated assault.

In what follows, a table representing the relative proportions of circumstances will be shown between injurious robbery and non-injurious robbery. The row "Stranger" indicates the offender was a stranger to the victim. The row "W: [X]" represents the weapon the offender used. The rows for marital status represent the victim's marital status.

Table 2.2.2 Not Injured vs. Injured, Robbery, 2015-2019

Measure	Not Injured (%)	Injured (%)
Stranger	52.81 (43.12 – 62.49)	38.00 (31.29 – 44.72)
W: Firearm	27.04 (18.91 – 35.17)	9.98 (6.13 – 13.83)
W: Knife	11.50 (8.44 – 14.56)	10.56 (6.62 – 14.51)
W: Other	4.19 (1.24 – 7.13)	14.43 (6.02 – 22.83)
W: None	44.91 (39.70 – 50.11)	51.84 (37.69 – 65.99)

Measure	Not Injured (%)	Injured (%)
Police Called	49.20 (42.90 – 55.50)	68.15 (59.75 – 76.54)
Male Victim	59.24 (53.99 – 64.49)	49.12 (42.13 – 56.11)
Female Victim	40.69 (35.57 – 45.81)	50.77 (43.77 – 57.77)
Never Married	57.16 (49.76 – 64.56)	48.43 (41.45 – 55.42)
Married	19.58 (13.44 – 25.71)	19.71 (14.45 – 24.97)
Divorced	14.87 (11.28 – 18.46)	17.12 (11.82 – 22.41)

For robbery, the location of incident works out as follows:[41]

Victim Not Injured

- At or Near Victim's Home: 44.6% (39.4%–49.8%)
- At or Near F/N/R Home: 4.9% (2.5%–7.3%)
- Public Areas: 28.5% (23.9%–33%)
- Apartment Complex Shared Area: 5.8% (3.6%–7.9%)
- Commercial Places: 4.9% (2.7%–7.1%)
- School: 3.8% (1.1%–6.6%)

Victim Injured

- At or Near Victim's Home: 38.5% (31.8%–45.2%)
- At or Near F/N/R Home: 7.5% (4.1%–10.8%)
- Public Areas: 31.7% (25.4%–38%)
- Apartment Complex Shared Area: 3.9% (1.5%–6.3%)
- Commercial Places: 4% (1.4%–6.7%)

Because the locations do not change much based upon whether the victim was injured, we can ask a few more questions. Unfortunately, due to

---

[41] F/N/R is shorthand stands for Friend's, Neighbor's, Relative's (home); Public areas are streets not directly adjected to the victim's home, and parking lots, or parking garages. If the victim lived in an apartment complex, the parking lot or garage of the apartment complex is included in the category "Apartment Complex Shared Area" rather than "Public Area." See Appendix B.

limitations with the NCVS query, these questions must be asked without differentiating between injurious and non-injurious robbery.

Table 2.2.3 Home vs Public Area, Robbery, 2015-2019

Measure	Home (%)	Public (%)
Stranger	28.03 (21.54 – 34.53)	68.60 (61.78 – 75.41)
W: Firearm	14.54 (9.30 – 19.78)	28.33 (19.77 – 36.88)
W: Knife	13.24 (7.45 – 19.04)	9.81 (5.28 – 14.34)
W: Other	10.22 (4.83 – 15.61)	7.86 (1.56 – 14.15)
W: None	50.79 (43.45 – 58.14)	34.78 (22.34 – 47.22)
Police Called	57.67 (45.91 – 69.43)	57.17 (49.96 – 64.39)
Male Victim	42.99 (36.80 – 49.18)	68.83 (61.99 – 75.67)
Female Victim	56.95 (50.64 – 63.25)	31.10 (24.54 – 37.65)
Never Married	49.30 (39.32 – 59.28)	58.54 (48.41 – 68.68)
Married	19.79 (12.56 – 27.02)	19.56 (14.08 – 25.05)
Divorced	17.63 (12.89 – 22.36)	12.35 (7.21 – 17.50)

Rape

UCR

- A male is the offender 93% of the time and under 40 years old 66% of the time.
- A woman is the victim 89% of the time and is under 30 years old 63% of the time.
- Seventy-one percent of the time, the rape occurred at a residential home.
- The offender was a stranger 8% of the time and 16% of the time, the relationship between the victim and offender was unknown. Hence, around 76% to 92% of the time, the offender was someone the victim knew
- Eighty-six percent of the time, the offender did not use a weapon. A firearm was only recorded at 1%.

NCVS

The NCVS combines sexual assault and rape into one category. Hence, I filter by injury to have the statistics more in line with the UCR. Because the circumstances for rape are very different than aggravated assault and robbery, I changed some of the rows to better show these differences.

Table 2.2.4 Injured, Rape, 2015-2019

Measure	Injured (%)
Stranger	10.25 (6.14 – 14.36)
W: None	84.95 (79.55 – 90.36)
Police Not Called	71.58 (65.41 – 77.76)
Female Victim	94.85 (91.77 – 97.93)
Never Married	60.54 (47.17 – 73.90)
Married	5.93 (3.10 – 8.75)
Divorced	16.53 (6.97 – 26.10)

For injurious rape/sexual assault, the location of incident works out as follows:[42]

Victim Injured

- At or Near Victim's Home: 53.7% (45.4%–61.9%)
- At or Near F/N/R Home: 22.8% (14.2%–31.3%)
- Public Areas: 5.1% (2.5%–7.7%)
- Commercial Places: 1.7% (0.24–3.2%)

Murder/Non-Negligent Homicide

As a reminder, the NCVS has no details on murders, so only the UCR statistics are used.

---

[42] F/N/R is shorthand and stands for Friend's, Neighbor's, Relative's (home); Public areas are streets not directly adjacent to the victim's home, and parking lots, or parking garages. If the victim lived in an apartment complex, the parking lot or garage of the apartment complex is included in the category "Apartment Complex Shared Area" rather than "Public Area." See Appendix B.

Murders from 2015 to 2019 typically involved a male offender, around 79 percent of the time, and a male victim, approximately 75 percent of the time. The participants are under 40 years of age the majority of the time. About half of the time, there was a single offender and a single victim. Firearms were the most frequently used murder weapons. It also appears that around 25 percent of the time, a murder occurred due to the escalation of some other type of crime.

Around 41 percent of murder victims were confirmed by law enforcement to have known their assailants. However, the police could not determine whether the murder victim knew the offender in 49 percent of cases. Strangers were confirmed to be the offenders in about 10 percent of cases.

Asymmetries between Reported, Unreported, and Unknown Crimes

We've covered the statistics and I'll summarize the results in Section 2.8, but there is more to discuss. Interestingly, violent crimes that are tallied in the UCR have circumstances that make it more likely that they will be reported to law enforcement. In addition, using the NCVS, we saw there was a large percentage of crimes that were not reported to law enforcement. These crimes *also* have circumstances associated with them regarding why they were *not* reported to law enforcement. Furthermore, there are crimes that are unknown because they are not gathered by any statistical method at all. This reporting bias impacts our perception of violent crime when we look at violent crime statistics.

2.5 The Reporting Bias

The actual proportion of violent crimes occurring among known parties is probably even greater when one considers the underreporting of crimes among intimates in police data and the typical exclusion of violent crimes by intimates in victimization surveys.

— Clayton Mosher, Terance D. Miethe, and
Timothy Christopher Hart, *The Mismeasure of Crime*

Whether the victim feels a crime took place and the seriousness of the crime are significant factors in whether the crime is reported to the police. It is also crucial to note that a crime victim seeks advice and emotional support to decide whether law enforcement should be involved. Depending on how well the offender and victim know each other, this process could be complex.[43]

Based on this deep dive into violent crime statistics, let's create a few reporting buckets to help us understand reporting bias.

- Bucket 1: The offender was a stranger, happened in a public area, the offender had a weapon, and the victim was not injured.
- Bucket 2: The offender was a stranger, happened in a public area, and the victim was injured.
- Bucket 3: The offender was a person the victim knew, happened at a familiar non-public place, and the victim was injured.
- Bucket 4: The offender was a person the victim knew, happened at a familiar non-public place, and the victim was not injured.

Buckets 1 and 2 also have other attributes that may influence whether the crime is reported to law enforcement. For example, corroborating witnesses are likely strangers, and there may be video footage of the incident (e.g., store cameras). Furthermore, if the crime was a robbery and the victim lost assets, reporting to law enforcement may be required for insurance collection. Finally, buckets 2 and 3 represent an injured victim, and thus, the seriousness of the incident is increased. The more the victim believes what happened was serious, the more likely they will consider it a crime and report it to the police.

Looking at buckets 3 and 4, we can see how a victim would have challenges to overcome:

---

[43] Greenberg (2015)

- The victim and offender know each other.
- Because the victim and offender know each other, there may be no corroborating witnesses since they could be enjoying time together without other company.
- If there are corroborating witnesses, these witnesses may know both the victim and offender.
- The victim's support group may know the offender.
- Other circumstances, such as alcohol or illegal drugs, could be present. These circumstances may result in the victim feeling that they somehow contributed to their victimization.

These challenges are formidable. We could speculate that bucket 4 is likely the least reported of all violent crimes because the incident may not seem as serious to a non-injured victim. Even though a victim injury occurred, bucket 3 is likely underreported because of the complex dynamic between the victim, offender, and the victim's support group.

In short, the reporting bias likely *contributes* to reporting violent crimes to law enforcement when the offender was a stranger to the victim, and the crime happens in a public area. This bias is present regardless of whether the victim is injured or not. Violent crime where the offender was someone the victim knew is known to be underreported using the NCVS (e.g., rape), especially when the victim is not injured (e.g., non-injurious domestic violence). This fact leads us to an **uncomfortable truth**: The amount of violent crime where the victim knows the offender is underreported in our crime statistics. This fact makes violent crimes where the offender is a stranger seem more significant in comparison.

There is still more to discuss. Let's explore the injurious violent crimes that are not reported to law enforcement. Is it possible they could reveal something important about violent crime and injured victims? It turns out they can.

2.6 Violence Against Women

It is essential to characterize some differences between the sexes in violent crime victimization:

- Men were victimized more in aggravated assault and robbery when the victim was not injured.
- Women and men are victimized about the same in aggravated assault and robbery when the victim is injured.
- Women are by far the majority victim in injurious rape/sexual assault.
- Men are by far the majority victim in homicide.

The elephant in the room is: how much injurious violent crime is violence against women? One way to estimate it is to apply NCVS percentages to UCR statistics. In doing so, we come up with these percentages for victim sex in injurious violent crime:

Men = 37.5%
Women = 62.5%

This result shows that injurious violent crime is predominately violence against women. The derivation of these percentages is detailed in Appendix A. Here is a short summary:

1. The UCR mixes aggravated assault and robbery with rape and homicide. Aggravated assault and robbery can be both injurious and non-injurious, while rape and homicide are always considered injurious (and fatal in the case of homicide).
2. Aggravated assault and robbery make up 89 percent of the violent crime in this period.
3. The NCVS says that aggravated assault and robbery result in victim injury around 33 percent of the time.

4. When the victim is injured in an aggravated assault or robbery, the victim sex percentages change from predominately male in non-injurious cases to about a 50/50 split for injurious.

5. There is considerable police reporting bias around crimes where the victim knows the offender. Rape is a crime where the offender is almost always someone the victim knows. Hence, the police reporting bias is more significant with rape (in addition to other factors, such as the humiliation of the victim and the prospects of a criminal trial). Compensating for the police reporting bias leads to a substantial increase in victims of rape.

6. Rape is a crime where the victim is predominately a woman.

7. Homicide is a crime where the victim is predominately a male.

8. Homicide is only 1.3 percent of violent crime in this period.

9. Hence, injurious aggravated assault and injurious robbery show the victim's sex to be about 50/50. However, compensating for the unreported nature of rape increases the victim's sex to female since most victims of rape are female. Even though homicide has predominately male victims, homicide is not underreported and is a much smaller percentage of overall violent crime.

Note that this estimate may be higher than actual because no statistical methods of violent crime capture a woman unwilling to report a crime to the police (which impacts the UCR) or admit that a crime occurred (which affects the NCVS). If a woman convinces herself that a crime didn't happen, there is no crime victim. This fact leads us to an **uncomfortable truth**: Women are the victims of injurious violent crime more than men. Men are victims of non-injurious violent crime more than women.

We've covered the statistics, the reporting bias, and how compensating for known issues shows that injurious violent crime targets women more than men. However, there is something else that influences these statistics. Did you know that drug dealers shooting it out and getting arrested is reported just like two neighbors beating each other up over a property line dispute? Failing to account for a crime conducted during another crime is one problem with the UCR. There are more.

2.7 Uniform Crime Reports and Its Problems

Because law enforcement is a trusted third party, there are more circumstances the UCR can account for if law enforcement agencies were tasked to account for them. This additional detail would greatly help self-defense training.

- The UCR needs to keep track of whether the victim was physically injured. Furthermore, I should be able to see the demographics and circumstances based on that selection. For example, the UCR should have "Injurious Violent Crime" and "Non-Injurious Violent Crime" selections where the demographics are appropriate to the selection. The UCR should have "Injurious Aggravated Assault" and "Non-Injurious Aggravated Assault," and "Injurious Robbery" and "Non-Injurious Robbery."

- There is no reporting on whether the victim and/or offender were engaged in criminality when the incident occurred. For example, a pimp beating up a prostitute on a street corner would count as an aggravated assault. While this is a crime and it should be counted, it is being committed within the context of other crimes. The UCR needs a way to filter these situations out to focus on threats to an ordinary civilian rather than those a criminal may face.

- There is no reporting on whether the victim and offender had previous criminal records, previous arrests, or had an active justice status (e.g., on probation) at the time. We know law enforcement runs checks based on identification, so this information should be available and included.

- There is no reporting of whether the victim or offender are illegal aliens.

- Toxicity levels of offenders and victims are not reported. If no toxicity tests are done, the law enforcement officer could certainly record their opinion on the matter. Our ability to understand how much violent crime is committed under the influence of drugs or alcohol is essential.

- There is no report on whether the offender was legally carrying a weapon nor if they had a permit to do so.
- There is no report on whether the victim was legally carrying a weapon nor if they had a permit to do so.

Luckily, we have the NCVS to help solve the first problem. However, there are no solutions for the other problems, some of which are serious and it lead us to an **uncomfortable truth**: UCR statistics do not distinguish between violent crimes occurring in the context of criminal activity and violent crimes involving non-criminals, do not account for whether the participants had previous criminal records, do not account for the toxicity level of the participants, and do not account for whether the participants are legally allowed to reside where the crime was committed. It is anyone's guess whether these situations significantly influence violent crime statistics.

2.8 Conclusion

While I did my own research in this section, other, more qualified data researchers have reached similar conclusions to what I've shown.

> Likewise, the vast majority of violent offenses in the United States are attempts or threats that involve little or no injury to the victim. [...] Although it is certainly true that the majority of homicides committed in the United States involve the use of firearms, contrary to the popular image of the nature of violent crime, the vast majority of violent offenses do not involve the use of deadly weapons.
>
> — Clayton Mosher, Terance D. Miethe, Timothy Christopher Hart,
> *The Mismeasure of Crime*

My research focused on understanding the circumstances of violent crime so that self-defense methodologies can be formed and evaluated. The crimes of aggravated assault, robbery, rape, and homicide all have differences in this regard.

Violent Crime Overall

- As I discussed in Section 1, an ordinary civilian's perception of violent crime is that it is always injurious to the victim. We bring this perception with us when we look at violent crime statistics. Without further enlightenment, ordinary civilians will assume that violent crime statistics are representative of victim injury. This assumption is very apparent with aggravated assault because there is a tendency to assume that the word *assault* means *physical brutality*. Hence, the perception that the world is full of violent crime and injured victims can be reinforced by a superficial look at violent crime statistics.

- Victims of injurious violent crime are more likely to be women than men.

- Contrary to television news, dramas, and movies, violent crime arrests by law enforcement represent only about five percent of the total number of arrests.

- Violent crime offenders are usually men under the 40 years of age.

- During Prohibition, the buying, selling, and distribution of alcohol was a factor in violent crimes.[44] Today, the buying, selling, and distribution of drugs is a factor in violent crimes. Unfortunately, the statistics cannot isolate and account for them.

- Violent crimes where the participants have criminal or arrest records, are under the influence of drugs or alcohol, and whether they are illegal aliens cannot be isolated and accounted for.

Injurious vs. Non-Injurious: Aggravated Assault and Robbery

Aggravated assault and robbery make up 89 percent of the violent crime in this period. Unlike rape and homicide, aggravated assault and robbery can be injurious or non-injurious to the victim. Let's work through an example to showcase how to interpret these two situations. Assume that

---

[44] https://clayeolsen.com/prohibition

100 aggravated assaults occurred and 70 of them resulted in the victim not being injured and in 30 of them, the victim was injured. Let's further assume in the non-injurious case, 35 of the offenders were strangers to the victim. In this example, this number would mean that 50 percent of the offenders in non-injurious aggravated assaults were strangers to the victim (35/70). In the injurious case, let's assume that 15 of the offenders were strangers, therefore, that percentage would be the same at 50 percent (15/30). You could easily think that injurious cases of aggravated assault were just the non-injurious circumstances escalating to victim injury. After all, the percentages where the offender was a stranger are the same.

Importantly, this relationship is not what we see in the actual data. The proportions between non-injurious aggravated assault are substantially different. Strangers, firearms, public areas, and male victims are the largest proportions of non-injurious aggravated assault. With injurious aggravated assault, strangers, firearms, public areas, and male victims decrease their proportions significantly. If the "offender is a stranger" proportion decreases, that means the proportion of the "victim knows the offender" increases. This fact strongly implies that these are not simply non-injurious escalations to injurious. Instead, they represent different circumstances. Injurious aggravated assault is more likely to involve people the victim knows, firearms are rarely used, the victim's home is the most common location, and male and female victims are much more proportionate

Aggravated Assault

Non-injurious aggravated assaults seem to be cases of weapons being used to intimidate the victim (remember, when the victim isn't injured, a weapon *must* be involved for the crime to be *statistically* classified as an aggravated assault). I suspect that many of these are situations between civilians that spiral out of control, such as road rage and a weapon being flashed. These situations are likely reported to law enforcement more often than the other situations, based upon the reporting bias. Injurious aggravated assaults look more like domestic violence situations. These are likely underreported to law enforcement. We should also remember that there are likely many non-injurious aggravated assaults involving intimates and the home. These would also be domestic violence situations and are even more likely to be underreported to law enforcement.

Robbery

The two most significant differences between the circumstances of robbery compared to aggravated assault are: (1) when the victim is injured, offenders being strangers are still significant, and (2) the location where the crime took place doesn't change much depending on the victim's injury status. Another consideration is that "no weapon" is the most common robbery weapon regardless of whether the victim is injured or not. This fact will become important when we look at Defensive Gun Uses (DGUs) later in the book.

Rape

Rape is a crime predominately perpetrated by someone the victim knew, it happened at a location where the victim felt comfortable, and the offender rarely used a weapon. Rape is dramatically underreported to law enforcement. Over 60 percent of the victims of rape are women under the age of 30.

Murder/Non-Negligent Homicide

Contrary to public perception, murder and non-negligent homicide make up only 1.3 percent of violent crime in this period. Men under 40 years of age are the primary offenders and victims in this crime. Some guesswork is required as this crime seems segmented across two very different lines: civilians killing other civilians in emotionally charged situations where the victim knows the offender, and possibly criminals killing other criminals where it is unknown to law enforcement whether the victim knew the offender. Firearms are the primary murder weapon.

Uncomfortable Truths

This research has covered a lot of ground and has some surprising insights. Let's put these insights into some **uncomfortable truths**:

- Aggravated assault and robbery, not homicide, make up around 89 percent of all violent crimes in the period studied (2015–2019). Homicide represents only 1.3 percent of all violent crime.
- Two-thirds of aggravated assaults and robberies do not result in the victim being injured.
- Firearms are rarely used in injurious aggravated assault and injurious robbery.
- Robberies tend to occur at the same places regardless of whether the victim was injured.
- The most common weapon robbers use is no weapon at all.
- Rape is almost always perpetrated by someone the victim knows. It happens in a place the victim feels comfortable, weapons are not used, the victim usually doesn't seek treatment for her injuries,[45] and the victim rarely reports the crime to law enforcement.

In Section 1, I showed how civilians erroneously believe an armed violent criminal is their greatest criminal threat. In Section 2, by researching actual violent crime statistics, I showed that the stranger who is an armed violent criminal is an unlikely civilian threat in injurious violent crime. Finally, in Section 3, we'll ask a question: Given the actual violent crime threats a civilian may experience, how does the Concealed Carry of a Firearm (CCF) rate for self-defense?

---

[45] See Appendix B. This fact is analyzed in using N-DASH for "Injured – Not Treated."

3. Evaluation

Based on what we've learned so far, it is time to evaluate a standard self-defense solution to combat violent crime, which is the concealed carry of a firearm (CCF). First, we generalize this evaluation method so that it can evaluate any self-defense method. Next, we'll do as much research as we can to populate the framework for CCF. The framework we will be using is called the fact box.

3.1 Introducing the Fact Box

Let's start with a Storytime, which is a short fictional story I use to illustrate concepts and promote thinking.

Storytime

A divorced woman named Shelly and her child live in an Arizona suburban cul-de-sac. She knows her neighbors and has great friendships with them. One day, the next-door neighbor's wife comes over and says that her husband was jumped and robbed on a business trip. He was in the hospital for a couple of days. Her husband plans to go around the neighborhood to sign up people for a concealed-carry class. He feels this is the best way to prevent his friends from becoming victims of violent crime like he was. However, Shelly doesn't own a firearm and is unsure what she should do when he arrives.

#

How does Shelly evaluate whether CCF is a suitable self-defense method for her? This question must be answered holistically. What do I mean by holistically? A clue comes from your health and your decisions around it, which most people try to do holistically. For instance, if your doctor tells you that your blood pressure is too high and gives you the option of losing weight or taking pills, you have to make a decision. If you choose to lose weight, you will need to make some lifestyle changes, such as eating healthier and making time for exercise. If you choose the pill approach, you need to understand the side effects of the medication and its impact on your life.

One of the best methods of evaluating health decisions is the fact box, a creation of the Harding Centers for Risk Literacy[46] that incorporates many insights to help civilians make choices about their health.[47] However, since the fact box concept is not specific to health, I've decided to create a fact box for CCF.

For now, let's get back to Shelly, designated by "S." Instead of waiting for her neighbor to come over, she goes straight to the CCF instructor, Mike, designated by "M."

Storytime

M: So you want to talk about self-defense? Do you mind if I ask what you do for a living?

S: I go to school part-time, and I'm a parts runner for an auto parts store.

M: Do you use your car?

S: Yes, I just slap a magnetic sticker on it when I'm working. Sometimes, I forget to take it off!

M: It sounds like you probably are in a lot of parking lots and see a lot of strangers.

S: Kinda.

M: Well, you heard on the news about the university student getting pulled out of her car, right?

---

[46] https://clayeolsen.com/hcrl
[47] This discussion is indebted to Gigerenzer (2014).

S: I heard something about it. I didn't pay attention. I don't watch the news much.

M: Yes, a stranger tried to rape her right in the parking lot.

S: Wow.

M: In our free self-defense class, we cover things you can do to protect yourself against just that situation.

S: Are the classes big?

M: At my school, we have ladies-only classes for physical self-defense. If you decide you would like to learn about concealing a firearm, we also have ladies-only classes for that. So you don't have to worry about guys who think they know everything bugging you.

S: Yeah, maybe I should learn about it. Sign me up.

#

The vast majority of self-defense instructors I've met have been great people. Many self-defense instructors are former law enforcement or former military, and they are experts in their line of work. They genuinely believe in what they do. Mike in the Storytime is no exception—he is genuinely trying to help Shelly.

Shelly doesn't know what her risk of rape is. However, she is aware that rape does happen, and it is covered in the news. She knows she doesn't want to be a victim, and she trusts an expert to help her in that endeavor.

In our next Storytime, Mike will be talking to Kelli, who is also interested in self-defense. Kelli is better informed than Shelly.

Storytime

M: Do you mind if I ask you what you do for a living?

K: I'm a direct primary care doctor.

M: Really? How is that different from a regular doctor?

K: I don't take insurance, and I focus on preventative care. By not taking insurance, I don't have conflicts of interest. I can focus on what is best for the patient.

M: Interesting. Do you have staff to help you?

K: No, I'm a one-woman show!

M: Well, are you ever alone with a new patient? That could be a situation where a patient might try to rape you.

K: It could be. According to the Uniform Crime Reports, there are about five rapes per 10,000 people in Arizona. Because rape is an underreported crime, we would have about one rape per 1000 people if we double it. I'm 35, and most rapes happen to women under 30.[48] For comparison, about five women out of 1000 aged 50-70 die of breast cancer[49] over an 11-year period.

M: Wow! You are well informed, but it sure seems more likely than that. I think there is a rape talked about on the news every week. Even if you think it may be unlikely to happen to you, it could still happen, though. So carrying a concealed firearm may be an option for you. You can think of it as a preventative measure, like a mammogram for breast cancer. You may never be a crime victim, and you may never get breast cancer, but carrying concealed and getting your annual mammogram are reasonable steps to keep worse things from happening to you.

K: Even with mammograms, the breast cancer death rate is still four out of 1000.[50] So, mammograms help one out of 1000 women. But, there are harms.

M: What do you mean harms?

---

[48] See Appendix A.

[49] https://clayeolsen.com/hcrl

[50] https://clayeolsen.com/hcrl

K: Well, 100 out of 1000 women are told they have progressive cancer when they don't.[51] Five out of 1000 have unnecessary invasive procedures done.[52] Unnecessary medical procedures are a big deal because medical errors can happen.[53] Mammograms aren't a slam dunk. I talk about them extensively with my patients, and they decide what is best for them. Speaking of harms, what are the harms of carrying a firearm concealed?

M: Harms? If you are trained well, there are no harms.

K: Well, that seems a bit silly. You are, after all, carrying a dangerous weapon.

M: As long as you follow your training, you'll be fine.

K: That is like saying if you decide to get a swimming pool, pay attention, and no one will drown. Yet, hundreds of kids drown every year. Having a swimming pool has benefits and harms. Your kids will learn to swim, but accidents do happen. What happens if my firearm accidentally goes off?

M: Hopefully, no one gets hurt.

K: Is that all that happens? I thought all gun crimes in Arizona have mandatory prison sentences.

M: For criminals, I'm sure. I doubt if that is the case for a concealed carrier.

K: You should probably research that. But, let's say I get your training, I successfully defend myself one day, and I mention your training on the news. You would probably get a big jump in business. However, if I follow your training and still become a victim, can I sue you?

---

[51] https://clayeolsen.com/hcrl

[52] https://clayeolsen.com/hcrl

[53] Estimated to be the third-leading cause of death (https://clayeolsen.com/jhme). Johns Hopkins researchers wrote an open letter to the CDC about it: https://clayeolsen.com/jhol.

M: Um, no. You wouldn't have been a victim if you had followed my training correctly.

K: Really. I think it is interesting that you and I receive the benefits of your training, but only I would experience the harms of your training. You are sheltered from any training mistakes you make, and you are sheltered from any mistakes I make due to your training. That seems off-balance to me.

#

Discussion

Let's walk through what Kelli did right in her discussion with Mike.

- *She skipped the news and went right to the relevant statistics.* Whether they are on television or the Internet, the primary purpose of news stories is to grow viewership. These stories may be about everyday events, or they may be about unlikely events. For instance, the news talks about murder quite often. However, homicide doesn't even appear on the CDC's 15 Leading Causes of Death from 2015 to 2019.[54] Pneumonitis,[55] a noninfectious lung inflammation typically caused by airborne particles, takes the number 15 slot (which means homicide was lower). When was the last time you saw a news report on pneumonitis?

- *She identified a mismatch between the instructor's harms and the trainee's harms.* As Thomas Sowell remarked: "It is hard to imagine a more stupid or dangerous way of making decisions than by putting those decisions in the hands of people who pay no price for being wrong."[56] For example, having concealed-carry

---

[54] https://clayeolsen.com/cdc-ucd—You can use the CDC WONDER utility to gather this information. Read and agree with the restrictions. Select 15 Leading Causes of Death, Years 2015, 2016, 2017, 2018, and 2019. Press Send.

[55] https://clayeolsen.com/pne

[56] https://clayeolsen.com/ts

instructors sign a contract with you that said they would pay your legal fees if you were ever charged with a gun crime would be an excellent first step to correcting this mismatch. You would see a very different type of firearm training using this approach, which would likely benefit the trainee.

What did Mike get right? Mike was right to focus on the circumstances, but neither he nor Kelli had statistics on the circumstances around rape. For example, in Arizona, 73 percent of rapes took place at a home, and 82 percent of the offenders were known to the victim.[57] Kelli's medical practice matches these circumstances well even though she isn't in the highest risk age group (69 percent of rape victims were under 30 years of age).[58]

What did Mike get wrong?

- Mike was using news reports to create concern because he doesn't understand how the news creates the perception that violent crime is a probable occurrence, as detailed in Section 1. The question is whether this fear is justified. Only by gathering reputable data and creating the appropriate statistics can we determine whether it is justified or not. We need to avoid unjustified fear as it impacts our ability to make good decisions.
- In 2013, a revised definition of rape was introduced that referred to a lack of consent instead of force, which significantly increased the rate of rape.[59] This change in definition covers cases of rape where, as an example, the offender drugged the victim without their knowledge. In Kelli's case, if she were in a situation where she was drugged, her self-defense capability would be limited, and CCF may not be the best defense.

---

[57] See Appendix A

[58] See Appendix A

[59] See Appendix A

- Arizona gun crimes have mandatory prison sentences.[60] A concealed carrier may be surprised at what constitutes a gun crime. For example, an accidental (i.e., negligent) discharge of a firearm in a municipality is a gun crime. Or, perhaps, a concealed carrier is charged with aggravated assault when they thought it was a case of self-defense, such as in cases of road rage.[61] If you commit a gun crime, the law doesn't care whether you are a criminal or concealed carrier.[62]

Parallels

I introduced a health decision—mammograms—into the discussion because of conceptual parallels with CCF. I'll use more information from the mammogram fact box in this section. Let's go through a couple of similarities:

1. Choices matter in health. Although no one gets out of life alive, choices can have an immense influence on the quality of life. Sadly, many individuals discount the impact of diet, exercise, and tobacco products on their health and instead feel that health screening can compensate. In short, they think if cancer is detected early enough, they can be saved regardless of their other health choices. This idea is mistaken. For example, while mammograms have some benefits, the mortality rate from *any* cancer for women over the 11-year period *is the same* for those who have mammograms as for those who do not.[63] This fact means that even though breast cancer is detected early by a mammogram, other forms of cancer did occur and

---

[60] https://clayeolsen.com/aff-5

[61] https://clayeolsen.com/rage

[62] See "Mandatory Minimum Sentences" at https://clayeolsen.com/aff-5. You can also search online for "Arizona gun crimes mandatory sentences." You'll see that it is a quite popular discussion item for Arizona criminal defense attorneys. There is a reason for that, and it doesn't involve violent criminals as much as you might think.

[63] https://clayeolsen.com/hcrl

killed the patients at the same rate as those women who did not get mammograms. For example, a woman smoker who is getting mammograms may have inflicted enough damage on her body via smoking that she is continually fighting different types of cancer after breast cancer was initially detected. Therefore, early breast cancer detection did not matter in the long run. Quitting cigarettes would have been a better first step. Similarly, a concealed carrier may feel that a firearm is all they need to be safe, and they ignore small lifestyle changes that could significantly reduce their chances of being victimized by a crime. I will substantially expand on these options later in this book.

2. *What is essential is that the person experiencing the benefits and the harms make the decision.* A healthy woman can decide whether to get an annual mammogram, and they would be better informed if they referenced the fact box for mammograms. For example, a woman familiar with the harms of mammograms would understand that false positives are much more common than true positives (100 versus 5 per the fact box). If she gets a positive, she may not be as psychologically devastated by the news, and she can have more tests done before undergoing any invasive medical procedures. By developing a fact box for CCF, the person deciding whether to carry a firearm can determine whether the benefits outweigh the harms. Each individual should look at the benefits and harms of any self-defense strategy and decide whether that defensive strategy is best for them. For example, after making lifestyle changes to reduce their chances of being victimized by crime, a bodyguard, armored truck driver, or former judge may feel that carrying a concealed firearm is still the best defensive option for them based upon their likely threats.

In the next section, we'll begin to populate our fact box for CCF. I'll start with the firearm injury categories that the CDC uses and evaluate them.

3.2 Fact Box Harms: Center for Disease Control and Prevention Injury Categories

Although I have concerns about the CDC's approach to firearm violence, it doesn't mean they do not have helpful information for our fact box. For example, on the Fast Fact page,[64] the CDC lists the types of firearm injuries, which can be fatal or nonfatal. This list seems like a good place to start so we can understand the benefits and harms of firearm ownership with the intent to carry one for self-defense. We'll start with the following terms:

- Intentionally Self-Inflicted
- Unintentional
- Interpersonal Violence
- Legal Intervention
- Undetermined Intent

Let's go through each item on the CDC's list, evaluate them, and determine if they belong in our fact box's harms section.

Intentionally Self-Inflicted

The question we are trying to answer here is that if I introduce a firearm into my household, does the firearm make it more likely that a person in my home will commit suicide? If true, this would be a substantial harm.

With the CDC WONDER tool,[65] we can investigate suicides from 2015 to 2019. It turns out that there were 232,186 suicides in those five years. Of those, 117,183 took their life using a firearm, or around 50 percent. Many civilians think that teenagers are the primary victims of suicide, due to the pressures of school, bullying, and budding adulthood.

---

[64] https://clayeolsen.com/vpf-2

[65] https://clayeolsen.com/cdc-ucd—Read and agree with the restrictions. Select ICD-10 113 Cause List, Years 2015, 2016, 2017, 2018, and 2019. Select Injury Intent and Mechanism. Then select Suicide, then All Causes of Death. Press Send.

However, using the same tool, we can also look at the age groups of the suicides that were committed with a firearm:[66]

- 5–14 years   861
- 15–24 years   13,898
- 25–34 years   16,810
- 35–44 years   15,558
- 45–54 years   19,095
- 55–64 years   20,924
- 65–74 years   15,067
- 75–84 years   10,327
- 85+ years   4,636

The people who committed suicide by firearm were primarily *mature adults* (73 percent were 35 years and older). Teenagers making rash emotional decisions do not dominate the statistics. Of the suicide victims, around 25.6 percent of them were on Medicare. For instance, due to the effects of smoking, my father was unable to do very much in the last two years of his life. He simply wasn't able to breathe. As someone active his entire life, this sent him into depression, and he seriously considered suicide. He would have used a firearm if he had chosen to end his life. Other people on Medicare, such as my father, may be experiencing terminal physical health problems that lead to suicide.

To determine whether this category belongs in our fact box, we would need a study to be performed. Here is what would be required:

- Control Group: People diagnosed as suicidal and live in a house with no firearm.
- Test Group: People diagnosed as suicidal and live in a house with a firearm.
- Test: Is there any difference in mortality for the two groups over ten years?

---

[66] https://clayeolsen.com/cdc-ucd—Read and agree with the restrictions. Select Ten Year Age Groups, Years 2015, 2016, 2017, 2018, and 2019. Select Injury Intent and Mechanism. Then select Suicide, then Firearm. Press Send.

I do not know of such a study. Given the mental illnesses linked to mass shootings and suicides, I'm not convinced that the presence of a firearm leads to more suicides *long-term.*[67] Until such information becomes available, it does *not* belong in our fact box as a harm. In other words, it is unproven that purchasing a firearm for self-defense will make it more likely that you or a loved one will commit suicide. That being said, it certainly makes sense to be attuned to any behaviors of your loved ones, regardless of their age, that may indicate suicidal thoughts and take the appropriate preventative measures. One of those measures could be to remove all firearms from your home if a loved one was diagnosed as suicidal.

Unintentional

Using the CDC WONDER tool, we can look at unintentional fatalities, which WONDER calls "Accidents."[68] From 2015 to 2019, 818,048 accidents were fatal. Of those, firearms were responsible for 2,414 (0.3 percent). Drownings constituted 18,499 (2.3 percent) and traffic fatalities 189,154 (23 percent) for the same period.

In 2020, there were an estimated 434 million guns in the United States, far more guns than people.[69] For comparison, the number of registered vehicles in the United States was around 287 million.[70] Given the numbers, unintentional *fatalities* with firearms were incredibly low. Safety is a major topic for those unfamiliar with firearm classes and is strictly enforced. Every hunting class and firearm class spends a lot of time on this topic. If you go to a gun range and handle a firearm in an unsafe manner, you will get kicked out and likely banned.

In contrast, many drivers on the road have only studied driving safely to pass the driving test, and they never look at it again. Imagine

---

[67] https://clayeolsen.com/mi

[68] https://clayeolsen.com/cdc-ucd—Read and agree with the restrictions. Select 15 Leading Causes of Death, Years 2015, 2016, 2017, 2018, and 2019. Select Injury Intent and Mechanism. Then select Unintentional, then All Causes of Death. Press Send.

[69] https://clayeolsen.com/nf

[70] https://clayeolsen.com/vr

not using your turn signal, getting pulled over by police, and then having your driver's license suspended. That would be the firearms equivalent.

What about unintentional firearm *injuries*? A study from 2015 showed that from 1993 to 2012, accidental firearm injuries continued to decline and remain very low.[71] *However, when deciding to go from being a household without a firearm to one having a firearm, given our Storytime example, unintentional injury/death should be a harm on our concealed-carry fact box.*

Interpersonal Violence

This item seems to be more of a catch-all. I would expect it to include:

- Firearm injuries and fatalities between criminals engaged in crimes.
- Firearm injuries and fatalities between private citizens and criminals, where the potential victims defended themselves against criminal activity.
- All other interpersonal violence causes.

The inability to distinguish between offensive and defensive uses of firearms makes this category unsuitable for a fact box.

Legal Intervention

This category records the number of firearm injuries caused by law enforcement acting in the line of duty. *This category isn't a candidate for a fact box for CCF.*

Undetermined Intent

This category indicates the firearm injury is under investigation and cannot be categorized more specifically at this time. *Therefore, again, not a candidate for the fact box.*

---

[71] https://clayeolsen.com/fi

3.3 Fact Box Benefits: Defensive Gun Use

Defensive Gun Use (DGU) is commonly understood as an armed civilian using a firearm to prevent a criminal victimization. The firearm does not need to be discharged for it to be classified as a DGU. As an example, if a robber tried to physically assault a victim and the victim pulled a firearm and the robber fled without the firearm being discharged, that incident is typically considered a DGU.

3.3.1 Commonly Cited Sources

CDC

The CDC has a separate section for Defensive Gun Use (DGU).[72] Unfortunately, this section changes quite a bit. Initially, it reported a range of about 500,000 to 2.5 million times per year. Then, they revised it to 60,000 to 2.5 million times per year. Now, they don't bother to report the range at all and claim more research is needed.

Let's look at other sources to see if we can get better precision on the range.

Gun Violence Archive

Another group that keeps track of DGUs, the Gun Violence Archive (GVA),[73] only uses verifiable DGUs, which are those reported to law enforcement. Here is an example of some of the statistics the GVA keeps track of, using the chart "GVA—SIX-YEAR REVIEW" available on their main webpage.[74] Verified DGUs numbered about 1,400 to 2,100 per year between 2015 and 2019. The average number of verified DGUs according to the GVA during this period was 1,788. That is a long way

---

[72] https://clayeolsen.com/vpf-2

[73] https://clayeolsen.com/gva

[74] https://clayeolsen.com/gva

from 60,000, the lowest range of DGUs previously reported by the CDC.

Given what we learned about violent crime, only using law enforcement reports would seem odd. So here is their justification,[75] with my emphasis in italics:

> "There are sometimes questions about Defensive Gun Uses which are not reported to police. GVA can ONLY list incidents which can be verified. Our policies do not take into account stories not reported, 'I can't believe this happened to me' scenarios, or extrapolations from surveys. *Our position is that if an incident is significant enough that a responsible gun owner fears for their life and determines a need to threaten lethal force, it is significant enough to report to police* so law enforcement can stop that perpetrator from harming someone else."

This justification leaves a lot to be desired. Using a similar approach for rape, many of the rapes in America would not be counted. This fact could be expanded to violent crime as a whole. The unreported nature of violent crime is the whole point of victimization surveys—to understand crimes that are not reported to law enforcement. As we saw in Section 2, aggravated assault and robbery are not reported to the police about 40 percent of the time. Rape is at 71 percent. The NCVS is a very reputable source for victimization data. The GVA's justification is too simplistic and offensive to victims who felt they would endanger themselves by reporting the incident to law enforcement.

UCR

Another option is to look more closely at justifiable homicides by private citizens. It turns out they are about the same as the number of justifiable homicides by law enforcement, according to the UCR.[76]

---

[75] https://clayeolsen.com/gva-methodology

[76] See Appendix A

Justifiable Homicide by Weapon, Private Citizen 2015-2019
Average of Total: 360
Average for Handguns: 225

Justifiable Homicide by Weapon, Law Enforcement 2015-2019
Average of Total: 424
Average for Handguns: 291

Justified homicides by private citizens are about 85 percent of the total justified homicides by law enforcement (360/424). Looking only at handguns, typical for CCF, we are at 77.3 percent (225/291).

Researchers have pointed out problems with how the UCR gathers data for justifiable homicides.[77] However, even doubling or tripling their number doesn't come close to even a quarter of the bottom range number once reported by the CDC of 60,000 DGUs.

Kleck and the CDC

In the 1990s, Gary Kleck and Marc Gertz published a study about defensive gun uses. They concluded that it could be as high as 2.4 million per year. In the late 1990s, the CDC did its research but did not publicize the results. Taking a look at the results of the CDC's survey around twenty years later (when he found out about it), Kleck concluded it supported about 1.1 million defensive gun uses per year.[78]

A recent new survey of DGUs lends support to Kleck. William English from Georgetown University is the author of "2021 National Firearms Survey: Updated Analysis Including Types of Firearms Owned."[79,80] I unfortunately was unable to review this survey in detail as I became aware of it while in the final edits of this book. However, English indicates that it will be part of a larger book project which I'm looking

---

[77] https://clayeolsen.com/jhp

[78] https://clayeolsen.com/drgo

[79] English (2021)

[80] https://clayeolsen.com/ppdgu

forward to reading. With apologies, here are some highlights from the abstract:

- […] in most defensive incidents (81.9%) no shot was fired.
- Approximately a quarter (25.2%) of defensive incidents occurred within the gun owner's home, and approximately half (53.9%) occurred outside their home, but on their property.
- About one out of ten (9.1%) defensive gun uses occurred in public, and about one out of thirty (3.2%) occurred at work.
- We estimate that approximately 20.7 million gun owners (26.3%) carry a handgun in public under a "concealed carry" regime.

Seventy-nine percent of DGUs happen in the home or on the property of the home. Almost 82 percent of the time, no shot is fired. These statistics will match well with other sources that we look at later in this section.

Sadly, DGU research is incredibly controversial.[81] Readers and researchers will need to scrutinize sources and methodologies carefully. I have made my readers aware of English's research and it lends support to already heavily scrutinized research. However, due to lack of time, I did not do a deep investigation of it. I encourage my readers to do so.

3.3.2 Uncommon Sources

When a Civilian Discharges a Firearm in Self-Defense

The only study I've seen that analyzed civilian DGUs when the firearm was discharged was done by Claude Werner and posted to The Thinking Gunfighter blog.[82] Here is an excerpt (emphasis in italics is mine):

---

[81] https://clayeolsen.com/reason

[82] https://clayeolsen.com/tgf

- If the defender fires any shots, most likely it will be two rounds.[83]
- Defenders frequently communicate with their attackers before shooting.
- *The firearm was carried on the body of the defender in only 20% of incidents.* In 80% of cases, the firearm was obtained from a place of storage, frequently in another room.
- The majority of incidents took place in the home (52%).
- Next most common locale (32%) was in a business. Incidents took place in public places in 9% of reports and 7% occurred in or around vehicles. The most common initial crimes were armed robbery (32%).

These statistics align well with our analysis in Section 2. By cross-referencing Werner's study with the survey reports, we can get an idea of how accurate these survey reports are.

Where Do DGUs Happen?

American Gun Facts has a useful website for guns used in self-defense.[84] Astonishingly, almost 80 percent of the time, the victim's home was involved, either inside the home or on the property of the home. This aligns well with English's research which showed 79 percent. Werner's research on when the firearm was discharged showed 52 percent for the home. A home is an unlikely place to be carrying concealed. Furthermore, American Gun Facts shows that only 9 percent of gun owners reported carrying firearms with them always or almost always. Almost 44 percent say they never carry a firearm with them. English's analysis showed only 26 percent operated under a "concealed carry regime."

These facts lead us to an **uncomfortable truth**: It is a mistake to assume that DGUs always involve someone who is carrying a concealed

---

[83] This fact has major ramifications for civilian firearm training, that to my mind have been unexplored.

[84] https://clayeolsen.com/gusd

firearm. It is correct to say that most DGUs do not involve someone who is carrying a concealed firearm.

When a Firearm Is Not Discharged

Another statistic from American Gun Facts shows that a firearm is *not* discharged almost 82 percent of the time. This percentage aligns well with English's research. Because of this high percentage, I will assume that the circumstances, such as the location of the incident, are more likely to reflect when the firearm is not discharged.

Of the 82 percent of the time when the firearm is not discharged, 31 percent of the time, simply telling the attacker they were armed was sufficient to prevent victimization. Around 51 percent of the time, the firearm needed to be shown.[85] This fact leads us to an **uncomfortable truth**: The vast majority of DGUs did not result in the firearm being discharged, and almost a third of the time, the firearm did not need to be displayed to be an effective deterrent.

Mass Shootings

Recently, there were three incidents where a CCF stopped a mass shooter. These courageous individuals saved many lives. Unfortunately, one of them was killed by law enforcement.[86]

Based on our analysis in Section 1, we know that two out of the top three mass shooting locations took place in gun-free zones. We also know that long-range sniping at open areas, such as mall parking lots or other open gatherings, limits the effectiveness of a CCF in stopping a mass shooter. However, in certain circumstances, CCF can save many lives in a mass shooting situation. Let's try and get a rough estimate on the percentage.

Schools were said to be a bit over 20 percent of all mass shootings. Let's call it 25 percent. If around 75 percent of the mass shootings were

---

[85] https://clayeolsen.com/gusd
[86] https://clayeolsen.com/jhu

at the workplace and open spaces, we only have open spaces to consider. If open spaces are 37.5 percent of the mass shootings, then we need to consider what percentage are sniper incidents. If we say 50 percent of the 37.5 percent were sniping incidents, then we are close to 19 percent of the time a concealed carrier could help in a mass shooting. In short, mass shootings are rare, and in these rare events, a concealed carrier will be unable to help 81 percent of the time. Obviously, more research is needed to pin down these numbers. However, these considerations do lead us to an **uncomfortable truth**: A person who lawfully carries a concealed firearm is likely overestimating the number of mass shooting situations they can successfully defend against.

3.3.3 Defensive Gun Use Example

There is a great deal of controversy over gathering DGU statistics. Let's walk through a Storytime and show why DGUs can be hard to track.

Storytime

It's about 11:30 pm, and you have dozed off in your chair. Your wife comes in and wakes you up. She says that the baby is not feeling well, and she needs you to hit the store and get some medicine. You run down to the local 24-hour convenience store. Two men rush up toward you from behind as you get out of the car. You hear their footsteps and whirl around with your hand on your weapon. You shout, "I'm armed!" They take off running. You get back in your car, go to a different convenience store, get the medicine, and return home. You tell your wife what happened.

"Did you call the police?" she asks.

"No. I didn't really get a good look at them. If I called the police and the police found them, they might just say they were trying to ask for directions or something like that."

"What if they were?"

"At midnight? No, they were going to rob me. Technically, because they didn't say anything about robbing me and didn't have any weapons, they probably would have had to throw a punch for the police to consider what happened a crime. But that would have been too late for me. Otherwise, I guess it was just suspicious behavior."

"Can they charge you with a crime?"

"Maybe. If they went to the police and falsely said I told them I was going to kill them and showed them my weapon, I guess I could be charged with aggravated assault. The cameras at the store don't record audio, so the police would just have my word against theirs. Look, I seriously doubt those boys will call the cops. They probably have outstanding warrants. In any case, I don't want you going to that convenience store anymore."

#

For various reasons, we can see that the man convinced himself that involving law enforcement would not accomplish much. As a result, the UCR will not have a record of this incident. As far as victimization goes, if the man happened to be part of a sample in the NCVS, no crime occurred, so he wasn't victimized. Therefore, there would be no report in the NCVS either.

Now, let's assume the man did call 911 and reported an attempted robbery. When law enforcement gets there, the man will basically explain he committed an aggravated assault with a firearm to avoid being robbed (i.e., self-defense is typically the admittance of a crime to avoid being victimized). The question then becomes: was it reasonable for him to believe he was about to be robbed? Furthermore, no experienced criminal attorney will want you making statements to law enforcement, especially when it comes to admitting crimes. So let's go back to the beginning and show what would happen if the man called 911:

- He or someone there would call 911 and report an attempted robbery of a person at that address.
- He would securely store his firearm so that it is not a threat to the law enforcement officer when they arrive.
- When the law enforcement officer arrives, he invokes his constitutional rights. He makes no statements, agrees to no searches, and so forth. Finally, he requires his attorney present for any questions.

It doesn't sound like he will get home soon with that medicine. It also looks like a costly trip to the convenience store. So, it is little wonder why this man convinced himself to do nothing. Just walking through this example leads us to an **uncomfortable truth**: The number of DGUs is not easily gathered with our traditional crime statistics reporting via the UCR and NCVS. Any source which claims to know the number of DGUs needs to be scrutinized extensively. In fact, changes to the law to encourage law-abiding firearm owners to report DGUs may be required.

3.3.4 Defensive Gun Use Conclusion

Although the CDC has indicated that more research needs to be done, their research and private researchers have found hundreds of thousands, if not millions, of DGUs per year. As our Storytime suggests, these are probably not reported by any of our current methodologies.

Unfortunately, many sources consider DGUs synonymous with CCF. As the cited sources indicate, they are not the same. Based upon this research, whatever DGU number we get in total, we should reduce the total by 70 to 80 percent to get an estimate of DGUs that happened while carrying concealed. It is an open question as to how many of those who were carrying fired their weapon, showed their weapon, or said they had a weapon to avoid victimization. More research is needed to determine if concealed carriers require the lethality of a firearm more often than say a homeowner or business owner.

Although there is work to be done here, DGUs do prevent criminal victimization. *Therefore, I consider DGUs to be a benefit for our fact box.*

3.4 Firearm Violence Consequences

The CDC has a section called "What are the consequences of firearm violence?"[87] Unfortunately, this section changes frequently, so I won't quote it directly in this book.

Ultimately, the CDC talks about firearm violence in terms of long-term consequences, the sense of safety and security, and economic impact. However, they do not provide any context or comparison with other datasets. The most obvious question is how does firearm violence compare to non-firearm violence? That would help us understand the context and whether these considerations are significant. Our deep dive into violent crime statistics shows that firearms are not used often *when the victim is injured* in aggravated assault, robbery, or rape. In fact, lethal weapons are just not that prevalent in our most common injurious violent crimes. As such, *non-firearm violent crime injuries would dwarf firearm injuries significantly*, which is a fact not mentioned by the CDC. Furthermore, even in non-injurious violent crimes, firearms are *not* used the majority of the time.

Mass shootings and suicides plausibly indicate mental health issues. It has been known for quite a while that detailed news stories on suicides can influence whether or not other people commit suicide. Mass shootings may also have a similar pattern where intensive media coverage motivates other mentally ill individuals to imitate these crimes.[88] The impacts of media reporting on violent crime may well be more important to study than firearm violence. Other unique criminal activity, such as terrorism, does not always employ firearms but instead involves bombs, vehicles, planes, and other more destructive weapons or weaponized

---

[87] https://clayeolsen.com/vpf-2

[88] https://clayeolsen.com/ms

objects. The impacts of terrorism on a community are substantial and comparing it with firearm violence would be valuable.

To the CDC's credit, they mention the health problems associated with experiencing violence. Many people know about Post-traumatic Stress Disorder, or PTSD, which has been the object of active research for many years.[89] The Bureau of Justice Statistics has also published data on physical and emotional problems due to the experience of violence.[90] These problems are significant and can last a long time. *However, these issues are not firearm specific.*

The fundamental question is this: *does owning a firearm incur more risk of violence that can be psychologically damaging?* We have listed some harms in our fact box, such as a negligent discharge, that are a part of firearm violence, but we also have the benefit of DGUs. If the potential victim of a DGU did not own a firearm, they would have been victimized, which can be psychologically damaging. By possessing a firearm, the DGU prevented a victimization, but the experience of violence can still be psychologically damaging for the potential victim. Here are the three outcomes:

- A DGU is just as psychologically traumatizing as a victimization.
- A DGU is more psychologically traumatizing than a victimization.
- A DGU is less psychologically traumatizing than a victimization.

If I were a betting person, I would bet on the last one being true. However, it does deserve to be an object of future study. Until a quality study contradicts my intuition, I won't list anything concerning psychological trauma and firearms ownership in our fact box.

---

[89] https://clayeolsen.com/ptsd-1

[90] https://clayeolsen.com/bjs-1

3.5 Centers for Disease Control and Prevention Benefits and Harms Summary

Let's go through what we found:

- Suicide by firearm—Around 50 percent of all suicides use a firearm, and the CDC includes these as instances of firearm violence. The CDC does not show that owning a firearm leads to more suicides. *However, if you have a family member who is suicidal, you should not introduce a firearm into the household. If you have a firearm, you should remove it from the home or securely lock it up.* Most importantly, you need to get that person some help. Remember, around 50 percent of suicides used something other than a firearm.

- Unintentional fatalities with firearms—Although tiny, this showcases the dangers associated with firearm ownership. Therefore, this statistic is a harm in our fact box.

- Unintentional injuries with firearms—This data is essential for the same reasons as unintentional fatalities data. However, many dangers remain in the gathering of this data. For instance, most emergency rooms must report gunshot wounds to law enforcement. This reporting could be problematic if many people were shot while engaging in criminal activity. They, of course, will not admit this criminal activity to law enforcement. In addition, the false alternative circumstances they give will likely cause problems with the data (e.g., "I was hit by a stray bullet" instead of "I was shooting it out with a drug dealer"). Researchers have also pointed out additional problems in how the CDC gathers information on firearm injuries.[91] This statistic is a harm in our fact box, but the caveat is that much better data is needed.

- Defensive Gun Uses—This dataset is essential for self-defense and is included as a benefit in the fact box.

---

[91] https://clayeolsen.com/fiep

- Psychological problems due to firearm violence—The CDC is correct that this is a problem with firearm violence. It also happens for self-defense. Even if you successfully use a firearm to prevent a criminal victimization, you could still experience psychological problems from the incident. However, non-firearm victimizations are the norm and can cause psychological issues that are just as significant. Besides unintentional fatalities and unintentional injuries, it has not been established that firearm ownership increases the odds of experiencing psychological trauma. Therefore, it is not included in the fact box.

Let's move on and look at other resources for our concealed carry fact box.

3.6 Criminal Charges

Attorney Marc J. Victor is the owner of the Attorneys For Freedom law firm in Arizona. A few years ago, he published a blog post advising concealed carriers not to carry a round chambered.[92] This post generated a lot of responses, some positive and some critical. The key point he was making is that the negligent discharge of a firearm in a municipality is a class 6 felony with a mandatory prison sentence in Arizona. Carrying a firearm with a round in the chamber will increase the risk of a negligent discharge. Therefore, a person should be well informed about the laws in their state before deciding how to carry a concealed firearm.

Because different states have different firearms laws, we will include the US state in our fact box. Furthermore, research analyzing the CDC firearm injury data[93] has pointed out substantial regional variations in the number of incidents of violence involving firearms. This fact is another reason to include the US state in the fact box.

However, Marc J. Victor pointed out a harm that doesn't get enough attention: a CCF inadvertently breaking the law and being criminally

---

[92] https://clayeolsen.com/aff-1
[93] https://clayeolsen.com/fiep

charged. So let's go through some Storytimes to see how easy it is for a CCF to get into trouble. For all these Storytimes, assume the protagonist has a concealed-carry permit and carries a concealed firearm.

Storytime

You and your wife are going to your local hardware store. A man approaches you smelling of whiskey and marijuana. He asks you for money, saying that he and his wife ran out of gas a few miles away. You refuse. He gets mad and begins insulting your wife in a very derogatory manner. You take offense; you grab him by the shirt and tell him he had better get lost. He attempts to push you away, and he feels your concealed firearm.

He panics and begins wrestling with you, trying to get away. You panic, thinking he is trying to grab your firearm. You use your close quarters combat training to draw your weapon and fire, wounding him. Law enforcement arrives on scene. A witness tells them that they heard yelling and saw you grab his shirt before you began fighting. In the hospital, he claims he feared for his life when he felt your concealed weapon. Your attorney tells you that you will likely be charged with an aggravated assault.

Storytime

You are waiting in line at the bank when the door opens, and a man wearing a trench coat walks in and pulls out something that looks like an AR-15. You draw your concealed handgun and shoot the man in the chest. The bullet passes through him, hits a young woman behind him, and kills her. Later, it was determined that the armed robber had a toy gun that he had used in three other robberies during the summer. No one had been injured in these robberies, and he had escaped with minimal cash. In fact, he was known as the "toy gun bandit."

Public opinion turns against you—if you had just left the situation alone, the woman would have lived, and the bank would have lost a few hundred bucks. A few days later, law enforcement arrests you at your home.

You are being arrested because it was your bullet that killed the young woman, and you are responsible for every bullet that leaves your firearm.

Storytime

You are out running errands around town when your wife calls. Your son is sick at school and needs to be picked up and taken to the doctor. Your wife has already set up an appointment and it is in 10 minutes. You drive to the school, but your son is not where he usually is. You figure he is in the nurse's office. You swing into the parking lot, but in doing so, you make an illegal turn in front of a law enforcement officer. He promptly follows you into the parking lot with his lights on. You show him your license, registration, proof of insurance, and your concealed-carry permit. He asks you if you are carrying concealed. You suddenly realize that you should not be carrying a firearm in a school zone.

In Arizona, you must answer whether you have a firearm truthfully. One of the problems over time with concealed carry is that your firearm becomes part of your "clothing," and you forget it is there in slightly abnormal situations—like picking up your sick son.

Storytime

You are out running errands around town when your wife calls. You have a package to be picked up at the post office. You pick up your package and get into your car. A law enforcement officer pulls you over on the way home. Someone in line at the post office saw the outline of your gun in your shirt and turned you in for carrying a weapon on federal property.

This situation could have happened on any restricted property, like the Social Security Administration, the Bureau of Land Management, or an election polling place.

Storytime

You and your wife are starting your vacation to the Grand Canyon. To get there, you have to drive across the Navajo Indian Reservation. Your car gets a flat tire, and you pull off the road at a safe place to change it. Arizona is a bit hot, so you strip down to your T-shirt while working. A tribal police officer shows up to see if you need some help. He can see you have a weapon under your shirt. You show him your concealed-carry permit. Too bad, he says, Navajo tribal law doesn't recognize your concealed carry permit. You can't have a loaded weapon anywhere on the reservation. You object and say you are on a federal interstate highway and are under the protection of the Firearms Owner Protection Act. He says that's not entirely true. The Interstate is on an easement granted to the federal government by the tribe, and tribal laws still apply. You are supposed to have your unloaded weapon in one locked container and your ammunition in another locked container.

Storytime

You and your wife are out and about on the town. Your wife says you never take her out to dinner anymore, so you immediately pull into a fancy steakhouse. To help with the romance, you have a candle brought over and order a bottle of red wine. You have a wonderful dinner. As you are leaving, you run into her ex-husband. Evidently, he and his new wife aren't getting along very well, and he is in a bad mood. He starts an argument with you, and the rising voices result in the young hostess getting scared and calling the police. When they show up, the police separate you and ask for identification. One officer comments that you have a concealed-carry permit. The ex-husband overhears that and begins yelling, "He was drinking alcohol! With a gun!"

Storytime

You and your wife are having dinner at a restaurant. You had worked all day in the yard and have been drinking water at the restaurant like a fish. Your body finally catches up, and you have to go to the bathroom three times. You and your wife laugh about it. When you get home, you realize that you left your firearm on top of the toilet in the restaurant bathroom.

#

All of these Storytime scenarios can result in criminal charges against you. Depending on the US state you live in, these could be serious charges with mandatory prison sentences. *Therefore, we will add the name of the US state where you live and "Criminal Charges due to Concealed-Carry" to recognize this risk as a harm in our fact box.*

3.7 Law Enforcement

Think back to all the times you have interfaced with law enforcement during your life. Now imagine those same incidents occurring again, except you have a firearm on your person this time. Do any of those experiences improve?

When you CCF, your relationship with law enforcement is altered due to your possession of a lethal weapon. Misunderstandings between a CCF and law enforcement can be fatal. These misunderstandings can happen in different ways. For example, while a traffic stop is somewhat expected, law enforcement arriving unexpectedly in these other situations can be deadly:

- When you are investigating a burglary or trespassing on your property while armed.
- During a violent crime, when you are armed.
- In the immediate aftermath of a violent crime, when you are armed.

I'll discuss all of these situations later in the book. The essential item for this section is that when law enforcement arrives on a scene, they often have imperfect information. They may even have conflicting information regarding what has happened. While you may be a licensed concealed carrier and a law-abiding civilian, the law enforcement officer does not know that. Until the law enforcement officer has determined that you are not a threat, you'll be handled like you are a threat. The more dangerous the situation is, the worse it is for the CCF.

Another interaction can be a big problem for someone who has used lethal means to defend themselves: talking too much to law enforcement after a self-defense incident and hurting your legal standing in the case. This issue isn't specific to CCF, but people who choose to CCF may be impacted more than others.

People who CCF are often strong supporters of law enforcement. Additionally, law enforcement usually supports law-abiding civilians and their self-defense initiatives. A big reason for this support is that law enforcement often deals with bad actors that have successfully victimized good people. When law enforcement gets to handle a bad actor that *unsuccessfully* tried to victimize good people, that is a better experience for everyone in the community. However, interactions between law enforcement and people who CCF are much riskier than interactions between law enforcement and an unarmed civilian. This fact leads us to an **uncomfortable truth**: When interacting with law enforcement, the possession of a weapon on your person will not result in any benefits for that interaction. It can at best be neutral and at worst be detrimental, even lethally detrimental.

As a result, I will add "Interactions with Law Enforcement" as a harm in our fact box.

3.8 Community Harms

If you decide to CCF and have not previously owned a firearm, you will be introducing a firearm into your household for the first time. We do have the harm of unintentional injury/death listed. However, there is another harm as well. If your firearm is lost or stolen, it will likely enter the illegal market and could be used in future criminal activity. We want to make sure that we list this as a harm, although it is more of a community harm than a personal harm. A new firearm owner must plan to protect their firearm from theft.

This protection is not just in your home but in your vehicle as well. You may end up going to a destination that is a gun-free zone. As such, you may need to store your firearm securely in your vehicle. Needless to say, the glove box isn't sufficient. Even if you store your firearm securely, your car may be stolen, and the thief will have all the privacy they need to break into your secure storage. I will cover ideas for both the vehicle and the home to safely and securely store your firearms later in the book.

3.9 Violent Crime Victimization Rate

DGUs vs. Violent Crime Victimization

On our conceal-carry fact box, we have DGUs as a benefit. However, that does not tell us the background rate of criminal victimization. We may want to use the violent crime victimization rate, but it is essential to understand that DGUs could occur in other situations. For instance, burglary is not considered a violent crime. However, if you happened to run into a burglar with your gun in hand and the burglar ran away, it would be classified as a DGU. At the time of the incident, the victim has no idea if the offender is a burglar or an intruder intent on harming them. The victim doesn't have the luxury of knowing in advance whether an incident will turn violent and be classified as a violent crime. A better indication would be something called "Interpersonal Criminal Victimization." This term would designate a situation where the victim and offender interact in a way comparable to situations where a DGU could occur.

Unfortunately, it won't be easy to gather this data. We would have to pull information on trespassing, vandalism or property damage, and burglary and somehow distinguish when the victim and offender meet, as well as information on other situations like simple assault. This research would be challenging to do with any degree of quality. As such, I will use violent crime statistics. However, remember that DGUs can be higher than violent crime victimizations for the reasons given.

Male vs. Female Victimization

There should be two different violent crime victimization rates; one for women and one for men. This difference is because rape victims are predominately female. Although murder victims are predominately men, murder is a rare crime compared to rape, especially considering the unreported nature of rape. In short, if you are a man, factor out rape in your fact box for violent crime victimization.

Age

Understanding that violent crime impacts young people more than older people is essential. As we shall see later in the book, 40 years of age is a good age to reduce violent crime rates for both offenders and victims. If you are over 40, reduce your victimization by 66 percent or two-thirds as a rough rule of thumb.

DGUs

As we are working on a fact box for the concealed carry of a firearm, we should reduce the total number of DGUs by 70 to 80 percent because that represents the number of DGUs that happen while carrying a concealed firearm.

3.10 Preliminary Fact Box

Based on what we have covered so far, here is what our preliminary fact box for concealed carry would look like:

US State:
Rate
Violent Crime Victimization:
Benefit
CC Defensive Gun Uses:
Harms
Unintentional Death by CC Firearm:
Unintentional Injury by CC Firearm (better data needed):
Criminal Charges due to CC Firearm:
Interaction with Law Enforcement:
Lost or Stolen CC Firearm:
I live in Arizona, so I'll give an example for this state.

State and Rate

The UCR shows the rates of violent crime by the state. Using 2015 to 2019 data, I would list approximately three aggravated assaults per 1000 people, one robbery, one rape (I double the rape rate because it is a crime that very often goes unreported), and a minuscule rate for murder. The total would be five out of 1000 for a woman and four out of 1000 for a man.

Harm: Unintentional Death

We can use CDC WONDER to get this information. Here is an example for Arizona,[94] whose population is about seven million, but the cumulative total over the five years is 35,225,769.

ICD-10 113 Cause List	Deaths	Crude Rate Per 100,000
#Intentional self-harm (suicide) (*U03,X60-X84,Y87.0)	3,865	11.0
Intentional self-harm (suicide) by discharge of firearms (X72-X74)	3,865	11.0
#Assault (homicide) (*U01-*U02,X85-Y09,Y87.1)	1,421	4.0
Assault (homicide) by discharge of firearms (*U01.4,X93-X95)	1,421	4.0
Events of undetermined intent (Y10-Y34,Y87.2,Y89.9)	76	0.2
Discharge of firearms, undetermined intent (Y22-Y24)	76	0.2
#Legal intervention (Y35,Y89.0)	75	0.2
#Accidents (unintentional injuries) (V01-X59,Y85-Y86)	44	0.1
Nontransport accidents (W00-X59,Y86)	44	0.1
Accidental discharge of firearms (W32-W34)	44	0.1

The rate per 1000 for accidental death due to discharge of a firearm would be 0.001 per 1,000 people.

We still need to research the rest of the values, which I will discuss in the next section.

---

[94] https://clayeolsen.com/cdc-ucd—Read and agree with the restrictions. Select ICD-10 113 Cause List, US State Arizona, Years 2015, 2016, 2017, 2018, and 2019. Select Injury Intent and Mechanism. Then select All Causes of Death, then Firearm. Press Send.

3.11 Data Gathering Methodologies

Unfortunately, gathering data on the harms of CCF is quite problematic for several reasons:

1. There are no "uniform judicial reports" to query for data on plea bargains or court cases and their decisions. Court cases must be researched by hand, and laws and their enforcement vary from state to state, so it would be challenging to generalize nationally.

2. Because the harms of CCF usually result from the negligence of the concealed carrier, and most people don't jump up and down with excitement to admit when they've made a mistake, asking concealed carriers themselves may not give us the most accurate data.

3. Any government-run entity, like the CDC or ATF, that attempts to get this information would likely be treated with suspicion and distrust by people who CCF for fear that the government was gathering data to ban or regulate firearms.

4. An entire industry supports CCF, including gun manufacturers, training organizations, ammunition manufacturers, and insurance providers. Unfortunately, this industry has a lot to lose if the harms of CCF are significant. Historically, it has not boded well for researchers who point out problems like these.

These are substantial problems. *Ultimately, it will be up to people and groups who care about effective self-defense to gather this data.* Here are some suggestions:

1. Because many states allow CCF without a permit, CCF trainers could be asked to do a yearly anonymous survey of their former trainees in that state. This survey would provide data on the number of CCFs, how often they carry, DGUs, whether a DGU was reported to law enforcement, etc. We

may find some details about harms, but I'm not sure if this is the best way.

2.   We could do an anonymous survey of the various criminal defense attorneys working in the state. This survey would gather statistics on (1) the harms of CCF—namely, whether a concealed carrier faced criminal charges due to the firearm; and (2) how many successful cases involved self-defense and CCF. Again, it would need to be general in scope to protect privacy, but we should learn a lot.

3.   All *civilian* DGU cases reported to law enforcement should be researched and their circumstances outlined. *I believe all civilian DGUs should be studied, much like traffic accidents are investigated.* Understanding how the firearm was used defensively will influence civilian firearms training. Also, the circumstances can shed considerable light on prevention techniques (i.e., how the situation could have been avoided or recognized before the DGU). For example, the victim/offender relationship, the location, whether alcohol/drugs were involved, the time and day, etc.

Ultimately, data gathering for our concealed-carry fact box is in its infancy, and there is much work to be done here. However, I hope that the fact box we've developed so far can be a starting point in this endeavor. Unfortunately, these facts lead us to an **uncomfortable truth**: Data and statistics around the harms experienced with the concealed carry of a firearm are not being researched and gathered.

3.12 Evaluating the Concealed Carry of a Firearm

In this section, I do not dispute the benefit of lethal weapons. Law enforcement carries lethal weapons because they are the primary weapon of their greatest existential threat: the stranger who is an armed violent criminal. What is up for discussion is whether an ordinary civilian needs to carry a concealed lethal weapon based upon the threats they face.

3.12.1 Benefits and Their Circumstances

Clearly, there are situations where carrying a firearm is required. Civilians stopping mass shooters is one such case. However, the data we have looked at shows that *the combination of carrying a firearm and requiring a firearm is much less common.* When I say requiring a firearm, I mean discharging the firearm. In short, lethal force was needed in the victim's opinion. Let's review:

- CCF is responsible for around 20 to 30 percent of all DGUs.
- Firearms are not discharged in about 80 percent of all DGUs.
- More research is needed to focus on the 20 percent that were carrying. How many discharged their firearm versus showing or telling their offender they were armed?

Also, there is an essential point about what we are comparing here:

- The main comparison isn't against unarmed civilians, but against civilians that have their firearm securely stored in their home or securely stored in their vehicle, *but not carried on their person.* Carrying firearms in this manner would still result in most DGUs (80 percent).

There seems to be *a minority of circumstances* where the combination of *carrying a firearm on their person* and needing lethal force *is required.* Stopping a mass murderer is an obvious one. I feel that this is a ripe topic for further research on DGUs.

Yet another factor that needs to be considered to further reduce these circumstances would be clarity about your mission. Here is what Varg Freeborn, author of *Violence of Mind*, writes:

The very first step in any training is to identify the mission you will train for. "What is your mission?" I always ask this question first thing in the morning for every level 1 course I teach. It is amazing how often people cannot clearly answer it. If you are not clear what your mission is, you have very little guidance on how to properly equip, train and prepare. I know this sounds simple, but in the hundreds of courses that I have taught, when I ask this question most people either cannot answer or get it completely wrong.

What is a wrong answer? It is wrong when it contradicts your OWN goals. For example, someone who trains to protect themselves and their family but intends to run head first into a fight for a stranger when neither that person or his or her family is endangered. Noble or not, if your mission is to protect yourself and make it home with your family every night, running into any random deadly situation you see is not in line with that mission. You could lose your life, and it would not have been in the defense of you or your family. Your family is left without protection.[95]

Many men who CCF feel they have an obligation to stop violent criminals in the community regardless of whether their loved ones are threatened. I think that is great if *that is your mission*. However, to understand Freeborn's point, let's use the following example mission: "*To protect and provide for my family while allowing us the freedom and resources to enjoy life.*" If this is your mission, it will prevent you from involving yourself unnecessarily in other people's violence. To understand this better, imagine if you are married with kids. You and your spouse both carry a concealed firearm. Now ask yourself, "what violence do I want my spouse involved in that doesn't revolve around protecting us or our children?" I suspect that would be a short list. This fact leads us to an **uncomfortable truth**: Clarity about your mission will likely reduce the number of violent situations you are willing to involve yourself in, which in turn, will reduce DGUs.

The main point is that if the circumstances for carrying and needing a lethal weapon are not very common, we must consider the harms. In short, if 99 out of 100 people CCF and never need to carry a lethal weapon, are these 99 needlessly exposing themselves to unintended consequences of carrying a lethal weapon? Let's look at the harms.

---

[95] Freeborn (2018)

3.12.2 Harms and Their Circumstances

Harms

Each self-defense method has benefits and harms specific to that method. It is also appropriate to recognize that the implemented self-defense solution should be justified based on the relevant risks. However, there is a widespread objection to this approach that I've heard in many firearm classes. It goes something like this: "Regardless of how likely being attacked by a violent criminal is, it does happen. Would you rather be armed or unarmed if it happens to you?" This question is conceptually similar to testing for a rare cancer: "This cancer is rare but extremely deadly. You likely don't have it, but why not be sure and test today?"

Both questions assume there are no harms to the rare cancer testing or CCF. This assumption is why we use a fact box so that the people who experience the harms can make the appropriate decision regarding risk. Most people don't ask what happens if the cancer test says I have cancer, but I don't, nor do they ask what the test exposes you to and what those risks are. For example, if the cancer test exposes you to radiation, the radiation exposure could equally cause a different rare cancer. The fact box provides the facts about benefits and harms and helps the person who will experience the harms make an informed decision.

The same is true with CCF. For example, if the violent crime rate is five out of 1000 and the harm rate of CCF is 10 out of 1000, then the fact box would say that you are twice as likely to experience a harm with CCF as you would be a benefit. If the rates were flipped, you would be twice as likely to need your firearm to protect yourself as you would be to experience a harm. This reason is why collecting empirical data on the harms of CCF is essential—*so an informed decision can be made by the person experiencing the harms.*

If you CCF to protect yourself and your loved ones and experience a harm listed in the CCF fact box, you've contradicted your own goals. In other words, you've failed at your mission. As I've stated previously, at least in Arizona, a civilian who carries a firearm and inadvertently commits a gun crime has committed a felony with a mandatory prison sentence.

This fact makes defendants seek a plea bargain, which could still result in a felony and prison time. Let's hear again from Varg Freeborn's *Violence of Mind* on what prison is like (language warning):

> A plea bargain means conviction, and conviction [maybe] means prison time. Prison is like dying, except you get to stay alive and watch what happens after you die, how everyone moves on without you, but you still get to hear all about it. It is truly a living death. Your friends will move on and forget you. Your spouse might hang in there for a while but eventually they will move on, too. You may not know the details either, you may have to just wonder. Did she meet someone else? When did it start? Was she already thinking about leaving before this? No one owes you any answers, and you will have all the time in the world to wonder about it all. It will drive you crazy. Everyone will move on with their lives just like you were laid in the ground. You'll live out your days in captivity with predators much meaner than you, while your spouse lays down with someone else and your kids get their school clothes from some other guy. Or maybe they don't get any school clothes. Hell, maybe they get beat and you do hear about it. But you can't do shit about it. Nothing. *You are powerless to protect them*, and they know it, too.[96]

There really isn't anything to add to that description.

The major problem is that many people who take self-defense training don't believe they can experience the harms listed in the fact box. Why is that? As I've touched on before, it is because they are being trained using a law enforcement curriculum, and they are usually trained by former law enforcement officers. So I will be very blunt here: Return to the Storytimes in Section 3.6 and substitute the ordinary civilian who is concealed carrying a firearm with a law enforcement officer that is open carrying a firearm. You'll find that it is highly unlikely there will be criminal charges levied against the law enforcement officer in these circumstances.

---

[96] Freeborn (2018)

I'm bringing up these points not to criticize law enforcement but to convey an **uncomfortable truth**: The reality is that ordinary civilians do not have the same legal protections as law enforcement regarding lethal weapons, and it is a fundamental mistake to think that they do.

A Commonsense Analysis

As I've indicated, we don't have a lot of empirical data on experiencing CCF harms. Unfortunately, some people believe that absence of evidence is the same as evidence of absence. That is not the case. Only by gathering data can we evaluate that data. If the data is not gathered, we cannot assume anything about it. What we do have is pretty tiny, like unintentional fatalities (i.e., negligent discharge or a child finding a loaded firearm). However, we can go through a commonsense circumstance analysis.

1. Ordinary civilians will interact with law enforcement more than they will be victimized by violent crimes. An ordinary civilian carrying a loaded firearm will not result in any benefits for this interaction.
2. Ordinary civilians will handle their firearms more than they will use them in a DGU. A firearm that has a chambered round is much more dangerous to handle than one that does not.
3. Carrying a loaded firearm on your person is more likely to violate the law, such as unknowingly going into a gun-free zone. These law violations could result in life altering criminal charges.

These three things explain why when I carry a firearm, I carry in a certain way, which I will describe in later sections. Given the DGU statistics we've went through, a less-than-lethal weapon is a valid option for carrying in public. These DGU statistics also show that a properly secured firearm is a valid option for the home and in your vehicle. Again, we shall discuss these issues in depth in later sections.

3.12.3 Conclusion

Let's review our mission for ordinary civilians: *To protect and provide for my family while allowing us the freedom and resources to enjoy life.* Given our definition of an ordinary civilian and the statistics we've covered, the circumstances where a lethal weapon is required to be carried on our person are not common. In addition, there seem to be far more common circumstances where a harm could be experienced, but unfortunately, there is not enough empirical evidence to decide.

Ultimately, the person experiencing the benefits and harms must make the decision, not someone else. I've provided the statistics and I'll describe what I do in later sections, but I certainly cannot speak for you.

Conclusion to Part I

Understanding Part I is vital to the rest of the book. Because we have covered a lot of ground, I'll provide the key takeaways for each section.

Section 1

Ordinary civilians are not experienced in violence and require someone or some group to explain what violent crime entails. The news media slants coverage toward injurious violence and firearms, as that style of story keeps people watching their channel or viewing their web pages. Self-defense classes bring in former law enforcement and military members to teach and develop their curriculum, which is again biased toward threats they most commonly face: strangers who are armed violent criminals. This two-punch combination leaves ordinary civilians believing that their greatest threat is a stranger who is an armed violent criminal, often acting in a public location.

Furthermore, self-defense training based on law enforcement curriculum leaves essential details out because it assumes the audience is law enforcement. Thus, an ordinary civilian is unprepared to interact with law enforcement while carrying a lethal weapon and untrained in how their legal standing is different than a law enforcement officer.

Section 2

A deep dive into violent crime statistics showed us that most violent crime does not result in a victim's injury. Also, the circumstances between non-injurious violent crime and injurious violent crime are usually different. Lastly, most injurious violent crime circumstances most often involve offenders the victim knew, locations where the victim felt comfortable, and lethal weapons aren't often used.

Section 3

Leveraging the fact box developed to evaluate preventative health screenings, CCF is evaluated as a self-defense method in terms of benefits and harms. An immediate problem is that we lack good statistical data around the harms. With regards to the benefits, we see that over 80 percent of DGUs happen when the victim is not carrying and, importantly, around 80 percent of the time, the firearm is not discharged. Lastly, when assessed against the injurious violent crime threats most ordinary civilians face, there is a minority of circumstances where the lethality of a firearm is *required*. The danger is that CCF is believed to be more effective than it actually is, and as a result, the harms may outweigh the benefits for most ordinary civilians.

The Uncomfortable Truths of Part I

These little tidbits are scattered throughout Part I. I've gathered them up and put them here in one place:

- If you were victimized in a violent crime and you were injured, the offender was likely someone you knew (from the Introduction).
- If your knowledge of violent crime comes from news programming, you will likely perceive murder as being far more common

than it is. In addition, you will probably assume that firearms are the most common weapons used in the commission of violent crimes.

- There is an unstated assumption in self-defense training that the predominant violence threat to law enforcement officers is the same predominant violence threat that ordinary civilians face.
- Ordinary civilians will interact with law enforcement more often than they will experience a violent crime. When you carry a weapon for self-defense, misunderstandings between you and law enforcement mean the primary threat to your well-being could very well be from a law enforcement officer rather than a criminal.
- The odds of dying from suicides, falls, and opioid overdoses, are far ahead of gun assaults. In terms of accidents, dying from an accidental gun discharge is rarer than having a fatal sunstroke.
- The amount of violent crime where the victim knows the offender is underreported in our crime statistics. This fact makes violent crimes where the offender is a stranger seem more significant in comparison.
- Women are the victims of injurious violent crime more than men. Men are victims of non-injurious violent crime more than women.
- UCR statistics do not distinguish between violent crimes occurring in the context of criminal activity and violent crimes involving non-criminals, do not account for whether the participants had previous criminal records, do not account for the toxicity level of the participants, and do not account for whether the participants are legally allowed to reside where the crime was committed. It is anyone's guess whether these situations significantly influence violent crime statistics.
- Aggravated assault and robbery, not homicide, make up around 89 percent of all violent crimes in the period studied (2015-2019). Homicide represents only 1.3 percent of all violent crime.

- Two-thirds of aggravated assaults and robberies do not result in the victim being injured.

- Firearms are rarely used in injurious aggravated assault and injurious robbery.

- The most common weapon robbers use is no weapon at all.

- Rape is almost always perpetrated by someone the victim knows. It happens in a place the victim feels comfortable, weapons are not used, the victim usually doesn't seek treatment for her injuries,[97] and the victim rarely reports the crime to law enforcement.

- It is a mistake to assume that DGUs always involve someone who is carrying a concealed firearm. It is correct to say that most DGUs do not involve someone who is carrying a concealed firearm.

- A person who lawfully carries a concealed firearm is likely overestimating the number of mass shooting situations they can successfully defend against.

- The vast majority of DGUs did not result in the firearm being discharged, and almost a third of the time, the firearm did not need to be displayed to be an effective deterrent.

- The number of DGUs is not easily gathered with our traditional crime statistics reporting via the UCR and NCVS. Any source which claims to know the number of DGUs needs to be scrutinized extensively. In fact, changes to the law to encourage law-abiding firearm owners to report DGUs may be required.

- When interacting with law enforcement, the possession of a weapon on your person will not result in any benefits for that interaction. It can at best be neutral and at worst be detrimental, even lethally detrimental.

- Data and statistics around the harms experienced with the concealed carry of a firearm are not being researched and gathered.

---

[97] See Appendix B. This fact is analyzed in using N-DASH for "Injured – Not Treated."

- Clarity about your mission will likely reduce the number of violent situations you are willing to involve yourself in, which in turn, will reduce DGUs.
- The reality is that ordinary civilians do not have the same legal protections as law enforcement regarding lethal weapons, and it is a fundamental mistake to think that they do.

Moving Forward

The rest of the book is about developing self-defense strategies for ordinary civilians that can be evaluated alongside other techniques, such as CCF. For example, making small lifestyle changes can dramatically reduce your chances of being victimized. Another example is taking a look at the people you are just starting to get to know and scrutinizing them to see if they may be a threat. Lastly, violent crime statistics show homes are a surprisingly popular location for violent crime. I show how to prepare your home against violent crime yet not leave you vulnerable to more common "uncommon situations," such as a house fire.

Planning, preparation, prevention, and avoidance are key themes throughout the rest of the book. I focus primarily on things an ordinary civilian has a large amount of control over, even if they may be only tangentially associated with violent crime circumstances. For example, I cover vehicle maintenance as it is something a civilian has a lot of control over. If your vehicle fails in a remote location, you can be at risk of robbery or rape. A properly maintained vehicle can reduce the likelihood of that event.

These are not mutually exclusive techniques by any means, and many people who CCF can benefit from the rest of the book, as well as those who do not feel CCF is right for them. Keep in mind that I continue to provide commentary on situations where the civilian may be armed with a lethal weapon. I also offer extensive advice for law enforcement interactions and legal implications when you have a lethal weapon, as well as if you have a less-than-lethal weapon.

PART II

Strangers, Criminals, and Public Locations

Most self-defense books and training, on the other hand, begin, for the most part, with the premise that you're already under attack and this is how you fight your way out. Wouldn't it make more sense to steal a page from the bodyguard's playbook and not get into trouble in the first place?

—Nick Hughes, *How to Be Your Own Bodyguard*

4.1 Preliminary Considerations

The rest of the book will cover a lot of ground. I don't expect these various preparation and prevention strategies to be adopted without a great deal of thought and consideration. I covered the fact box so extensively in Section 3 because many of you reading this book will need to develop your own fact boxes for other defensive methods. There are subjective considerations that will vary from person to person. To be sure, I'll point out obvious benefits and harms. However, everyone will need to be honest about their abilities and needs. Using the fact box is an excellent way to do just that. Let's go through a Storytime to see what I mean.

Storytime

Georgiana is in her late seventies and a widow. She lives in a retirement community and has a wonderful network of friends. She spends most of her time doing activities with her friends within the community. Once a week, she does her errands and grocery shopping. One day, she was loading the trunk of her car with groceries when a woman took her purse out of her shopping cart and started running away. Georgiana yelled for help, and another patron gave chase. The woman dropped her purse and continued running. Georgiana was sitting in the car when the patron returned with her purse. The whole episode made her light-headed, and she almost fell.

#

Although not a victim of violent crime, Georgiana could become very afraid of being victimized by crime. Unfortunately, the elderly often overestimate the likelihood of being victimized by crime, probably because of their vulnerability and fragility. In fact, with a bit of reflection, Georgiana may realize that grocery shopping in general, with different people bustling around and kids running through the store, could be the most dangerous thing she does. She could have an accidental collision while shopping, which could cause a fall. Falls are a top threat for the elderly, far more dangerous than violent crime for their age group.[98]

As an alternative, Georgiana may ask her kids to do her grocery shopping for her, or she may decide to have her groceries delivered, or she may shop online and then pick them up at a designated location. All of these things reduce her risk of crime (and falls). There are a lot of benefits, and the only harm for her may be learning how to online grocery shop.

This type of decision making is what falls under the umbrella of holistic self-defense. Almost becoming a crime victim made Georgiana think about her vulnerabilities. She may decide to get her groceries a

---

[98] https://clayeolsen.com/falls

different way to reduce the likelihood of crime as well as the likelihood of falling. However, someone other than Georgiana may have a different lifestyle. They may be widowed and not be in a retirement community. Perhaps they dedicate a whole day to running errands and shopping because that is their socialization time. Getting rid of that socialization time could cause depression or make life a lot less fun.

All in all, it would be a mistake to read through this section of the book and simply implement what is discussed without thoroughly evaluating the harms or downsides, which can differ between individuals.

Legal Issues

In what follows, we apply what we've learned from the statistics on violent crime to develop strategies to help us prevent becoming a victim. We will also discuss defenses we can use should our efforts at prevention fail. Many of these self-defense strategies will require legal consultation before implementation. An attorney on retainer is a good option for these consultations. You must consult your attorney about various defensive strategies to ensure they are legal in your state. You don't want those defensive strategies to get you into trouble with the law or have evidence thrown out of court. Let's work through a Storytime as an example.

Storytime

Rebecca is a single woman who lives in an apartment downtown. In her job, she meets a wide variety of people. Sometimes, there is a man that sparks a dating interest, and she would like to get to know him more. Anytime a man is over to her apartment for the first time, Rebecca turns on two hidden cameras in the dining room and living room; the rooms she will be in when entertaining a new guest. Outside her apartment, she has a sign that says the premises are under audio and video surveillance, so she believes she is legally covered. One day she is getting to know a man better over lunch, and she suddenly falls ill. Luckily, a friend arrives unexpectedly, and they convince the man she is in good hands and he can leave. When she recovers, she remembers that she has camera footage of the lunch. She reviews it and discovers the man put something in her drink while she was getting food from the fridge. She decides to contact an attorney to press charges against the man. However, the attorney says her evidence is inadmissible because she needs written permission to audio and video record someone in the state she resides in.

#

I chose to go through an audio and video recording example because there are substantial legal and privacy issues. All in all, these issues could lead to a much different strategy for Rebecca to get to know people.

You don't want to be like Rebecca and learn about these things later. You want to know them before spending time and money on them. The best approach for these issues is to have an attorney on retainer. Usually, you'll get steep discounts on their hourly rate just by having them on a retainer. In addition, you can consult with your attorney about the prevention and protection strategies you are considering and they can provide legal advice. I live in Arizona and have been using the law firm Attorneys for Freedom, which has an excellent retainer program.[99] However, even if you are not in Arizona, you can review their plans and compare them to what attorneys in your state may offer.

4.2 Defenses Against Robbery

Our analysis of robberies in Section 2 concluded that robbery is a violent crime where a stranger can injure you in a public location. We will treat robberies committed by someone you know and robberies that occur at or near your home in later sections. In this section, we will look at protecting yourself against strangers who seek to rob you in a public area. Public areas are places like highways, alleyways, parking lots, parking garages, parks, etc. If you notice something, you'll see that many of

---

[99] https://clayeolsen.com/aff-3

these areas have something in common: vehicles. *Walking to and from your vehicle is a time when you are the most vulnerable to robbery in a public location.* Obviously, driving to places and doing things is a fundamental part of American life, whether for fun, chores, or business. We don't want to forgo those things because we are worried about a robbery, but we do want to handle ourselves more carefully. These changes are typically small and can drastically reduce our chances of being victimized by robbery.

When many people imagine being robbed, they think of their robbers as being masked and having firearms. However, most of the time, robbers use close-quarter weapons or no weapons. This fact means the robbers have to get close to you. *Therefore, how you approach strangers or let strangers approach you is critical in mitigating the risk of robbery.*

Vacations are also a fun part of life. Many of us pack up the family and take a road trip. As a result, I'll also cover proper vehicle maintenance, safety kits, and travel tips for staying safe. Many of us have cell phones, and when we travel, we no longer have to look for "call boxes" in case we break down on the freeways. However, I recently finished a 2,500-mile road trip and was shocked at how often I didn't have cell phone reception. I'll cover an alternative way to communicate in these circumstances. With that in mind, I'll also discuss other technologies you can use to help you avoid being robbed and track your valuables if they are stolen from you. These tracking devices can help law enforcement get your valuables back and get the robbers off the street.

Regardless of our prevention steps, we may find ourselves in a robbery situation. You'll need to ask yourself whether fighting to protect your valuables aligns with your mission. This decision is personal and needs to be addressed on an individual-by-individual basis.

Let's get started.

4.2.1 The Concealed Carry of a Firearm and Robbery

In this section, we are looking at robberies where the offender is a stranger, and the location is a public area. With this background in mind, three common situations could occur:

1. Confrontation/Refusal/Running: The robbers confront the victim and demand the victim's items. The victim refuses and is injured. Alternatively, the victim takes off running, the robbers give chase, and catch the victim.

2. Confrontation/Compliance: The robbers confront the victim and demand their items. The victim complies, but the robbers injure the victim anyway.

3. Surprise/Jumped: The robbers surprise the victim, injure the victim, and take the victim's items. This situation could be a stranger who can get close to you and then surprise you, or it could be you never saw them coming. The assumption here is that the robber did not use a weapon like a firearm but used "no weapon" based upon our statistical analysis.

Confrontation/Refusal/Running is mainly about your mission and how it relates to your valuables. In short, it is your choice to refuse or run. For Confrontation/Compliance, we do not have statistics indicating how often robbery victims complied and were still injured. I suspect this is not common in dealing with strangers and public areas simply because robbers are after your valuables and not you. If they get your valuables, any more time they spend on you increases their chance of being caught and injured. The last item, Surprise/Jumped, is what I will focus on as I feel it represents the most likely of the three situations that you have little to no control over.

We can speculate that many robberies are committed by individuals addicted to illegal drugs. They don't have any weapons because anything of value they likely sold. So, it is possible that many unreported DGUs were from addicts trying to jump a victim. When the victim turns out to be armed, they flee. Thus, the argument might go, simply CCF, and don't worry about where you park or what time it is.

This technique is fine and dandy as long as you see the robbers before they hit you. If you don't, you could be in a lot of trouble. You will need to defend yourself, and *you are starting at an incredible disadvantage*. Even if you CCF, you need physical defensive skills to prevent "weapon overreliance." For example, if your assailant is hitting you in the face while you are still trying to draw your weapon, you will likely get knocked out before you can use it. So instead, your focus should be on blocking those strikes and separating yourself from your attacker. Unfortunately, many concealed carriers I know do not have physical defense training, and some do not have the health for it.

Once you have fought back and kept yourself from being knocked out, you'll need to create some separation between yourself and your attacker. The next skill set you need is Close-Quarters Combat Training—the ability to draw and use a weapon in close quarters against a determined foe. Unfortunately, many people who CCF have never had this training either.

The point is that CCF is not as easy of a solution as it may seem to be for these types of robberies. Luckily, the self-defense methodologies we employ against robbery are not mutually exclusive. They can be used in conjunction with CCF if desired. So, let's cover some of the things you can do to make your risk of robbery plummet.

4.2.2 From the Vehicle and Back

> Morons. I've got morons on my team. Nobody is going to rob us going down the mountain. We have got no money going down the mountain. When we have got the money, on the way back, then you can sweat.
>
> —Percy, from the movie *Butch Cassidy and the Sundance Kid*

One of our most vulnerable times for robbery in a public area is when we leave or approach our vehicle. This vulnerability is exposed in parking lots, parking garages, streets that take us to/from parking, alleyways as shortcuts to/from our destination, etc.

Let's go through a simple Storytime.

Storytime

A petite lady leaves a bar alone around midnight to walk to her car. She is on her cell phone, laughing—she seems like she has been having a good time. She ends her call, walks to a nearby ATM, and withdraws some cash. She is walking to her car and begins texting on her cell phone.

#

Even for an unarmed robber, this lady is an easy victim. She has cash, is likely not armed (as bars typically don't allow weapons) and is distracted. A robber can simply punch her out as soon as she enters a darker part of the parking lot or gets close to her car. Even if the robber is armed, why should he bother talking to her? So she can be a witness at his trial? It is less risky to knock her out. Her phone goes flying and her purse is ripe for the picking (perhaps some jewelry). The robber will be long gone before someone finds her (or she wakes up) and calls law enforcement. What is she going to know about the robber to help law enforcement? *Nothing*.

Here are some additional Storytimes. In what follows, ask yourself how these situations could have been avoided or prevented. I'll add my two cents in italics after the story.

The Pizza Place

You are having a party at your house. It is almost 10 p.m. and everyone is hungry. They pool their money and have enough for five large pizzas. They call the pizza place downtown, but they won't deliver because it is too late. They will allow someone to pick them up if they can arrive by 10:30 p.m. You draw the short straw and have to run downtown to the pizza place. You park next to a car, get out, and shut the door. As soon as your car door closes, a person hunched down in front of the car next to you gets up and walks between the two vehicles, blocking you from going forward. You hear something behind you and see another person between the two cars, blocking you from behind.

#

The combination of being alone, at night, with money is what got you into trouble. First alternative: you could have called Grubhub or DoorDash, where someone else picks up your food and delivers it to you. Second alternative: proper planning—knowing you were going to have a party, you could have stocked up on some cheap frozen pizzas, which would have been less expensive and less risky. Third Alternative: proper planning could have allowed you to get your food delivered earlier and safer from the pizza place you wanted. Last and least desirable: recognizing the potential danger of going alone to the pizza place late at night, you could have taken several bigger and tougher people from the party. A larger group would make a more challenging target for unarmed robbers.

Asking For Directions

You dress to impress and you have a nice car. You go to the mall and park in the back of the parking lot so you won't get any door dings. As you leave your vehicle, you notice a guy approaching you. As he gets closer, he says, "Excuse me, sir, I'm a bit lost. I'm supposed to meet my girlfriend, and I'm late. Could you direct me to the AMC movie theater?" The theater is directly behind you, about a mile away. You say sure and turn to point toward where the theater is located.

#

You have a nice car and it looks like you have money. Unfortunately, you are in a remote location of a parking lot. Many of us like to be helpful, but this guy knows exactly where the theater is. Either he will slam the back of your head with a weapon, or when your eyes swing back around, you will get a right hook to the face. Your wallet, cell phone, jewelry, and possibly your car will be gone when you regain consciousness. Parking closer to the entrance where there are more people and security is one better alternative. Taking an Uber/Lyft for errands like this is also an option. If you can't avoid this situation, always keep your eyes on the stranger and maintain an appropriate distance. If he starts to get too close, be polite but assertive and back up if you need to so you can maintain distance. You should stand in a way that allows you to defend yourself against a sudden attack. If he begins to get hostile, he may be trying to get his adrenaline going for an attack. At this juncture, you may have to put your hand on your weapon (or pretend to if you don't have a weapon) so it is clear you are armed and ready. If he leaves you alone, wait until he is far away, get in your car, and go elsewhere to shop.

Late Work Night

Your kid had a doctor's appointment in the morning. By the time you got to work, the parking lot was full, and you had to park across the street. To make up for the time you missed in the morning, you work until about 10 p.m. that night. You step out of your work; the parking lot is empty. You can see your car across the street and start walking toward it. You start to text your spouse that you are on your way home.

#

Recognizing the danger in this situation is essential here. If your job allows you to get away for a couple of minutes, you could have moved your car closer to the entrance earlier in the day. If your job has security personnel, you could ask the security guard to escort you to your vehicle. Having your spouse pick you up at the entrance is another option. You can then decide whether there is any risk of getting into your car from your spouse's car. If you are distracted, like texting on your phone, your instincts are in hibernation. You must stay aware.

The Concert

One of your favorite bands is playing at a small venue in town. Unfortunately, parking is a nightmare; you have to park a couple of blocks away. You are running a bit late because it took so long to find a parking spot, so you decide to take a shortcut through an alleyway. You come across a large dumpster rolled into the alleyway about halfway there. There isn't much room to get by.

#

The dumpster acts as a funnel, forcing people to take a specific path to get around it. That path has plenty of advantages for potential attackers and zero advantages for you. There is no good choice here except avoidance. Being dropped off and picked up in front of the venue, either by a rideshare or friend, would be a much better choice.

The Late Flight

Your flight was delayed and came in much later than expected. It is around midnight when you get to your car in the airport parking lot. You haven't seen a soul since you got off the airport tram. You look around, unlock your vehicle, and get in. As you back up, you hear a thump and see a man on the ground writhing in pain. You are scared that you hit him and quickly get out to see if he is okay.

#

Civilians are much easier to victimize when they feel they've done something wrong. If you've been in a large city, you know that homeless people can store things under your car or even sleep under your vehicle, depending on the situation. You don't know whether you are being set up to be robbed or whether you hurt someone. Again, nighttime, remote parking, and no people make a recipe for disaster. You could have asked airport security for an escort or contacted a rideshare, friend, or spouse. Your car will still be there tomorrow at noon when it would be much safer to pick up.

The Late Dinner

You are having dinner at a fancy restaurant with your spouse. You are the last couple there when you pay the bill. You head out to the far reaches of the parking lot where your car is parked. You notice another car parked within inches of the driver's side door. You can't believe it. What moron would park their car in an empty parking lot right next to yours?

#

Here is a situation where someone is hoping to escalate a situation. As soon as you complain about the vehicle, suddenly the "owner" of the car appears and says something, "What did you say???" While arguing with the driver, his buddy gets you from behind, and they both beat you (then take your stuff). Or his buddy puts a weapon to your spouse's head and they take your valuables. Again, avoiding this situation is the key.

In these Storytimes, I've tried to showcase the vulnerability of walking to and from your vehicle. In some cases, you may have an opportunity to defend yourself. But, in other cases, you'll likely be knocked out before having the opportunity to defend yourself.

Ride Sharing

One way to avoid robbery situations, like the combination of nighttime activities and remote parking spots, is to use a ride-sharing service like Lyft or Uber. If you are using these services to pick you up at a place of business, you can stay inside among people and employees and watch the driver's approach on your phone. When they get close, you can step outside right in front of your location and get into the car. Also, you must make a conscious effort to be a great passenger because Lyft/Uber drivers will rate you on this. If your rating dips too low, you may find that no driver wants to pick you up. If you are partying with friends and some have had a bit too much to drink, make them use their Lyft/Uber application rather than you! Don't forget that a ride from a reliable friend is also an option and cheaper! They can text you when they arrive.

Planning

Planning is another excellent way to avoid these situations. For example, I've found that Sunday morning is the best time to grocery shop and fill up your gas tank in my town. It isn't crowded, it is easy to park where cameras are located, and the parking lots are empty. In addition, you can approach your vehicle from multiple angles and see anyone around it.

Many grocery stores now allow you to shop online and pick your groceries up in a designated location. This option is reasonable because the pickup location is usually close to the entrance and in view of many security cameras. In addition, many store employees will be milling about that area.

You could have groceries/food delivered to your home. However, you should review Part V: Home Defense to ensure you aren't opening yourself up to any attacks or delivery drivers "casing" your house for themselves (if they entertain burglary side work) or their burglar buddies. Of course, this is also true for Lyft/Uber drivers who drop you off at home.

Work

Ride-sharing services are not economical to take to work every day. However, a job that allows you to work from home a lot or even occasionally will help to reduce robbery opportunities, especially if you don't work the standard 9 to 5.

Carpooling seems like another good option because carpool locations at a job site are often close to an entrance, and there is safety in numbers. However, your fellow carpoolers could be people you don't know well. They could learn a lot about you in six months just by listening to what you say during the commute. Be sure to read Part IV: The People You Know.

Carrying Valuables

A wedding ring is usually the most expensive (and irreplaceable) valuable we carry on our person in everyday situations. This wedding ring is fine if you are at a friend's house for an afternoon barbecue. If you are going to be having a late-night dinner at a place you have never been, however, you may want to temporarily replace it with a simple gold band to reduce the chance of robbery. It gets the point across but has little monetary value. You should use a similar approach for all your high-dollar jewelry—consider where you are going and when and plan accordingly.

There are other, less common situations. For example, we may need to withdraw cash from an Automated Teller Machine (ATM) instead of making an electronic transfer. Going to/from an ATM can immediately put a target on your back. If the amount isn't large and you don't need it immediately, you might consider withdrawing some extra cash using your debit card each week while grocery shopping.

What goes for a bank also goes for a jewelry store or any place where you might purchase a "highly valuable, easily stolen" item, although these are less common situations. When they do occur, the combination of a friend and a rideshare service is often a good approach. When the rideshare approaches, you and your friend can get in together. Also, if what you bought can be concealed rather than showcased in a bag with a high-end name on it, do so.

In these situations, you must put yourself in a robber's shoes. Am I making it obvious that I am carrying valuable items? Am I making it easy for someone to rob me? If I needed money to feed my child and was desperate to rob someone else to get it, what would I look for in a potential victim?

Awareness

We focus on reducing risk, but that is not a substitute for awareness. Several self-defense books have been written about awareness, and you can find a lot of good information online. I recommend reading *Left of Bang* by Patrick Van Horne and Jason Riley.[100]

Awareness is essential to reducing your risk of robbery. However, your ability to maintain heightened awareness is limited. When combined with steps to reduce your risk, the amount of time you need to maintain a heightened level of awareness drops significantly and is much more sustainable. For example, parking and walking to a concert requires a very different heightened awareness duration than taking an Uber/Lyft.

---

[100] Horne and Riley (2014)

Summary

The combination of nighttime, a remote parking location, and a lack of people should be an immediate red flag for a potential robbery. Planning to avoid those situations is the best. If you cannot avoid the situation, don't hesitate to call a spouse or friend to pick you up or schedule a Lyft/ Uber ride. You can always pick up your vehicle later when it is safer to do so. When carrying valuables, don't make it obvious. Use common sense, friends, and rideshares.

4.2.3 Strangers and Help

What does your mission say about accepting help from strangers? What does your mission say about helping strangers?

Sometimes we take road trips that require jumping on the highway for several minutes or several hours. One of the worst things that can happen in this situation is for our vehicle to fail. Sometimes it is simply a flat tire. Other times, it may be more serious. Unfortunately, these are situations that robbers can exploit. Let's talk about the first thing you can do to help prevent this from happening.

Prevention: Good Vehicle Maintenance

Your local dealer's service department probably has a comprehensive service schedule for your vehicle. Unfortunately, these dealer services are usually above and beyond the manufacturer's recommendation. You don't need the dealer to tell you what maintenance your vehicle needs. The manufacturer already does that. Simply open up your owner's manual and skip to the maintenance or routine maintenance section. Usually, there is a "normal" use and a "severe" use schedule for routine maintenance. Follow what the manufacturer recommends and avoid the extra (and unnecessary) dealer services for regular maintenance to save some dollars. You can use these saved dollars to buy some roadside equipment to help you.

Here are a couple of more tips I've used:

- Any time you purchase new tires, get a front-end alignment.
- Rotate your tires every oil change. Specifically, ask them to inspect your tires and point out any problems.
- You may want to upgrade your spare tire from the one that comes from the factory (which is probably a "doughnut"). You may even want to check if you have a spare tire—not all cars come with them anymore.
- If you have a key fob, ensure the batteries are good before going on a road trip. Try taking the battery out of the key fob to simulate a dead fob battery. Then, make sure you can get in and operate your vehicle manually without the fob. It would be best to practice this *without* the owner's manual in hand. If the manual is locked in your car and you can't get in, the manual will not do you any good.

Of course, even if you properly maintain your vehicle, bad luck can still rear its ugly head, so you'll want a roadside maintenance kit. You also should be able to use everything in your kit. Ask a trusted friend or family member to teach you if you don't know how. Here are some things you should include in it:

- A self-contained battery jumper lets you jump-start your car without asking a stranger for jumper cables. Just make sure it is charged before you leave.
- 12V DC air compressor. I usually carry a Ryobi 18V portable compressor as well.
- A reflector and flashing light kit. Assume you'll break down at night. If you have lights that require batteries, do not install them. Instead, simply buy a big pack of batteries and leave them in the packaging. Then, when it is time to use them, you can pull them out and install them. Just make sure you test your lights with some batteries around the house first to make sure they work. Then, uninstall the batteries—you don't want them

to leak and ruin your lights. Even if they didn't leak, they would slowly discharge while installed, leaving them dead when you need them.

- Flares. These are helpful but be careful with them because they can start fires. You may want to use lights and reflectors instead.
- Handyman toolset.
- The necessary tools to change your tire.
- Miscellaneous items you may need to get your car on the road: duct tape, oil, water, antifreeze, Fix-A-Flat, etc.
- Gas, if you can store it properly. I have a gas can for emergencies in the truck but be careful with gas if you can't store it in a properly ventilated compartment. The fumes can cause significant problems. You should also use any stored gas before the year ends and refill it because gas does expire.
- AAA membership or equivalent.
- Emergency medical kit—including things like a tourniquet and standard items like adhesive bandages.
- Important documents. I travel with my mom, so I have a copy of her healthcare power of attorney, living will, and contact information for all her children. You may want to carry some similar documents for yourself and your loved ones.

Bad Luck: Broken Down

Let's assume you had some bad luck and your vehicle failed. If you have prepared for the possibility of breaking down, you will not need any help from strangers. First, however, you must be smart about getting to a safer place.

I've driven a lot during my life. I started driving tractors when I was twelve years old. I've lived in rural areas and congested urban areas. I've seen a lot of accidents and vehicle failures. Consistently, the dumbest thing I witness is when people have a flat tire or vehicle that can still make it a mile or two, but they park on the shoulder of a busy road. This location is the most dangerous place to park, especially in this age of distracted driving. If you need to, slow down, turn on your hazards, ruin a rim if you have to, but get to a safe place. Your life and the lives of your loved ones are worth more than a wheel. If your car has overheated, let it cool down a bit, then drive slowly to a place where it is safer.

If you dropped a driveline, ruined a transmission, or froze the engine, you will have no choice but to stop on the shoulder. If so, don't get out on the driver's side, which will put you in the way of passing traffic. Instead, move over and get out on the passenger side. Many people recommend staying in your car with your seatbelt fastened. I do not. I get out of the car and walk about 100 yards to the rear and then another several hundred yards away, perpendicular from the vehicle (if possible). You don't want to be near your car if it gets hit by another vehicle!

You can contact AAA or your preferred roadside service if you have cell phone reception. If you use WAZE for navigation, start reporting that law enforcement is in your area. Even though that is a lie, a potential robber using WAZE to locate broken-down cars on the highway will think law enforcement is there.

If you can park far away from the interstate/highway, don't bother to put your hood up. Don't bother putting your hazard lights on if you are way off the road. That just tells people you are broken down and attracts people who may want to rob you. A car just sitting there without any apparent problems may have an owner that could return at any time. This worry may give a robber pause.

When you are sitting far away from your vehicle, if someone stops to check it out, don't let them see you. Just watch. If the person looks around and then leaves, it may have been a helpful person, or they may be returning with more people. If they look around, don't see anyone, and then start trying to get into your car, you know what kind of person it is. Review your mission. If your vehicle isn't as important as you and your loved ones, leave them alone. Call your roadside service and let them know what's happening. Call law enforcement and report them. If you don't have cell phone reception, you can take a picture of them and their car, zoom in, and provide law enforcement with valuable information when you do get reception. Use all of these precautions regardless of whether you are armed or not.

A Stranger Needs Help

When I was little, I used a cardboard box, stick, rock, and bait to catch critters. Unfortunately, this is reminiscent of what some robbers do.

Storytime

You are driving on the interstate late at night. You see a vehicle pulled off the road with the hood up and its hazard lights on. A cute young lady is sitting on the bumper, looking disgusted. You pull in to ask her if she needs help. You look at your cell phone and realize that you don't have reception.

#

It could be true. It could be bait.

Because I'm usually traveling with my mom, I never stop and help people because that would be counter to my mission. If someone looks like they are in a bad way, I simply call 911 and report their location. If there is no cell phone reception, I note their location and wait until I have cell phone reception.

If your mission is to help people, then help them. Remember, though, if the person genuinely needs help, how you appear could scare them. For example, getting out of your vehicle with a gun on your hip may scare a young lady to death. The same thing would happen if a car pulled up with four twenty-something-year-old males—a group like this would not be comforting for a young lady. Keep in mind that scared people don't make good decisions.

Also, just because you are armed doesn't mean you are invulnerable. For example, if you pull up to help a young lady, you and your wife get out, and the young lady's boyfriend throws down on your wife with a shotgun, your firearm may not be a lot of help.

Robbery may not be the only threat to consider. Let's continue our Storytime about the young lady with the broken-down car.

Storytime

The young lady asks if you could give her a ride to a police station so she can call for help. You say sure and notice that she may have been physically abused. You give her some advice on the way to help her get out of a bad situation. You drop her off in front of the police station. On your way home, law enforcement arrests you for assault.

#

In this Storytime, her boyfriend abused her, she took off, and then the car broke down. The broken car was legitimate. However, by the time you got to the police station, she realized that she would be out on the street if she reported her boyfriend to the police. So, she decided it would be better to blame you and use "your crime" to get back with her boyfriend. Here, your instincts were right that she needed help, but you are still in a bad way.

Trust me—nothing bothers me more than not giving help to people who need it. But the interstate and highway are not my community, and some people have bad intentions. All I can say is: make sure you fulfill your mission in all aspects. My mission does not allow me to pull over and help someone when my mom is in the car or when I'm alone. If I have a couple of friends with me, then, depending on the situation, I am much more likely to help.

4.2.4 Hotels/Motels

Robberies in hotels and motels don't show up much in the violent crime statistics. Since these robberies would likely be quickly reported to hotel management (and law enforcement), they don't happen very often. However, many people pick hotels based on how close they are to different attractions or venues. This means that the hotel functions a bit like a vehicle where individuals are walking to and from their hotel. As such, there are opportunities for robbery going to and from the hotel room just like there are going to and from a vehicle.

We can try and reduce our risk by doing several things:

- Plan trips several weeks in advance so you can research things like quality hotels and restaurants.
- When planning a trip, ensure all your stops are in a good part of town.
- Plan on arriving during the daytime.
- When checking into a hotel, park in front of the lobby and check-in, move your luggage to your room, and *then* park the car. Avoid the tendency to have your spouse check in while you park the car and bring the luggage.
- If it happens to be late, after checking in and moving your luggage, have your spouse stay by the lobby doors, cell phone in hand, and watch you park the car.

Here are some more tips for when you are in your hotel room:

- Get the front desk number and store it on your cell phone when you check-in. Then, if you get any calls to your room phone from the "front desk" asking you to do something like open the door, you can tell them that you'll call them back on your cell phone.
- Cover the peephole to prevent people with "peephole reversers" from seeing inside.
- Place a towel between the door handle and the door. Hotel doors generally don't fit the doorjamb very well. As a result, devices can be inserted above, below, and around the door to circumvent security. For example, these devices can push the security latch aside and then loop the inside door handle and open the door.
- Use a strap between the handle and the deadbolt lock to secure it. If you have a patio door, make sure it is locked and do the same thing to that door.
- Use a doorstop wedge. Carry a set of door wedges of different heights because the gaps on hotel room doors vary. They even make wedges that can sound an alarm.

- I always put the privacy sign out and leave sports on the television to provide the appearance that I'm in my room even when I'm not.
- If you are only staying a couple of days, do not get housecleaning services. After COVID, many hotels will only clean after you leave or if you request it. If you need towels or other items, just go down to the front desk and request them.

Secure Storage

Talking about secure storage and hotel rooms may seem a bit like an oxymoron, and it is. However, there are a few things in your favor:

1. If you picked a good area for your hotel, you are primarily worried about current and former hotel employees. Secondarily, with many hallway cameras around, another worry is about a guest who will "hop patios" and try to get in that way.
2. Usually, you will only be gone at most a few hours from your hotel room as opposed to a weekend as you would be with a home.
3. Your hotel room is not the only place you may have secure storage. Your vehicle may be more secure depending on your features and where your vehicle is parked.

I'm a big fan of decoys, hiding things in plain sight, and hidden cameras. Here is a good decoy. Find yourself an inexpensive lockbox, something like the hotel room ones, but it is small enough to fit in your luggage. What you are going to do is fill it with junk. Things like a money clip holding pieces of paper about the size of money, old jewelry from the pawn shop, and some change. When your hotel room thieves shake it, they'll think they hit the jackpot. You'll want to figure out how to permanently close the box so that it cannot be opened except with a pry bar (i.e., no batteries, manual lock set up so that it locks but doesn't unlock even if you have the key). You'll hide this lockbox under the pillows, between the mattress and box spring, under your pants in the dresser—

you know, the familiar places people hide things. Its only purpose is to make a thief think they hit the jackpot and leave your room to go open it in a better location (for them).

Wherever you put your decoy lockbox, you should put a hidden camera. They make all kinds of hidden cameras these days. For instance, let's say you put your lockbox under your pants in the dresser drawer. On top of the dresser, there are often A/C outlets that allow you to plug in things, most notably phone chargers. Guess what? They make hidden cameras that look like phone chargers. Whatever you do, you don't want your hidden camera to be obviously out of place for a traveler. Some of these thieves are hotel employees or former employees and will spot something obviously out of place. You also do not want your hidden camera to represent something valuable, like a watch. That might get stolen.

If you get back to your hotel room and your decoy lockbox is stolen, and your hidden camera is still there, you may have vital evidence for law enforcement. I would only hand over footage/pictures to law enforcement, not hotel employees. The thief may have a partner or may even be the person you are giving the evidence to.

If you are interested in secure vehicle storage, jump ahead and read the Section 4.3.6 and then come back here. You can store your valuables in your car rather than in your hotel room. This option depends on your hotel's area, secure vehicle storage, theft protections, and where you are parked. For instance, let's say you are going to go to see your daughter's college game. You have valuables you don't want to leave in the hotel room, but you have secure storage in your car. You might want to leave your valuables in your car in front of the hotel and take an Uber/Lyft. Here is a tip, though: keep in mind that hotel employees are part of the group you are worried about. If there is plenty of parking in front of the hotel, use this opportunity to take a travel bag with your valuables and other stuff (like a hotel pillow—keep reading until the end!) to your car and go get a soda at a fast-food place. Then, find a parking lot that doesn't have any people and transfer your valuables to secure storage (this is also a good time to enable your kill switches in your car if they are hooked to the starter—see the Section 4.3.7!). Finally, go back and park in front of the hotel. Make sure that the travel bag you brought your valuables out to your car with is taken back to your hotel room along with your soda. Here is where having the hotel pillow in your travel bag comes in handy—it still looks like you have all your stuff.

What if you must store valuables in your hotel room? Most places people put things will be searched. Remember, you may be dealing with current or former hotel employees—they know where stuff gets hidden. In addition to the decoy lockbox and hidden camera, here are some ideas to hide smaller items:

- Old Hairdryer. Take out the heating elements and store stuff in there.
- Outlet Box. My grandfather used to remove the covers of outlets and store money in the box. You can do something similar in your room, although I would pick a non-electrical cover, such as a cable connection.
- That tiny bedspread on the foot of the bed. These usually get thrown on the floor. In the folds of this material, you can pin something that holds credit cards or cash.
- Hollowed out wooden pant/skirt hangers. You can buy a couple of these hangers and hollow out a part of the wood inside to store things when the hanger is closed. Carry some old slacks that still look nice but don't fit and hang them on the hanger.
- Night-light. Many older people bring their own night-lights to hotel rooms. You can remove the bulb and store stuff in there.
- Ironing Board. If your room has one of these, check it out. You may be able to pop off the rubber caps on the stand and store items in the hollow tubes.
- The Extra Toilet Paper. Unwrap the wrapper, put some items in the hollow tube, put back the wrapper, and put it back where you found it.
- You can lift up the plastic bag in the bathroom trash and put some items between the bag and the container. You will then

want to put things in the trash that are a bit disgusting. Gauze with fake blood, toilet paper with something resembling poo, or whatever. Use your imagination. If you do this, you'll want to make sure housecleaning services are not coming.

It is complicated to hide larger items unless they can be broken down into smaller ones. In any event, should you choose to hide things, don't forget to get them when you leave!

4.2.5 Carjacking

A carjacking is a robbery during which your vehicle is directly stolen from you. Here are some common situations:

- You are driving and another vehicle hits your car from behind. You pull over to talk to the driver. He pulls a weapon, and his buddy gets in your vehicle and takes off; he gets your cell phone and drives off.
- You are at a stop sign or stop light when a man with a weapon suddenly pulls you out of the car.
- You are driving on a highway or interstate in a remote location when a car passes you, pulls into your lane, and slams on the brakes. You slam on your brakes, and before you know it, there is a man with a weapon pointed at you.
- You are in a parking garage; you have just opened your car door and sat down when a man suddenly appears with a weapon.

Many people throw their cellphone and wallet in the console when driving. You'll likely lose those things in a carjacking. You'll also lose your cell phone if you use it for navigation on a trip, as it is probably not on your person.

Like all forms of robbery, avoiding situations where a carjacking is likely to happen is best. However, your defense options are limited once you are looking at the wrong end of a gun. Here are some tips:

- Check out the top 25 stolen vehicles for your state. If you drive one of those vehicles, you are at increased risk. You may want to get a beat-up car (that is not on the stolen vehicle list) for most of your errands and around-town driving. You can drive the other vehicle when the conditions are safer.

- If you are slightly hit from behind in a desolate area, put your hazard lights on and drive to a more populated place before talking to the person who hit you. If the person who hit you were a carjacker, they would likely leave. However, if it was a genuine accident, they will follow you so they can exchange information with you in a safer location.

- Use the tips in the From the Vehicle and Back section to help you avoid carjacking in a parking garage or lot.

- Recognize that you will likely be left without your cell phone after a successful carjacking. Review the tips in the Preparation and Equipment section to help law enforcement.

- Driving with the top down and the windows down is fantastic on a beautiful day. However, if thieves highly desire your car, you may want to do this only in rural areas. Before getting to an urban area, roll up the top, roll up the windows, and lock the doors.

- Don't drive alone. The more adults in your car, the less likely you'll be carjacked.

- Avoid nighttime, bad parts of town, and unnecessary intersections.

- At an intersection, always stop and leave plenty of room between your car and the car ahead of you. This space may allow you to drive away from a carjacking situation.

- Get into the habit of immediately closing and locking your car doors as soon as you get in your car.

- Recognize that some cars automatically unlock the doors when you put the vehicle in Park. While convenient in most cases, it allows someone to open the door while you are distracted gathering your things. See if you can disable this feature. If not, get into the habit of immediately locking your doors when you put the vehicle in Park.

4.2.6 Conclusion

In most situations, some combination of these factors will dramatically increase your chances of being robbed:

- Nighttime
- Remote location
- Lack of people
- You are alone
- You appear to have valuables
- You are unaware or distracted

For many civilians, nighttime activities will take place on Friday or Saturday. Using ride-sharing services or friends can reduce our chances of robbery.

For daytime activities, we can schedule favorably by planning to do things on specific days and times when the likelihood of robbery is much smaller or by using services like grocery store pickup. If our activities involve carrying valuable items, taking friends and family along can help reduce the risk

Accepting help from and offering help to strangers can be a vector for robbery. Having a clear and concise mission is your top priority before getting involved in these situations. Preventative care and maintenance for your vehicle, accompanied by a well-stocked roadside kit, are your best options to avoid needing help from strangers. Whether you offer assistance to strangers is entirely up to you.

Be smart when traveling; plan to avoid troublesome areas and nighttime hotel check-ins. Always unload your valuables right in front of the hotel. Follow the guidelines for securing your hotel room and avoiding robbery scams that involve opening your hotel room door.

And don't forget that your car may be highly sought after by thieves. You can have a nice car and be safe, but you must plan well. Alternatively, your car may not look nice but be a parts bonanza for a thief! Your car may be an attraction or may have valuable parts, either way, it can also attract a lot of unsavory characters.

4.3 Preparation and Equipment

Let's review our example mission: *"To protect and provide for my family while allowing us the freedom and resources to enjoy life."*

Based upon this mission, unless you believe the robbers will murder you or your loved ones, shooting it out with them is not in line with your mission. If you are endangering your loved ones for the sake of valuables, then you are acting in opposition to your mission. Following your mission means the robbers get away with your stuff. Those things may reveal information about your life: who you are, where you live, your house key, etc.

Although you were unable to stop a robbery from impacting your life, if you prepare correctly, you can:

- Prevent the robbers from learning details about you and your loved ones.
- Prevent further crimes, such as the robber gaining entry to your home with your house keys.
- Help law enforcement catch the robbers.
- Help law enforcement get your valuables back.

The tips in these sections are helpful whether you CCF or not. For example, if you have to give up your car keys and wallet, do you want your robber to know you have a concealed-carry permit? Do you want him to have your home address where more firearms may be located? Probably not.

These sections also detail equipment that can help you notify law enforcement quickly, which may help law enforcement track down and catch your robber, get them off the streets, and get your valuables back. Consider this equipment helpful, but don't rely on it entirely.

If your mission is such that you won't be shooting it out with the robber over material items, you'll want to give the robber what they want and get out of there. You should carry a set amount of money with you to encourage the robbers to leave thinking they scored. If you hand over an empty wallet, the situation could escalate further. However, if you hand over a wallet with $80 in it, that may be enough for the robbers to take off and leave you and your loved ones alone. Unfortunately, there are no hard and fast rules for handing over valuables. Some people say throw your wallet and car keys and then run. Others will tell you to "just do what he says." A robbery is a dangerous situation, especially if the robber is armed, nervous, on drugs, etc.

One hard and fast rule is that you never leave a public area to go to a private place with a violent criminal—in this case, your robber. The private place he wants to take you to is just another word for Hell. This situation will mean it is time to fight—to the death, if necessary.

4.3.1 Identification and Keys

Here are some things that will likely be taken from you in a robbery:

- Wallet/purse
- Jewelry
- Cell phone
- Car keys and any other keys on the keyring
- Gun/weapon if they find it or realize you have one

Just thinking about all these things being taken from you—especially in the middle of nowhere—is disheartening and scary. However, we can try to offset the blow by properly preparing.

1. We do not want our home address in the car. Many car insurance companies no longer put your home address on their insurance cards. I cross mine off on my registration as well. Simply going through your car and discarding or crossing out anything with your address is an excellent first step.
2. We want to separate our identification from our wallet. This separation comes in handy for robbers as well as law enforcement. I have three IDs: my driver's license, concealed-carry permit, and passport card. I keep those separate from my wallet.

In addition, I copy my vehicle registrations and insurance cards and keep those in there too. This "packet" is my law enforcement packet because *being stopped by a law enforcement officer is more common than being robbed.* You still want those IDs available and in a location that is not suspicious to the law enforcement officer.

Here is what I did: I took an armband designed to hold your IDs and keys while you exercise. I gave it to my sister, who went to work on it with a sewing machine to transform it from a bulky item to a slim one. Now, I can put this armband under my shirt sleeve and separate my IDs from my wallet.[101] The IDs remain hidden from robbers but are easily accessible if I get pulled over by law enforcement. As I am being pulled over, I can easily remove the armband and set it on the dash. If I don't want to do that, I always tell law enforcement where my IDs are, ask permission to get them, and move slowly.

3. You should always have your credit cards and around $80 in cash in your wallet. Have two $20s on the outside and various smaller bills in the middle. If a robber thinks they made a good score, they will hopefully take off and leave you alone.

4. You should separate your house key from your car keys. Carry that key in a different location. I carry mine with my IDs.

5. Your car keys, cell phone, and wallet should be able to be removed without revealing your IDs, house key, or weapon.

6. You need to be familiar with where you keep all of these things. Essentially, you should always carry your stuff in this systematic manner. A robbery will be a stressful event, and you don't want to be fumbling for your things and finding the wrong things. Therefore, you should be very familiar with where everything is located. This familiarity lets you quickly surrender what is most valuable to the robber.

---

[101] This location works well in the spring, summer, and fall. I haven't found a similar location that works well in winter, so I tend to use my jacket front pocket. Thank goodness I don't like the cold so I'm often a homebody in winter!

7. Your apps on your cell phone, like banking apps or home alarm apps, should not have any information like your username pop up automatically or things along those lines. They should all be PIN protected when launched. While your robber may unlock your cell phone, he may not be able to access anything important. They will likely take the cell phone, remove the SIM card, and then erase it over time.

4.3.2 Cameras and Trackers

While many people who CCF look at state laws regarding firearms restrictions and even move to those states with minimal restrictions, another law they should consider is *one-party consent for audio recording*. A one-party consent law gives you more flexibility to protect yourself using video and audio recordings. However, even if you live in a state with one-party consent, you should consult with an attorney to make sure you do it legally. Otherwise, it may be inadmissible as evidence. Worse, you could have charges brought against you for illegal recording.

Body Cameras

One item that you should consider is a hidden body camera that records video and audio. It should not be a fancy watch or something that may be taken from you. Instead, have a discrete device that you turn on whenever you are going to or coming from your car or in other high-risk robbery situations that you cannot avoid.

I can't say I've found a hidden body camera that does everything I want. I feel like the best bet is some sort of fake eyeglasses, a baseball hat, or perhaps a fake button/snap that doesn't have a bulky accessory. You may wish to consider two separate devices—one for video recording and one for audio recording. Essentially you want something with the following specifications:

- Concealable and unlikely to be found and stolen.
- Able to be turned off/on easily.

- A clear indication for the user that recording is happening.
- A wide-angle lens.
- 720p at 60fps or better.
- Audio recording.
- Low light capability at least, nighttime if the battery life and concealment are still acceptable.
- Long battery life.
- Ample storage and automatic file overwrite.

I'm not suggesting you use a body camera 24/7. However, it would be best to consider it when your robbery risk is greater than usual. For instance, anytime you go out in your car at night, you should be recording when you walk to and from your vehicle and when you use Lyft/Uber.

Law enforcement officers in the United States are increasingly wearing body cameras, and you should too, especially if you CCF. A good body camera with audio will be significant evidence if you use your gun defensively, even if you don't fire a shot. Getting video/audio of bad guys doing bad things can help law enforcement get them off the street before they hurt someone.

Car Camera

Previously, we've covered how walking to and from your car is a prime opportunity for a robbery. There is a product called OwlCam[102] that seems promising in response to this. It is a dashcam with the smarts to detect bumps and record video when you are not in the car. Furthermore, you can connect to it with your cell phone to see what the camera sees—both the exterior and interior of the vehicle. This feature can help you survey what is happening in and around your car before leaving a safe location. Unfortunately, it doesn't have 360-degree views around the vehicle yet, but I hope a future product will provide that functionality. In any case, it is another tool in the toolbox to help you avoid violent crime.

---

[102] https://clayeolsen.com/owl

Speaking of car cameras, you may want to consider a rear-facing camera with GPS. This camera isn't much help for robberies but can help you get out of a speeding ticket if you feel you were given a ticket unfairly. Businesses often use these cameras to monitor the vehicles in their fleet for speed and location. Make sure your speed is recorded. If you feel you were given a speeding ticket unjustly, don't harass the law enforcement officer about it. Instead, let the traffic stop continue as if nothing happened. You can review the footage later and talk to your attorney if you wish to fight the ticket.

4.3.3 Tile and the Global Positioning System

There is a product called Tile[103] that is composed of two things:

- A small Bluetooth device (the Tile)
- An application (the TileApp)

You attach the Tile to something valuable, like your wallet or car keys. Then, you can use the application on your cell phone to ring your Tile, which prompts the device to play an audible tone. This feature is great for when you've misplaced something with a Tile attached (and you are in Bluetooth range). For example, if you've lost your car keys somewhere in your house, you can ring the Tile from your cell phone. Of course, the opposite also works—you can find your cell phone from a Tile.

Tile also works great if it is attached to a device that gets stolen. For example, I have a TilePro hidden in both of my cars. If someone happens to steal my car, I can open the TileApp and hit "Find." If the robber who stole my car is at a faraway intersection, and a random person in a vehicle next to them happens to be running the TileApp on *their* cell phone, here is what happens:

---

[103] https://clayeolsen.com/tile

1. Their TileApp recognizes my car's Tile beacon and then updates its location in the Tile database.
2. The TileApp on my cell phone pulls from the Tile database and gets the updated location of my Tile.
3. I can now tell law enforcement where my car is.

This physical device and social network combination are more effective in urban areas. The likelihood of running into another person with a TileApp is much higher in urban areas than in rural areas.

The company makes Tiles in various sizes and shapes. So, for example, if you have a rifle with a hollow pistol grip, you can put one in there. You can put one in your wallet, on your key rings, in your camera equipment bag, etc.

GPS Tracker

Another option, probably more helpful for road trips and vacations, is to hide a GPS tracker in your vehicle. These usually last for several days on a single charge. If your vehicle is stolen, you can use the GPS tracker application to find it. GPS trackers have legal issues, so consult with an attorney to determine if you can deploy one in your jurisdiction.

4.3.4 Garmin InReach

The Garmin InReach[104] is a satellite uplink device that I carry when hunting or in remote locations outdoors. As long as you can see the sky, you can get an SOS signal to their satellite network. For instance, if you get stuck in the snow and have no cell phone signal, you can use InReach to send an SOS. You'll need a subscription, but they have many different plans that are reasonably priced.

The InReach also can send preset text messages to contacts. The benefit is that you can use the satellite network when your cell phone

---

[104] https://clayeolsen.com/inreach

network is unavailable. For instance, I have my sister's cell phone number with a preset text message indicating that I've broken down, my AAA number, and my GPS location, which can be added when I send the text. She would be able to call AAA and get someone dispatched to my location. You may also consider having a preset text message for a robbery/carjacking, which would enable you to notify someone quickly.

Because the InReach can protect you in various ways, it makes sense to conceal it so it won't be stolen. You may want to carry the InReach in an ankle holster, as fast access is not required. If you are carjacked or otherwise robbed, you most likely will lose your phone as it will either be taken from you or will be in the vehicle. If the robber doesn't see your InReach, you have an option to text someone to help you after they leave.

4.3.5 Backup Cell Phone

We've talked about a couple of pieces of equipment that can help you if you are the victim of a robbery/carjacking. However, what makes everything come together is a backup cell phone in a safe location that can be used by someone you trust.

This backup cell phone needs to have your credit card information so you or your family members can put holds on them or cancel them. This information would include the card itself and the telephone number to call to report the card lost or stolen. The backup cell phone would also have the Tile application that your family member can use to help law enforcement locate your belongings. If you have a GPS tracker on your car, your backup phone should also have that application. Map applications, such as Apple Maps, can be used to input the GPS location given by the Garmin InReach to locate where you have broken down or where you were robbed. You can also have the OwlCam application if your car has an OwlCam.[105]

---

[105] https://clayeolsen.com/owl

You can find quality refurbished cell phones on eBay. This phone doesn't need to look the best—it will just be at home, plugged in. You don't even need a cell phone plan if you have wireless at home; just set the phone to use your home network. Hopefully, your family or friends will never need to use it.

It would be best to consider upgrading your backup cell phone to a newer model when you upgrade your primary cell phone. This upgrade strategy helps ensure that your operating system and the apps on your carry phone are still compatible with your backup phone.

4.3.6 Secure Storage Inside Your Vehicle

This section and the next section are primarily about theft but can help in robbery situations too. Many people have multiple destinations when they run errands. Having secure vehicle storage allows you to store valuable items securely and not have to carry them on you. Also, you may CCF and have multiple destinations. What if one of those destinations doesn't allow firearms? These options give you the flexibility of storing a firearm without having it easily stolen.

What people cannot see, they don't want to steal. However, if they do break into your vehicle, you don't want to make it easy for them. In my travel vehicle, I use a product called Console Vault.[106] This product has worked well for me over the years. The company is coming out with a line of elite locks for the Console Vault that I'm following closely, and existing customers can install these locks.

When I carry a firearm for protection, I carry a 1911 in condition 3.[107] This condition is a very safe way of handling a 1911 when carrying yet can be ready to fire in short order using the Israeli method.[108] The 1911 with no magazine and no round in the chamber goes into the Console Vault. To ensure I'm legal in my state when I travel, I supplement the

---

[106] https://clayeolsen.com/cv

[107] https://clayeolsen.com/c3

[108] https://clayeolsen.com/idic

Console Vault with a VaulTek Lifepod.[109] This product goes underneath my console and stores my 1911 magazines.

While this setup is slow if you need your firearm in a hurry, statistics tell me that it is unlikely that I would need my firearm while driving. I highly suspect readily available firearms are more likely to result in aggravated assault charges due to road rage incidents.[110] In addition, this setup allows me to interact safely with law enforcement. If a law enforcement officer feels more comfortable removing my firearm from my vehicle, it can be done extremely safely, and I do not have to physically handle it. In addition, the firearm can be returned in a highly safe manner, again without me having to physically handle the firearm in front of law enforcement.

These are the only two vehicle storage products that I have direct familiarity with. However, an internet search will reveal many more options. If you need more capacity or just have differing needs, look for concealability and security. Both are required for secure vehicle storage.

4.3.7 Vehicle Theft Protection

If thieves find your secure storage, they might just steal your vehicle rather than try to break into it. Or, they may have stolen your vehicle and found your secure storage later. In any case, there is an effective technique to keep your car from being stolen.

One may guess I'm talking about car alarms. I actually don't think very highly of car alarms. Car alarms go off so much now, mainly because of false positives, that no one even turns their head to look anymore. Perhaps some of the high-end alarms have some valuable features when professionally installed, but I'll leave it to others to toot that horn.

What I'm talking about is a vehicle kill switch. A kill switch disables either the fuel pump or starter. It must be enabled before the car can start. Unfortunately, many people hide the switch where they are easy

---

[109] https://clayeolsen.com/vtlp
[110] https://clayeolsen.com/rage

to find for someone with a bit of experience. The other problem is that they do not bury the wires sufficiently, and someone simply splices them and bypasses the switch.

One option that you could try is to have a two-switch kill. Both switches have to be enabled for the car to start. One switch is on the driver's side, somewhere hidden but easy to find. The other switch is in plain sight, but the thief doesn't know it is a switch. Here is an example: If you do not use your 12v DC accessory port (i.e., cigarette lighter), you can rewire it to become the second switch. You can modify an old cigarette lighter plug that provides the switched connection when pushed in. When parking your car, remove the lighter plug and disable the other switch. Another option is to put your second kill switch inside your secure vehicle storage. In any case, this setup is good against both these types of thieves:

- The beginner thief who doesn't know about kill switches.
- The advanced thief who finds the first kill switch and uses up the time they have to steal the car messing with it.

An advanced addition to this setup is to wire up a 12V home alarm siren in your car's engine compartment. Suppose someone tries to start it with the kill switch engaged, and the siren screams. This scream isn't some sissy car horn. The home sirens have major decibels. Every time the thief turns the key, it screams. Bad news for a thief trying to figure out the kill switch. Just make sure the thief can't splice the siren wires and start the car.

For safety reasons, I prefer bypassing the starter solenoid rather than the fuel pump (unless you have a manual transmission). That way, if you accidentally disable a switch, the car doesn't stop. This functionality is also helpful because you can enable the kill switch before reaching your destination. Potential thieves watching you park won't notice anything out of the ordinary. When you get back into your car to go somewhere (besides home), you usually have some stuff to put away. You can enable the switches while you are storing your stuff, and no one will know any different.

These switches can help you get your car back if you are carjacked. If the carjacker stops the vehicle for any reason, he won't be able to start it again.

Although the kill switches are helpful for the entire car, they don't protect your tires from being stolen or your catalytic converter. They also do not stop smash and grab attacks. However, when combined with concealed secure vehicle storage, you have a much more formidable way of taking care of your valuables in a vehicle.

4.3.8 Conclusion

Robbery is a violent crime where someone uses force or threatens to use force to take items from you, like your wallet or car. Robbery, in my opinion, represents a violent crime where an ordinary civilian is most likely to run into a veteran violent criminal. We want to fulfill our mission in all aspects. If our mission is to reduce the risk of injury or death to ourselves and our loved ones at the expense of our valuables, we should be willing to give up our valuables. That doesn't mean we've lost; on the contrary, we've fulfilled our mission.

We first started with the basics—how we carry our identification. I suggested that you separate your identification and keys from the main target of a robber—your wallet or purse. In addition, your car should not have your address in it if the robber also takes it. These techniques help minimize the damage. Also, walking around with an empty wallet or purse may make you feel better if you lose it, but it also doesn't have anything of value for the robber. I suspect many robberies are fueled by drug addiction. If the robber gets enough cash to score drugs, they have an incentive to leave you alone (or not chase you if you drop your wallet and run). If they don't get any money, an ugly situation might escalate into something uglier.

We also covered technology solutions that can help. For example, a hidden body camera can capture details of the robbery to help law enforcement. Make sure you can legally record by consulting with an experienced attorney in your state before purchasing one. If law enforcement captures the suspect, your footage may provide the evidence to get that robber off the street. Also, our valuables can contain technology that helps law enforcement track the items and, hopefully, catch the robbers and get us our stuff back.

If you travel around quite a bit, you may want to invest in a Garmin InReach to provide communication with a trusted friend or family member. This device is a lifesaver if you've broken down where there is no cellular service. Also, if you've been robbed, use it to notify your friend or family member, who then can notify law enforcement, lockdown credit cards, and track your valuables, all using your backup cell phone.

Finally, we cover ways to protect your belongings inside your vehicle and simple protections against vehicle theft. These protections can come in handy when traveling or just around town. If you CCF, for instance, and you find your destination does not permit firearms, these protections can help you store your firearm securely in your car and keep your vehicle from being stolen.

4.4 Defensive Skills Training

So far, we have looked at the following:

- Reducing the risk of situations common to robbery.
- Adding equipment to help law enforcement catch the bad guys and get our valuables back.

If you do the first item well, your risk of robbery probably decreases to the same odds as "getting hit by space debris." However, if you are incredibly unfortunate, you'll get jumped: the robber will attempt to surprise you, knock you out, and then rob you. We will discuss this situation here.

I've been to a lot of self-defense training classes. Of course, some are better than others. I've talked with people who seem to be in training classes most of the year. These classes cost a lot of money and take lots of time. I look at training similarly to how I look at knowledge. As Nietzsche once said, "Wisdom sets limits even to knowledge."[111] If you want to be a contestant on Jeopardy, remembering many facts about the world would be pertinent. However, there is a difference between answering Jeopardy questions about military tactics and applying military tactics on the battlefield. The Ancient Greeks distinguished between "Know-What" and "Know-How." In general, you are limited in the number of fields of *applied* expertise ("Know-How") you can develop. Self-defense training should be about "Know-How." As such, you should train *and limit training* accordingly.

A robbery situation where we are jumped is when our physical defense training can help us. However, there are a couple of caveats here.

- Remember that you will always be at a tremendous disadvantage in such a situation. You are under a *surprise* attack, after all. All the training and skill in the world may not help you. This disadvantage is why your focus should be on avoiding these situations.
- You also need to be in good physical shape to do this training and be effective at self-defense. Unfortunately, there are many physical defense dead-ends. For instance, if you want to learn physical defense, do not spend your time in classes geared toward exercise with some fighting moves thrown in as part of the workout. That will leave you unprepared. Also, physical defense "boot camps" without any scheduled follow-up training are of highly questionable value.

This training requires a commitment of time and money. You won't learn physical defense by watching a YouTube video. Instead, you need to go somewhere and train in person and you'll need to practice that training frequently with other people.

---

[111] Nietzsche, *Twilight of the Idols*

4.4.1 Physical Defense

Most people, probably because they are out of shape or a bit lazy, will forgo physical defense training and just carry a firearm. I feel this is a mistake. You may succumb to weapon overreliance, which will leave you attempting to draw your weapon while you're being beaten. You'll get knocked out or killed before you get your weapon out.

Rory Miller is the only person I've seen offer surprise attack defense training. I think highly of Miller's work, but I haven't gone through this training. Nevertheless, it is something that you should investigate. His program is called Training for Sudden Violence. Miller also periodically offers a seminar called Violence Dynamics.[112] If you are working with a self-defense group in your area, bringing Miller in to help "train the trainers" in some critical areas of self-defense would be wise.

In short, this training is designed to help you stave off an initial violent attack and still be able to fight back. This counterattack does not mean chasing down your would-be robber and committing battery. Instead, it means switching your focus to landing strikes instead of blocking strikes during an ongoing attack. As they say, sometimes the best defense is a good offense.

I believe the best counterattack for real-world violent crime is survival martial arts, which best represents the skills you will need against a violent criminal. Reality Defense[113] in Arizona, founded by Troy Coe, has excellent training in this area. I only wish I lived closer to their training facility. Survival martial arts is about survival and the techniques you learn are brutal. However, brutality is necessary when you are up against a violent criminal. Regardless of my opinion, you may believe a different martial art is best. If you do, you must train as though your attacker fights without following any rules—because that is how they will fight. Also, be aware that you often train on mats but fight on hard surfaces like pavement or cement. There are a variety of attacks that use the hard ground as a weapon.

---

[112] https://clayeolsen.com/vdyn

[113] https://clayeolsen.com/rdef

Also important, I do not recommend taking a class and never looking at training again. On the contrary, I would highly recommend that you practice weekly drills. You'll often find someone in the training class who is as interested as you are and you can keep up with sparring or other drills to sharpen your skills. As an added bonus, it's great exercise!

4.4.2 Weapon Defense

After hearing many training attendees talk about their experiences, I concluded that civilian Defensive Gun Uses (DGUs) seem to happen with robberies more than other *violent* crimes. However, following the guidelines in the section Defenses Against Robbery should be enough to prevent many of these situations. You still could get jumped by robbers, which requires a more physical defensive strategy to avoid becoming incapacitated. These considerations lead to a question: if I am still concerned about robbery after reducing my risk, preparing correctly by taking physical self-defense training, and continuously working on my physical defense skills, what weapon should I carry?

I recommend that the majority of ordinary civilians consider carrying a less-than-lethal weapon. Specifically, I would recommend the Piexon JPX4 Compact 2[114] or the JPX6.[115] These weapons use a technology that allows a non-aerosol Oleoresin Capsicum (OC) pepper spray to be deployed effectively up to around 18 feet away (by my testing—the company claims 23 feet). Furthermore, *this weapon is not classified as a firearm by the Bureau of Alcohol, Tobacco, Firearms, and Explosives (ATF)*, which means that firearm laws do not apply. As a result, many firearm-related harms in our fact box can be avoided.

Over time, when traveling with my mom, I've moved from carrying a firearm to carrying a JPX4 Compact. Now, I mostly take a JPX6. Of course, there are times when I still carry a firearm, but it depends on

---

[114] https://clayeolsen.com/jpx4
[115] https://clayeolsen.com/jpx6

where we are going. If you are interested in the JPX4 or JPX6, I review the JPX6 in Appendix D: JPX6 Review. Some improvements can be made to this weapon, but I feel it is a quality defensive product that avoids many pitfalls of firearms while still providing adequate protection. However, if you want to CCF, a ton of defensive training is available. Gunsite[116] is considered by many to be the standard, but you'll find a whole lot of high-quality training available. So do your research and practice!

Given that we know most violent crime comprises aggravated assault, robbery, and rape, would using a JPX4 or JPX6 put you at a significant disadvantage? I would argue not, especially when many civilian DGUs do not discharge their weapon. Murders involve significant firearms use, but murder is rare overall. Sadly, I have taken several self-defense courses and have never seen less-than-lethal solutions presented in a good light. They are simply not seriously considered—which is a mistake. A CCF proponent will usually describe cases when less-than-lethal weapons failed. However, they never give any statistics about how often less-than-lethal weapons are used compared to how often they fail—and they never discuss how often they succeed. Such a complete examination is necessary if you want to determine a weapon's effectiveness. You'll also never hear the stories about violent criminals who took a lot of bullets and kept going—these stories do exist. If such a story does come up, it is usually in the context of cartridge selection. Look at the ink spilled in the 9mm versus the .45 ACP cartridge debate. Realize that whatever your favorite concealed-carry cartridge is, it has had its fair share of failures stopping violent criminals.

As pepper spray technology was deployed in the 1980s and 1990s by police departments, its effectiveness became apparent. Law enforcement usually deploys less-than-lethal weapons, pepper spray, or Tasers to restrain people with less danger to the suspect and the arresting officer. Physical force introduces the risk of injury for both the arresting officer and the suspect. Given a Taser versus pepper spray, law enforcement

---

[116] https://clayeolsen.com/gunsite

officers would likely prefer the Taser. A pepper-sprayed suspect has to be handcuffed and loaded in a car, which may contaminate the officer. Tasers are way less messy for an arresting officer.

Civilians don't have to worry about handcuffing a suspect and taking them back to the station. What civilians care about is accomplishing their mission. We should use whatever weapon is capable of fulfilling that mission *in all aspects*. For example, unintentionally hitting an unintended target because of over-penetration, accidentally carrying a firearm in a place you are not supposed to, or a negligent discharge can all lead to a felony conviction, which would be disastrous to your mission. Carrying a JPX6 avoids firearm-related harms in our fact box. Furthermore, since most DGUs did not require the firearm to be discharged and most injurious violent crime doesn't involve weapons, you should still be in good standing to defend yourself with a JPX6.

Unfortunately, I do not know of any training classes focusing on the JPX4 Compact or JPX6. There are training classes for Tasers. In my testing, though I feel Tasers are more appropriate than pepper spray for law enforcement, I think the opposite is true for civilians. Therefore, in my opinion, the JPX4/JPX6 is superior to the Taser when used by civilians in a violent crime situation.

Regardless of my recommendation, the weapon you carry is an individual matter. You may prefer to get a concealed-carry permit and carry a firearm. I certainly have no objection to that—I have done that myself and continue to do so in certain situations. For instance, if I'm out in a very rural area, the limited effective range of the JPX6 is such that I'm more likely to carry a firearm. The point of my recommendation is to make sure everyone has as many viewpoints as possible and is aware of the various harms.

The JPX products are still weapons and all less-than-lethal weapons can still result in death. This lethality is primarily an issue for law enforcement as they use these weapons to arrest suspects safely. Civilians in a violent crime situation want to accomplish their mission. A civilian isn't using the JPX out of concern for the violent criminal. They're using it because it helps accomplish their mission in all aspects.

4.4.3 Close-Quarter Combat Defense

We've covered the defensive skills you will need if you are jumped and the types of weapons you may want to carry. However, there is a gap between the physical defensive skills required to avoid getting knocked out and accessing your weapon during a physical onslaught. That skill set is typically called Close-Quarters Combat (CQC) training. For example, Independence Training in Phoenix has a Close Contact Handgun[117]course. Here is the course description that can help you locate similar training classes in your area:

> This course will teach you to work verbal, physical and gun handling skill sets at close contact distances. Scenario based training is used heavily throughout this program, and the entire course is hands on. Students will learn how to consistently engage live fire targets at arms' length, and also use UTM and demo guns to engage in force-on-force training with role players at close contact distances, out of vehicles and inside structures.

Remember the civilian DGU analysis done by Claude Werner that we covered earlier. The distance between the offender and victim was just over arm's length. This type of training is likely more valuable than other types of firearms training that emphasize distance and reloading speed.

People who CCF rarely take this type of training. The basic idea of this training is about creating enough space to draw your weapon and fire when you are physically engaged in a fight with someone else. If you can find CQC training, it will be with a firearm rather than a JPX or Taser and will require you to have firearm expertise before you start— which is unfortunate as it may require much more firearm training than you will probably ever need.

---

[117] https://clayeolsen.com/cch

4.4.4 Conclusion

Robbery seems like the point where violent criminals and civilians will most often meet in violent crime—and the violent criminal has significant advantages against a civilian. We want to avoid these encounters if at all possible.

We've talked about physical defensive skills, weapons, and CQC for those who feel risk reduction isn't enough. However, the amount of time and training required to be proficient in these areas is extensive. Therefore, they represent the least "bang for your buck."

Everything we've covered in these sections is related to your mission. Clarity about your mission is vital before you do anything. I encourage you to think through and commit yourself to a mission you can accomplish with focus and passion.

PART III

Strangers, Civilians, and Public Locations

5.1 Aggravated Assault

Aggravated assault is the most common violent crime. When no injury was reported, we saw that strangers and public areas were quite common. Per the definition of aggravated assault, we can assume the offender had a weapon. For instance, during an argument over a parking spot, the offender pulled out a collapsible baton. The offender may have just held it at their side or swung at the victim and missed. It doesn't matter—injury is not a necessary condition of aggravated assault when there is a weapon and threats are made around using it.

Based upon our statistics, I feel that civilians are most likely implicated in aggravated assaults when the parties are strangers in a public area and *no injury results*. Basically, a minor conflict or argument escalated, and a weapon was deployed. When injury does occur in public place, the confrontation could have led to the weapon being used to injure the victim. Alternatively, the victim could have been injured via personal weapons (e.g., hands, feet, and so forth), and the injury was severe, so the crime was categorized as an aggravated assault.

In most cases, I do not feel that these are situations where the offender was a violent criminal, and the victim was an ordinary civilian. I feel that robbery in a public area is much more likely to involve a violent criminal. Hence, in this part, we take a different approach to handling these situations because they likely involve ordinary civilians whose emotions have gotten out of control.

5.2 Potential Aggravated Assaults: Storytimes

Each of the following Storytimes describe situations where an aggravated assault can occur. Think about how you would handle the situation to prevent a violent escalation.

Traffic Escalations

The Accidental Cutoff

You saw that you were in the wrong lane to turn left and quickly changed lanes, accidentally cutting off a car in your blind spot. The driver had to slam on their brakes to avoid an accident. The light is red, so you stop in the turn lane. Behind you, the driver that slammed on his brakes stops too. The driver's side door opens, and a large red-faced man gets out and walks toward your car.

The Impatient Driver

You are in the right lane, just minding your own business. You need to make a left turn in about half a mile to get into the left lane. A car appears out of nowhere and tailgates you. The driver honks their horn and gives you a "California Howdy." You get into the turning lane and the car goes by. You drive a short way and pull into your driveway. A car pulls up, and the window rolls down. A man starts shouting profanity at you in your driveway. It is the same guy who was behind you on the highway.

The Deliberate Cutoff

Your car is at the service center for repairs. They call and say it is ready. Your wife takes you to the service center to pick up the vehicle. You both leave at the same time and drive back on the highway together. You and your wife are in the right lane in tandem; a car in the left lane is going just a little faster than your wife. He gets barely ahead of your wife and swings into her lane, cutting her off and making her slam on the brakes.

Parking Escalations

The Parking Lot

You just bought a new car and decided to stop by the grocery store on your way home. You park and finish up a phone call with your friend about your new car. A junky-looking vehicle pulls up next to you. The car door swings open and hits your vehicle hard, making a dent and scratch. The man doesn't even seem to notice.

Parking Lot Vulture

You are circling the parking lot looking for a space close to the store. A car starts to back out; you give him some room and put your blinker on to let everyone know you've called dibs on that spot. As he pulls away, another car—going the wrong way down the parking lot—speeds up, turns directly in front of you, and takes the spot.

Movies, Bars, and Restaurants

The Movies

Someone is on their cell phone during the movie.

Someone is constantly talking during the movie.

Someone is behind you, throwing popcorn in your hair.

Someone's kids are running around without supervision.

A tall person decides to sit directly in front of you in an empty movie theater.

The Bar

You are a Green Bay Packers fan at a bar watching the Packers-Cowboys playoff game with many of your coworkers. You and a coworker, a Dallas Cowboys fan, start to give each other a hard time. As the beer flows, it becomes clear the Packers are winning. The Cowboys fan begins to get upset at your teasing. He tells you, "You need to shut up, or you are gonna get hurt." Because he is your coworker, you don't take him seriously. You continue to tease him, and he continues to remind you to shut up. Everyone is a bit buzzed and thinks it is funny. Then, another good zinger pops into your head.

The Restaurant (Language Warning)

You are eating alone in a restaurant after a long day at work. You stand up to go to the bathroom, and your elbow accidentally hits the arm of a woman walking by, spilling the glass of red wine she is carrying all over her white dress. She flies into a rage and begins shouting at you.

She says, "You stupid fucking asshole. What the hell is wrong with you? Do you know how much this fucking dress cost? You just ruined it! You fucking idiot."

Her husband rushes over.

He says, "What the fuck did you do to my wife?"

She says, "He fucking made me spill wine all over myself. Clumsy fuckhead. He just ruined my $300 dress!"

He says, "I'm gonna kick your fucking ass."

#

There is a good chance that the situation will escalate to violence in these Storytimes. However, that escalation need not happen. We are in control of a couple of things—ourselves and our ability to de-escalate.

5.3 Controlling Yourself

One of my first CCF instructors taught me something significant: *CCF is a lifestyle change.* He couldn't have been more right. If you consider all the benefits and harms of CCF, you will become a very polite person, even when insulted. Being calm and even-tempered in the most stressful situations is necessary because CCF adds another level of consequences to confrontations. An individual who wants to CCF must understand the danger of violent escalations. Whether you CCF or carry another type of weapon—or no weapon at all—we can all learn something from a calm and even-tempered person.

Road Rage

I spent several years commuting in some big cities. Road rage is terrible and at the root of many civilian escalations. Unfortunately, I've seen a lot of these escalations take place as drivers pull over and confront each other. I suspect some of the aggravated assaults in parking lots and on streets are people who pulled over due to road rage.

Being calm and even-tempered helps tremendously when driving and what is nice is that it is something you can control. Many folks believe being a good driver is all about skill, but it is mostly about your mental approach and planning. Plan so that you never have to be in a hurry. If you aren't in a hurry, you will naturally be more courteous and won't try to exploit every opening regardless of safety.

Impatience and frustration are your enemies when driving. If you recognize these emotions building in yourself, pull over for a bit to take a break. I remember one time I caught myself muttering about another driver—something I usually do not do. But the week before, an elderly friend of mine unexpectedly died while I was out of town. It bothered me that I had missed seeing him before he died. Unconsciously, these feelings caused a change in my mood. I was more easily frustrated and irritable. This frustration came out at another driver. Once I recognized what was causing my bad mood, I was able to control my emotions.

You will be surrounded by impatient, angry, frustrated, and distracted drivers. Once you understand that, you can prevent them from getting to you. You aren't going to make someone a better driver by insulting them for a wrong decision on their part. Instead, learn to recognize and control your emotions. You'll reap the benefits of that in all aspects of your life.

The Time Trap

People often believe that driving fast will help them reach their destination sooner. If you are traveling from end to end on Interstate 5 in the middle of California, driving fast makes sense (although not from a legal or safety perspective). There are no stoplights or stop signs. It is a long, open highway. Assume you have to drive 360 miles. If you go 120 miles per hour, you'll get there in 3 hours. If you go 60 miles per hour, you'll get there in 6 hours. This is a meaningful difference in time. It doesn't mean you should do it, but if you were only concerned about making up time, this would be the road to do it on.

Unfortunately, many people take this same attitude toward driving around town, which is responsible for a lot of road rage. You are not going to make up a lot of time in the city. Stoplights, stop signs, railroad crossings, crosswalks, and most importantly, traffic congestion, mean it is not worth driving at a high-speed rate on city streets. Depending on the day, the traffic signals, and traffic congestion, you might save a few seconds over someone who drives safely. Also, the sheer number of other things going on around you makes this a hazardous proposition. For instance:

- Motorcyclists
- Bicyclists
- Pedestrians
- Cars pulling out suddenly
- Cars slamming on their brakes suddenly
- Cars obscuring other vehicles or motorcycles
- Trucks pulling trailers smaller in width than their truck

Let's face it, if you're in a hurry, you aren't that efficient with your time. You probably sat on the pot for as much time as you made up (if you made up any time at all) because you were watching a video on your cell phone. That is not worth the risk you pose to yourself or others behind the wheel of your two tons of steel.

Parking Spaces

The same disease that makes people want to hurry through town also makes them want to park in the closest spot possible to the store they want to visit. I call these folks "Parking Lot Vultures," or PLVs.

There is bound to be conflict when many PLVs shoot for a few spaces. The best thing to do is take a safe parking spot away from the commotion. This approach may mean you have to park a bit out (where there are plenty of spaces) and walk to the building. However, you'll get some exercise, sun, and fresh air. You'll even save time, as the time spent walking to and from your destination is usually shorter than the amount of time you would spend searching for the perfect parking space. You'll also be less stressed.

Body Cameras

When you are in control of yourself, you will not be afraid of being caught on audio and video. When you feel that you are in a situation that could escalate, you should turn on your body camera or vehicle camera (again, assuming you've consulted with your attorney before buying one). Should the situation escalate into violence, this footage can be critical to your case.

5.4 De-Escalation

Even if you have done everything to avoid it, you may still find yourself in an argument where someone is angry or emotional. Luckily, there is good de-escalation training available. De-escalation training was primarily popularized by George J. Thompson with what he called Verbal Judo.[118] He was quite the character. Their website has classes and a store.

There are other options too. For example, Rory Miller and Marc MacYoung do a program called Conflict Communications.[119] They have an excellent description of conflict on their website:

> We know that not everything can be talked down.
>
> We know that not all conflict comes from the same motivation.
>
> We know that the tactics a clinical psychologist uses in his office will not apply to an EDP in crisis in the street—and we know why and what tactics might work.
>
> We know that it is unreasonable to believe that there is always a reasonable solution.
>
> We know that if someone's definition of a "win" includes seeing you bleeding and humiliated, there is no win-win.
>
> We know the differences between an indignant citizen, a panicked mental, a professional criminal, a hustler, and a predator who enjoys creating victims.
>
> We don't pretend that the same tactics will work on all those groups.
>
> We know that even if you can't always control the threat, there is one factor you can control: yourself.

De-escalation training is a must. I always recommend in-person training. If you can find it, get it scheduled. It should be part of everyone's self-defense training. It is far more critical than firearms training for the majority of civilians.

Once you have taken this training, go back and review our Storytimes. When you initially read them, you probably assumed most of them would escalate and end in violence. However, after this training, you may be surprised by what you can do to avoid that outcome.

---

[118] https://clayeolsen.com/vj

[119] https://clayeolsen.com/concom

5.5 Defense

Let's move to a Storytime that shows a failure to de-escalate.

Storytime

You are at a home store to buy a bunch of 10-foot-long PVC pipes. You get all the pipe you need and roll your cart carefully to the checkout. As you round a corner, a kid around five years old comes hauling butt from the other side and runs smack into your PVC pipes. She gets a black eye and she is screaming bloody murder. The mom comes rushing over and yells at you in a language you don't understand. You take a couple of steps back with your hands raised by your chest to show that you are not hostile. Her husband shows up, yelling and pointing at you, but you have no idea what he is saying. The husband begins an unhesitant advance toward you with clenched fists and a rather mean look. You continue to step backward slowly with your hands raised but then back into a wall. You have nowhere else to go. He steps toward you, raising his right arm back in preparation for a punch.

#

Although it may not have worked anyway, the lack of a common language has prevented de-escalation. Unfortunately, your body language has not stopped it either. His child is in pain and his wife's hysterics created a situation where he feels he needs to act against you.

Ending 1

You step in and counterattack before he can throw a punch, knocking him down in front of his family. He is embarrassed; he grabs an iron pipe from the shelf and advances on you, swinging away.

Ending 2

You step in and counterattack before he can throw a punch. You knock him down. His brother tackles you from behind and they both start beating you.

Ending 3

You flash the firearm in your holster, still raising one hand upright at chest level. He stops at first, then reaches for his gun. Shots are exchanged.

Ending 4

You run. He catches you and beats you.

Ending 5

You step in and counterattack before he throws a punch. Store employees step in and stop any further violence. A few days later, you look out your window and see a car across the street. He is in it, watching your house.

Ending 6

You pull your JPX6 and pepper spray him. He tries swinging at you, but he can't see. Store employees step in and stop any further escalation. A few days later, he and his friends figure out you are a jogger and where you like to run. They wait until you get done with your exercise—when you are the most tired—and jump you as you get into your car.

#

As you can see, this is a Storytime without a happy ending. This is an important lesson in actualized violence between civilians. If you "succeed" in this example, it will likely lead to resentment and future escalations—which is not in line with your mission. In sum, short-term success may cause long-term failure. *This relentless cycle of violence is why you want to work on yourself and your de-escalation skills.*

In the section about robbery, we talked about how reducing your risk is your best defense strategy. When dealing with civilians, getting yourself under control is, first and foremost, the best way to reduce your risk. Human beings are social animals, and you will sometimes find yourself in social situations that take a turn for the worse. Avoidance isn't the correct strategy here, as most people don't want to live life in their personal bomb shelter. Instead, the right approach is to master yourself and master de-escalation techniques.

What defensive skills do you need after you master de-escalation training?

Today, many people have trained in martial arts, with the UFC and MMA being so popular. Unfortunately, one of the things that people with such training do is try to take people to the ground. In a street fight, the last place you want to be is on the ground—where you may find that your opponent's friends are happy to jump in and help. You could get a work boot in your liver, a knee in your kidney, a rock smashed against your head, etc. If you are otherwise occupied, like trying to choke out your opponent (their friend), they will have the tremendous advantage of making a surprise attack with the weapon of their choice.

Even if your opponent has no friends and you have the upper hand in a fistfight, no referee will stop you from giving him a severe beating. From a legal perspective, excessive use of force will probably get you an aggravated assault charge. This charge would be a disaster for your mission.

In the robbery section, we discussed defense against a surprise attack, followed by a counterattack to create space. Counterattack skills are good to have in these situations. Remember, assume you are on camera (hopefully, you have a body camera rolling). You want to be on the right side of the law; otherwise, it will be a disaster for your mission. If de-escalation fails and an attack is imminent, your counterattack skills can surprise and put a civilian down to the ground. However, the fight may not stop there.

What weapon should I use?

If de-escalation fails, you may have to resort to using your physical defensive skills or even a weapon. I recommend the JPX6 here as the weapon that will allow you the best chance of success in the encounter and the legal world after the situation is over.

The trouble with using any weapon in these encounters is the possibility of being charged with excessive use of force. For example, getting into an argument with someone and then using a weapon against them when there was no direct threat to your well-being would be excessive use of force—another disaster for your mission.

Alternatively, for example, let's say you were physically attacked, you counterattacked, and he fell to the ground. He decided to try and get back up and come after you. You pull your JPX6 and put a "stop" signal hand in the air. He continues to come at you again, and you pepper spray him. You made sure he knew what the ramifications would be if he attacked. You are likely in better legal standing here, especially with your body camera.

In any case, should you have to use violence to protect yourself against a civilian, you need to be extremely prepared against future escalations. You should assume the civilian will try to get even, and you need to prepare accordingly. Document and record any future encounters or conversations. Get a restraining order if you feel threatened or believe your family is at risk.

5.6 Conclusion

The self-defense plan of most civilians is pretty simple: learn to shoot a gun that you can carry concealed. Some may focus on physical self-defense skills later, but it is rare to see anyone take de-escalation training. This emphasis is the total opposite of how it should be.

What you should do: Master yourself and your attitude toward others. You can make choices about how your day goes. You are in control and you should showcase it. Next, master de-escalation techniques.

These two skills are the best way to accomplish your mission. Finally, if you feel more is required, get in shape and take suitable physical defense classes.

A side effect of physical self-defense skills is confidence. Good training and practice will lead to feeling confident that you can defend yourself if needed. In addition, this confidence can help you to de-escalate. If you can de-escalate a situation so that the potential offender leaves feeling like they are the bigger man and you are a weakling, then fantastic! They'll forget about it after a while and because you have self-esteem, you won't worry about their opinion.

In the rare case where avoidance and de-escalation fail you, you may have to use your physical defense skills or a weapon. I am a fan of the JPX6; of course, lethal weapons also work, but as we've discussed throughout this book, they can impact our mission in various negative ways.

When dealing with civilians and violence, recognize that winning in the short term doesn't mean you will win in the long term. Some civilians who come up short in a fight will internalize it, and it will gnaw at them for the rest of their lives. They may choose to end that gnawing by later coming after you or the people you love.

PART IV

The People You Know

Aggravated assault has an interesting flip. When the victim isn't injured, people who are strangers to the victim are the common offenders. However, when the victim is injured, the offender is usually someone the victim knew. Even in robberies, where we believe civilians will be up against violent criminals more than any other crime, offenders who are strangers to the victim are not as common when an injury is reported. With rape, strangers barely make an appearance—the victim almost always knows their offender. In the case of murder, we have a large percentage of "relationship unknowns." As discussed previously, we need more data to characterize this, but I suggest that it represents violent criminals targeting other violent criminals. When civilians kill other civilians, the offender and victim likely know each other, and these crimes are solvable by law enforcement in most instances. We should also remember that murder represented only 1.3 percent of all violent crimes in this period. Therefore, even if strangers accounted for all of the "relationship unknowns," being murdered by a stranger wouldn't impact ordinary civilians as much as injurious aggravated assault, injurious robbery, and rape due to that lower percentage.

The people you know are incredibly significant in injurious violent crimes involving civilians. So, to help prevent becoming a victim, we want to investigate any clues that someone we know may become violent before developing any sort of relationship with them.

6.1 Criminal and Personal History

Knowing about the criminal histories of the people you know is essential. For example, one Bureau of Justice study[120] examined people convicted of a violent felony in the 75 most populous counties from 1990 to 2002. From this source:

"About half of all reported violent crimes nationwide occur in these counties. In 2002 these counties accounted for—

- 61% percent of robberies
- 51% percent of murders and nonnegligent manslaughters
- 47% percent of aggravated assaults
- 36% percent of forcible rapes"

These counties make an excellent benchmark given our focus on injurious aggravated assault, injurious robbery, and rape.

Let's summarize the demographics from this report:

- 91% of violent felons in the 75 largest counties were male.
- Only 19% nineteen percent of rapists were 40 or older.
- Only 6% of robbers were 40 years or older.
- Only sixteen percent of assault offenders were 40 or older.[121]

Basically, we are looking at men under 40 as our primary violent criminal threat. However, there is more:

- "Thirty-six percent of violent felons had an active criminal justice status at the time of their arrest.
- Seventy percent of violent felons had a prior arrest record, and 57 percent had at least one prior arrest for a felony. Sixty-seven

---

[120] https://clayeolsen.com/bjs-2
[121] https://clayeolsen.com/bjs-2

percent of murderers and 73 percent of those convicted of robbery or assault had an arrest record.

- A majority (56 percent) of violent felons had a prior conviction record. Thirty-eight percent had a previous felony conviction and 15 percent had a prior conviction for a violent felony."[122]

Another BJS study shows that most offenders had not completed a high-school education and did not grow up in a two-parent household.[123]

How can this information help us? We want to know if the people in our lives have a criminal history. How do we do this? *We hire a competent private investigator.* Even if you think you know someone's criminal history, hire a qualified private investigator to do an extensive background check.

The first problem is that we know many people and private investigators cost money. The more background checks you do, the more money it costs. How can we limit the number of background checks to be efficient with our money?

Well, men are much more likely to be violent offenders. We can see from the previous statistics that men under 40 years old are our primary threat. Here are five good rules to determine who is a good background check candidate:

- If you are a female under 40 years old, any male under 40 who might be a dating interest.
- Any men under 40 who have been to your house.
- Any men under 40 who are planning on going to your house.
- Any immediate neighbors of yours who are men under 40.
- Anyone your instincts are warning you about.

If this still results in too much money, look at men under 30 years old. Violent crime is more likely to be a young man's game.

---

[122] https://clayeolsen.com/bjs-2

[123] https://clayeolsen.com/bjs-4

Please remember to use good judgment if you find something in these background checks. If you're in your 40s and a person your age was arrested at 18 for marijuana possession and no other record, you may say that is not a big deal. Not everyone is perfect. However, a history of domestic violence should be concerning. Anyone with an active criminal justice status, such as probation, parole, or pending deposition, would also be a concern.

Even with these filters, won't it still cost a lot of money to hire a private investigator? Yes. But how much money might you spend on firearms, ammo, and training? If you are more thoughtful about that aspect of your self-defense, you'll have more cash to spend on something that, quite frankly, is more likely to be a benefit to you.

Other concerning statistics from the BJS:[124] "Fifty-six percent of all jail inmates said they had grown up in a single-parent household or with a guardian. About 12 percent had lived in a foster home or institution. […] Thirty-one percent of the jail inmates had grown up with a parent or guardian who abused alcohol or drugs, and 46 percent had a family member who had been incarcerated."

This report only considers federal prisoners. However, I suspect it can be extrapolated to state prisoners as well. *Having the private investigator check for family incarceration, parental drug use (e.g., criminal drug charges), not graduating high school, and growing up in a single-parent home (probably fatherless) is also a good idea.* When combined with a previous criminal arrest record, this person could be a risk as they may use violence against you.

Does that mean this person is "bad"? No. This person may be an outstanding citizen who will never get into trouble again. You simply don't know. Your treatment of them needs to be a risk management decision. Some criminals are very personable and your instincts can be fooled. Use a background check to help balance your instincts. Be sure to *trust your instincts* if your instincts warn you about someone and their background check comes back clean.

---

[124] https://clayeolsen.com/bjs-3

6.2 Association and Attraction Principles

When someone starts smoking cigarettes, they end up with many new friends who are smokers. How does this happen? Our new smoker now steps outside to light up when they are out on the town. They strike up a conversation with another smoker doing the same thing. Over time, they start becoming friends with people who smoke simply due to this segregation and the social nature of people. You can call this the Association Principle. When our smoker later decides to quit, he has a real problem: His "new" friends still smoke. It makes quitting much harder.

Here is another example. You have a childhood friend who ended up serving some time in prison. After he got out, you remained friends and hung out with him quite a bit. You met some new people through him and became friends with them. Who are these people? Likely, they are people he met in prison. This is another example of the Association Principle. Is that such a bad thing? Let's hear from Varg Freeborn's *Violence of Mind* about prison inmates:

> The worst part about being with the worst of the worst is not the direct violence, it's the constant manipulation and deceit that make up 90 percent of transactions and communication. These are predators, con artists, and vile creatures with no moral compass.[125]

It sounds like these new friends may have an advantage in taking advantage of someone.

Let's examine another principle—the Attraction Principle. Say you have a friend who does illegal drugs. You don't have a problem with it because you don't do illegal drugs, and you have been friends with this guy for years. However, keep in mind that you are now one degree of separation from those who sell your friend drugs. These people are much more likely to be criminalized than your friend. If your friend is a talker, they may even know who you are by now. If your friend loses his job or his habit gets out of hand, these people may come knocking at your

---

[125] Freeborn (2018)

door, looking for you to pay up for your friend. You can call this the Attraction Principle—you end up attracting people you don't want in your life.

But you can use these principles to your benefit too. First, become friends with people you admire or have traits that you find admirable. Since many become friends with people similar to themselves, you could find yourself introduced to other people with similar traits. Second, if you become friends with these respectable people, you will find that they will discuss you with other reputable people you haven't met. These other people may enjoy being introduced to you. In short, it is a positive feedback loop rather than a negative one.

6.3 Violence Drama

You must have zero tolerance for violence. Any family, friend, or lover who uses violence against you is someone you need to remove from your life. It will only get worse. Intoxication doesn't excuse it. Mood swings do not excuse it. It is simply inexcusable. Get that person out of your life.

Other situations almost lead to violence—but don't quite get there. I call this "violence drama." Let me explain through a Storytime.

Storytime

You are relaxing one afternoon, having a drink with your beautiful girlfriend. Unfortunately, one of the other patrons eyeballed her and sent her an expensive drink. You confront him and almost get into a fight.

Days later, you are talking to a friend about the incident. Your friend says, "Don't take this the wrong way, but your girlfriend seems to love making you jealous. You were almost in three fights this last year, and you weren't in any before that! So for safety's sake, you may want to reconsider your relationship with her."

#

The friend is almost right—don't reconsider, just get this gal out of your life! Continuing this line of thought, think about the people you know and see if they fit these examples of people who like "violence drama":

- Got a friend who wants to fight when they drink?
- Got a friend who drives like a maniac, constantly cussing and flipping people off while they're on the road?
- Hang out with a couple who are always yelling and screaming at each other?
- Got a friend who hangs out with criminals?
- Got a friend in and out of jail or who is arrested often?
- Got a friend who gets kicked out of bars and restaurants repeatedly?
- Got a friend who always has illegal drugs?
- Got a friend who isn't very honest about money?
- Got a friend who gets drunk every day?

At some point, "violence drama" will end in violence. Recognize that and wean yourself away from these individuals.

6.4 Under the Influence

Ask any cop how many of the calls they get are alcohol related and you'll get estimates ranging from 50 to 90 percent.

—Adam Plantinga, *400 Things Cops Know*

In the last section, we saw how other people could get us into trouble. One of those people would be a friend of yours who can't handle their liquor, and you have to back them up after they started trouble with others. The one good thing about those people is that it only has to happen once and you know to stay away from them. However, other people have trouble with alcohol and drugs and you may not realize that they can also cause you many problems. What I'm talking about here is dependency.

Are there people in your life who have a drug or alcohol dependency? Sometimes it isn't easy to tell. They may be a joy to be around, fun, and cool. A quick test is whether your friend can have fun without alcohol or drugs. If you can, try to plan activities with your friends that don't include alcohol or drugs. You'll gradually figure out who can have fun without them. People who cannot have fun without drugs or alcohol may have a dependency problem.

We also saw in an earlier section how the Attraction Principle could easily lead to criminals knowing more about you because of your friend's drug habit. That is never a good thing. So here are some more eye-opening statistics from the BJS around drugs and alcohol:[126]

> Two-thirds of the 2002 jail inmates said they were regular drug users. More than half of those inmates who had been convicted reported having used drugs in the month before their current offense. Almost a third said they were using drugs at the time of their offense. An estimated 66 percent of the jail inmates reported using alcohol at least once a week for a month, and 35 percent were under the influence at the time of the current offense. Three out of every four convicted jail inmates were alcohol or drug-involved at the time of their current offense.

These statistics clearly point to a dependency issue and crime. However, these individuals can appear quite normal and it can be hard to tell. Understand that someone who has a dependency problem will make some bad decisions at some point. Unfortunately, you may be involved in one of those bad decisions. The best thing you can do is to get your friend some help. Many communities have local resources to help with addiction. These resources can also help friends understand the recovery process and what their dependent friend will go through. However, if your friend chooses their dependency over help, you should not let them pull you down with them.

---

[126] https://clayeolsen.com/bjs-3

6.5 Consent

In what follows, I'll discuss situations where civilians misunderstand sexual consent—in other words, rape. Whether the victim brings charges against the offender or not, recognize that this is a traumatizing experience that must be avoided. This discussion will not be about physical assault that leads to rape or date-rape drugs. Instead, this section is purely about misunderstanding consent between civilians.

Consent may seem straightforward, but it is an ongoing agreement that can be communicated in different ways depending on the individual. Voluntary intoxication can further complicate the issue. I'll bring up an example of non-sexual consent to show how even it could have caused significant problems.

6.5.1 Example

I would like to relay a story that happened to me while on vacation in Hawaii. I was walking around the beach about mid-morning when I decided to have a couple of piña coladas. I stopped by a small beach bar setup and chatted with the bartender. About that time, two 21-year-old women stopped by. They were also on vacation and were getting ready to head to the airport. I overheard a portion of their conversation:

Brunette: We had a lot of fun last night.

Blonde: Hell yeah. We were drunk!! You definitely had a lot of fun. The guy you were dancing with was OLD! Hahaha.

Brunette: How old do you think he was?

Blonde: Like 30. OLD.

Brunette: I can't believe he tried to kiss me.

Blonde: I know, right.

[a short period of silence.]

Blonde: Weren't you kissing him while you were dancing?

Brunette: Oh my god—I forgot about that. Well, he still shouldn't have tried to kiss me.

If it weren't for her friend, she would have entirely forgotten about kissing the old guy while dancing. The old guy probably thought that the first kiss while dancing implied consent to his kissing her again later. He was wrong. He was lucky, though. His night could have ended a bit differently than it did. She could have:

- Slapped him, drawing the attention of men keen on defending her. If there was a bouncer, perhaps drawing that attention as well. This interaction could have led to a trip to the emergency room for him.
- Officially accused him of sexual assault.
- Both.

These aren't good outcomes and will likely result in a failed mission. Ultimately though, the root cause isn't dancing or even kissing. What happened was a misunderstanding of consent due to voluntary intoxication. After all, I bet most people remember when they kiss someone for the first time and don't forget about it a few minutes later. Going out and having fun is a common Friday and Saturday night activity for young people, but the social interactions can get complicated when both people are under the influence. Is there a way to avoid this complexity?

6.5.2 Intoxication

Law Enforcement uses Blood Alcohol Content (BAC) to charge people with Driving Under the Influence (DUI). BAC readers (breathalyzers) are often installed in the vehicles of people who the courts feel are at risk for another DUI. In addition, some companies make personal breathalyzers and many people use them to determine if they can drive home from a bar or party so they don't get a DUI. You might think that you can also use BAC to determine consent—if your BAC is low enough to drive, you might think it is low enough to consent to sexual activity.

Unfortunately, BAC is not a good factor for determining the ability to consent. People handle their alcohol differently, and those drinks may not catch up with them until after leaving the party or bar. So, let's try a different approach. Here are a couple of designations you may find helpful:

- Functional Intoxication: These folks are laughing, dancing, and having fun.
- Impaired Intoxication: These folks are no longer having fun. They are likely nauseated, slurring their words, falling asleep, etc.

The most significant factor I've seen in the transition from functional to impaired intoxication is hard liquor (i.e., whiskey, vodka, tequila, and the like). Also, if someone goes outside or to the bathroom a lot, they may be doing recreational drugs. When combined with alcohol, this is another fast way to get to the impaired intoxication level.

You could be doing fine at the functional intoxication level; however, you take another shot of hard liquor with friends, and 25 minutes pass. In those 25 minutes, you also have another beer or cocktail. While you are having fun, what gets said during that time may no longer be valid at the end of those 25 minutes. You could reach the impaired intoxication level as those drinks catch up with you.

It is easy for someone who doesn't drink to say: If you drink, don't have intimate relations. For sure, that is the safest way to avoid misunderstanding consent. However, the open secret is that people can have exciting, wild, and fun intimate relations at the functional intoxication level. Another open secret is that people are often more sociable and friendly at the functional intoxication level. Unfortunately, almost everyone knows these "secrets," and it often becomes challenging to follow such a hard-and-fast rule as "if you drink, don't have intimate relations."

For ordinary civilians who are decent people, here are some more practical rules of thumb:

1. You are the one responsible for your decisions—no one else. Do what you need to do to make good decisions. Here's a question to ask yourself: Can I stand before a jury and say that I made a responsible decision?
2. No means No. It never means "maybe." It never means that the person is playing "hard to get." Imagine standing in front of a jury and having to tell them, "She said 'no,' but she didn't mean it."
3. Never have intimate relations with someone who is at the impaired intoxication level.
4. Even if the other person is at the functional intoxication level, do not have intimate relations with them if you haven't already established an ongoing sober relationship.
5. If they are still at the functionally intoxicated level, pay attention to what they have been drinking and doing (shots, hard liquor drinks, going outside or to the bathroom with a lot of friends—where they may be doing recreational drugs). *If they are at risk of transitioning to the impaired intoxication level, do not have intimate relations.*

Waking up with someone who barely remembers you, let alone the night before, is not an accomplishment. It is more like kicking a snowball down a mountaintop toward a ski lodge labeled "Our Lives" at the bottom. It is a bad situation for both of you.

6.6 Conclusion

We learned in this section how people you know could be very much implicated in exposing you to violent crime. You can choose to spend tremendous amounts of money on training, ammo, and firearms, but in the end, that money may be better spent on a private investigator doing extensive background checks on the people in your life.

You may have friends with no criminal history but with troublesome habits or behaviors. Don't get caught up in their drama. Stay away from people who are dependent on drugs or alcohol. Stay away from people who always seem to cause trouble or be in trouble. The life you save may be your own.

Understanding how alcohol and recreational drugs can influence consent is essential. Avoiding situations where consent can be misunderstood will allow you to fulfill your mission.

PART V

Home Defense

The most common location for a violent crime to occur is in or near the victim's home. Weekends and evening hours are the most frequent times for violent victimization.

—Clayton Mosher, Terance D. Miethe, Timothy Christopher Hart, *The Mismeasure of Crime*

One's own home is involved in a staggering amount of violent crime. Who are the people that are usually in your house? People that you know. So, in the last section, we talked about doing extensive background checks on the people you know as the primary way to protect yourself from violence. This section will discuss preparing your home to defend against people you don't want to be there. Sometimes you will know them and sometimes you won't. We will cover three attack vectors:

- Opportunistic Theft
- Burglary
- Psychotic Ex-Boyfriends

Later in this section, I will offer some tips to defend against rape in your home. Rape is especially difficult to defend against because the offender is usually someone you know and it usually happens at a home.

We'll also discuss property damage that escalates into aggravated assault (around 28 percent of cases, as shown by the UCR statistics).

Theft and burglary are covered even though they are not violent crimes. However, home defenses are set up with the worst situation in mind, and if they are deployed correctly, they will be effective against such nonviolent crimes. Keep in mind the theft of a firearm is a harm in our fact box because it becomes part of the black market and may be used in crimes. We'll cover properly securing our weapons.

Before we get started, there are some essential points to consider when discussing home defenses:

- *All home defenses can be breached.* It is just a question of time and effort. Unfortunately, many homeowners are surprised by how ineffective many standard security measures are and how quickly they can be breached.
- *What keeps bad people out can also keep you in.* Home security can be problematic if you are injured. Home fires and carbon monoxide alarms are more common than home invasions. We don't want to secure our home so well that we die because we can't get out.
- *What keeps bad people out can also keep good people out.* For example, your security measures can delay first responders or family responding to a help call. Please don't assume you'll be able to let them in. You may be hurt or unconscious.

Our goals with home security are:

1. To prevent our home from becoming a target. We want criminals to look at our home and say, "Not this one."
2. To slow down the offenders and make them work under pressure knowing law enforcement is on the way.
3. To keep the offender who wants to hurt you at bay until law enforcement arrives.
4. To make it possible to defend yourself if the offender does breach your home defenses before law enforcement arrives.

I will analyze the standard home protections many people deploy and showcase their weaknesses against our three threats. Then I'll start talking about how we can do better. Fundamentally, my strategy is about "Defense in Depth"—we don't want to be like a turtle you can turn over to expose the soft underbelly. Instead, we want to be like the turtle you turn over and find another shell protecting the belly. If you get through that shell, there is another shell. In short, there never is a soft underbelly. It's hard-shelled turtles all the way down!

Every home is different, the values of the people inside are different, and the budgets are different. But, given your constraints, you can scour this section for ideas and figure out what works best for you and your home. Some of these ideas may work for apartments, but not all of them (unless you want to lose your security deposit!).

7.1 My Background

I grew up on a cotton farm in a rural area in Arizona. When I was a young teenager, our family was sitting in the living room, and we heard something that we hadn't heard in fourteen years—a knock on the door. A couple of weeks before, our watchdog died. He lived a long 14 years and kept everyone away from our farmhouse. We felt safe with him and we hadn't quite processed what it meant when he died. When we heard that knock, we no longer felt safe.

My father immediately had our entry doors fitted with deadbolt locks. If you can believe it, our entry doors weren't even machined for deadbolt locks. Our screen doors had the simple hook-in-the-hole latch that kept them from banging in the wind. A strong pull would ruin it, or you could open the door by simply popping the screen, reaching in, and lifting the hook. Also, because we lived on a farm, there were a lot of tools and equipment around the house that an enterprising burglar could put to use.

Our vehicle security was similarly weak. I can't even remember locking our car doors (well, until one day, I fell out of the truck while it was rounding a corner—I made sure my door was shut and I locked them religiously after that!). Often, when we got done rounding up cattle on my grandfather's ranch, we would head down to the local coffee shop. Our trucks unlocked, gear including firearms inside, keys inside, and so forth. Others in our rural community had similar security measures, even if they weren't farmers and ranchers. For example, deer season would always start on a Friday. On Thursday, the high school parking lot was full of guns and gear as eager high schoolers headed out to the hills to join their families right after school. Deer season Friday should have been a school holiday.

The death of our watchdog seemed to coincide with a new era emerging in our community. That new era was the methamphetamine era. Highly toxic and highly addictive, it could be snorted and smoked. Dealers weren't dependent on plants from other countries. Just a bathtub and off-the-shelf chemicals from the store could make a large batch to sell. It was one drug where you didn't need to photoshop the before and after pictures of addicts. After a couple of years of use, the "after picture" was simply horrible.

Needless to say, the amount of theft skyrocketed. We had to worry about all of our valuables, no matter where they were. Later on, when I moved from a rural area to live in urban areas, not much changed. I learned to evaluate my home, vehicles, and valuables with the eyes of a thief; particularly someone who needed quick money to score drugs. As I gained more experience, I helped many friends and family members design their security.

In what follows, I'll cover three threats your home could experience, the typical defenses used, the vulnerabilities in those defenses, and discuss better defenses.

7.2 Where You Live

You may have been in your house for twenty years. You may enjoy your neighborhood. However, you may notice that the "crime line" is gradually moving toward your home. A few miles away, crime rates are higher, and cars and housing start to look run down. You can remember going on jogs in your younger years through this area where you now wouldn't feel safe after dark.

Looking at this situation with an open mind is tough when your emotions about your home are involved. But, at some point, you must ask yourself a question: do I pack up and move to a neighborhood that will likely be safer in five years? This is an important decision. How do you protect your home if you are increasingly likely to have criminals as neighbors casing your house?

Even if you live in a great area, you should still consider these things. In most places where civilians live anyone in the world can pull up and park in your driveway. That is great if your friend from Europe wants to surprise you one day with a visit. It is bad when a violent criminal who has targeted you can do it. You can find yourself in an existential crisis trying to keep a balance. We want to find that happy medium.

An excellent location improvement is finding a home in a gated community with a staffed entrance complete with cameras. Sometimes these communities have walls around them with specific entry and exit points. All visitors must check in with ID and have their license plates recorded. Additionally, a gated community with a few roads to get to the community itself is even better. Criminals like corner convenience stores for a reason—many escape paths exist. A community with fewer paths to escape means the criminal will likely find another neighborhood to target.

Such a community offers a good initial defense against threats that are external to the community. However, there are internal threats, and our first example will showcase such a threat.

7.3 Opportunistic Threat

Storytime: The Neighbor's Friend

Your neighbor has a teenage son who has a friend over one evening for a barbecue. You come home from the grocery store with bags and the kids in tow. Because your garage is full of stuff, you park in the driveway. The neighbor's friend notices something most people miss—you weren't carrying your purse. From the backyard barbecue, he can watch your house without being noticed. The barbecue ends and he pretends to head home. However, he stops a short distance away and comes back under cover of night. It turns out you didn't lock your car doors, so he easily enters your car and takes your purse.

#

People have an excellent security device for their vehicles—their garage. But unfortunately, they don't use the garage because their garage is usually filled with junk! *Parking your vehicle outside the garage makes it a prime target for an opportunistic attack.*

Some folks think a motion-sensing light will act as a deterrent. The problem with that is false positives. Neighborhood dogs, cats, raccoons, coyotes, and other animals always set them off. The first time you installed your motion light, you were probably checking every time it went off. After seeing 10 different cats and dogs for a week, you no longer even notice when it turns on.

What is true for motion lights is also true of doorbell cameras. If your phone goes off five times a night because of cats and dogs, it won't be long before you simply ignore it or disable notifications.

Let's look at another opportunistic threat that uses a different approach.

Storytime: The Jogger

Your house backs up to a walking trail. Every morning, there are joggers, cyclists, dog walkers, and so forth out and about. One day, one of our more criminally minded joggers notices your awesome new mountain bike on your backyard porch. Over the next few days, he changes his jogging time to figure out your schedule and the traffic on the trail. He picks a day, jumps the fence, gets your bike, and off he goes.

#

Always keep your valuable possessions locked up and out of sight. *What people can't see, they don't steal.*

7.4 Burglary Threat

Burglars prefer not to confront homeowners. If such confrontation occurred often, our violent crime statistics would show it because burglaries far outnumber violent crimes. This observation is further confirmed by residential daytime burglaries happening more often than nighttime ones. It is easier to tell if you are gone during the day.

Most residential burglars don't roll up with a team of specialists like in the movie *Ocean's 11*. They also don't want to be stopped by law enforcement while in possession of crowbars, picking tools, and so forth, which would be rather incriminating. Let's walk through an example where talking too much and standard home security cause massive problems.

Storytime: The Coworker

One of your coworkers likes to spend money and have a good time. Although no one at work knows, he usually needs some extra cash. Luckily for him, you enjoy talking about your money and the cars you drive. He takes note. Once he has your work schedule down, he takes early lunches to case your home and neighborhood. It turns out that all your neighbors are gone during the Monday through Friday workweek too. He picks a particular day to call in sick at the office. Wearing a hoodie, mask (thank goodness for the pandemic!), and gloves, posing as a jogger, he hops the fence to your backyard. He gets to your backdoor and with one swift kick, he splits the doorjamb and is in the house. The entry/exit alarm goes off, waiting for the PIN to be entered. He ignores it. He moves right to the master bedroom, searches a few locations, and hits the jackpot. He is out of the house in two minutes. The alarm system monitoring company is notified when the PIN is not entered after around three minutes. They try to call you. You are in a meeting and don't have the alarm system company on your contact list. You think it is a telemarketer. It goes to voicemail. After the meeting, you listen to it and hurry back to your house where law enforcement is waiting.

#

This Storytime describes the method of many burglaries. The entry/exit delay, the monitoring station delay, the homeowner delay, and the law enforcement response time add up to quite a duration. Our burglar is taking a shower in the comfort of his own home before anyone knows what happened.

The weakness that was exploited is typical: the doorjamb. Residential entry/exit doors open to the inside. Although you have a deadbolt, what secures the deadbolt is the doorjamb, which, as it turns out, is usually weak. A good solid kick between the deadbolt and the door handle will likely split the doorjamb. Most alarm systems cannot detect whether a key opened the door or if an intruder kicked the door down. All they know is the magnetic door sensor showed an opened door.

We could go through more examples of windows being left open, doors being unlocked, the alarm system not being set, and so forth, but you get the idea. Also, be aware that if you have tools lying around, burglars will put them to work if needed.

7.5 Psycho Ex-Boyfriend

The real danger of this offender is that he doesn't care about being caught.

Storytime

You met a guy you thought was sweet, but he became obsessive about you after a couple of months, so you ended the relationship. He is upset and harasses you. Finally, after a couple of months, he quits, and you think things are okay. You go out on a date with someone new. One of your ex-boyfriend's buddies happens to see you two. He runs into the ex-boyfriend at a party about a week later and tells him about your new boyfriend. The ex-boyfriend freaks out, gets into his car, and heads to your house.

You have just gone to sleep. Your ex-boyfriend pulls up to your place, gets out, and walks to the porch. Your phone buzzes that motion was detected by your doorbell camera. You are half asleep, wondering if you should bother to check it. He grabs a metal patio chair on the porch and throws it through your large front window. The house alarm goes off, but he doesn't react to it. Instead, he climbs through the window and marches right to your bedroom. One easy kick, and the door breaks open. He flicks on the light. There you are, searching for your phone in an absolute panic.

#

These actions took about fifteen seconds, if that. The behavior of someone who wants to hurt you more than they fear getting caught (or killed) is incredibly different from someone who fears getting caught more than they want to hurt you.

Would the homeowner having a gun help here? It might. However, at some point, one person will have a strong advantage. Let's look at the situation:

- The victim was half-asleep without any knowledge someone wanted to hurt them.
- The offender was wide awake with the explicit goal of causing harm.

How little time is necessary before the intruder has a significant advantage? Does it take fifteen seconds from being startled awake to being dead? Ten seconds? How can we swing those odds in our favor?

7.6 Better Home Preparation—Outside

The Perimeter

Many homes have a fence around the property, which is a good idea. It would be best if the fence could also contain a large dog, which makes an excellent addition to your home security. However, you need to know your state's laws before putting up a "Beware of Dog" sign. Depending on your state, you may get into more trouble if your dog bites someone.

This sign is a critical issue to discuss with your attorney. Michigan State University has a website[127] showcasing the complexity of various state laws. Also, keep in mind that dog doors, especially for large dogs, are a significant security risk. *Do not use them.*

Another excellent addition to your fence is a sign: "Warning: Premises Protected by 24-Hour Audio and Video Surveillance. By Entering, You Consent to Be Recorded." You can have this on the front gate. If you have a back entrance, put it there too. Most criminals will assume you have a home security system if you have 24-hour audio and video surveillance. *Audio surveillance is full of legal issues, and you should not do something like that until you consult with your attorney.* Although there are open questions that you need to resolve with your attorney before recording audio, this sign effectively lets people know you are security-conscious without letting them know what security system you have.

The next step is to clear the area around your windows. You don't want someone to be able to hide behind a bush while they're breaking into your home. You want them to be in full view of the street, neighbors, yourself, and your cameras. Strangely, some people recommend planting cacti or other prickly plants by your windows. That is great until you have a house fire and need to jump into them to escape!

The next step is to add powerful exterior LED lights. If you hear something outside that concerns you, you can flick that switch and light up your house and yard like a stadium.

If you have an outside dog, any motion lights will become problematic as your dog will set them off at night. However, you can work around this problem by setting up a different trigger mechanism. For example, you can use break beams throughout the yard that are high enough for your dog not to trigger them. If something breaks the beams, the receiver can activate the lights (you'll want to disable the motion detection setup for these lights or get non-motion detection lights). This trigger mechanism means you won't be bothered with false positives nearly as much. If a motion light comes on, something bigger than your

---

[127] https://clayeolsen.com/dog

dog is in the yard. I've had good luck with Dakota Alert[128] products, but I'm sure there are other vendors.

Lastly, park your cars in your garage and lock up any valuables in the yard when you are done with them.

The Home Exterior: Doors

The first upgrade to your exterior should be metal security doors with double-cylinder locks. High-quality metal security doors are an extra level of protection. Unfortunately, high-security double-cylinder locks are expensive—look for ANSI Grade 1 ratings, such as the BiLock.[129]

These security doors should have smaller built-in portals you can open up to hand stuff to people at the door. For instance, if you have something delivered that you need to pay or sign for, you won't need to unlock the security door. Instead, you can pass money or whatever back and forth to the delivery person through this slot. The slot should be a little bigger than the size of the handheld devices the USPS and UPS carry. My security doors have an insect screen that I can remove to pass things back and forth in this manner.

Don't expect too much from these security doors, though. A couple of guys with crowbars can get through your door faster than you think. Still, security doors and locks are the first physical defense on your entryways. If you set them up correctly, getting through them will take time and make noise, which should get your attention.

Behind the metal security door is your entry door. Because of weather and fire codes, these doors are usually pretty solid. However, your entry doors can also be upgraded to ones made with steel reinforcement, metal/composite, or other higher security options than the standard ones that came with the house. Your entry door should also have no glass. I recommend having a peephole that you can cover up when not in use. You can use that peephole should your door camera fail for some reason. However, don't get into the habit of using it unless absolutely

---

[128] https://clayeolsen.com/da

[129] https://clayeolsen.com/bilock

necessary. It is best to utilize your cameras or your doorbell camera as someone at the door can usually hear or detect a lighting change when you are using the peephole.

For entry doors, I recommend Master Lock NightWatch[130] deadbolts. At night when you are home, you can set them so that they will not open even with the key. This feature is beneficial to protect against angry ex-lovers, lost keys, or lockpickers. This feature should only be used while you are home. If you have multiple doors, be sure to disengage the NightWatch feature on all doors before leaving the house so you can reenter your home.

Many people make the big mistake of hiding a spare key outside their house. Unfortunately, finding someone's hidden house keys is usually straightforward, especially for an experienced burglar. Never hide your house key outside your home.

The next upgrade to your entry doors is to add doorjamb reinforcement. I use Armor Concepts,[131] but others are available. These protect hinges, the doorjamb itself, the doorknob, and the deadbolt. This reinforcement keeps simple brute force attacks from being successful. The primary benefit is to protect the doorjamb from being split, which can happen with a brute force kick to the door. They also offer more protection from crowbars against the deadbolt lock and hinges.

Fire and weather resistance is required of entry doors, and usually, contractors make sure that the doors are well sealed per building codes. However, be aware that one avenue of attack is to force tools between the door and the jamb to open the deadbolt and the door handle (similar to attacks on hotel room doors). One simple thing you can do to counter this is to use a knob on the inside door handle rather than a lever, which will be tougher to get ahold of and turn with a tool if the intruder has already opened the deadbolt. *However, be aware that knobs are much harder for the disabled and elderly to turn.*

Just as you can get a tool between the door and doorjamb to lift a lever, so can you turn a deadbolt. To protect your deadbolt from these

---

130 https://clayeolsen.com/nw

131 https://clayeolsen.com/ac

attacks, you can put straps around your deadbolt and the doorknob to secure the deadbolt handle.

Sliding glass doors are a favorite of criminals because of the many easy ways to attack them. Armor Concepts makes an effective physical device that shuts down many of these attacks.[132] I'm sure there are other solutions available too. Always look for solutions that screw into the door or house. Some of the pressure security bars on the market can be manipulated via door movement.

Garage doors are another mechanism for easy entry. Your garage door itself should be metal and insulated. It needs to seal well with the ground as well as the sides. Garage doors typically have cables that dangle down so you can pull on them to open the door in case of a power failure. A simple wire loop can break the garage door seal, and anyone can reach in and loop this handle. You should make sure you secure this handle to prevent such an attack.

I don't have a lot of confidence in the security of garage door remotes nor in the manual locks on these doors. A better way to handle this is to control your garage door using a smart outlet connected to your wireless network and managed via an application on your phone. You can put a smart outlet on your garage door motor, then use their simple application on your phone to turn on the smart outlet, which provides power to your garage door motor. Next, open your garage door using the supplied door remote or wall-based switch. Once the garage door is shut, you can use the application to shut off power to your garage door motor. This process is an extra step, but it is more secure than keeping your garage motor on all the time. You will need to test this out to ensure your garage door opener doesn't lose connection to the motor: Get your garage door working with the remote, unplug it for a few days, plug it back in, and make sure everything works. If it does, a smart outlet should work for you.

The interior door that seals the garage from the house should be treated just like an exterior door. While you may not need a metal security door here, you should have the same protection on that door as on any other entry door.

---

[132] https://clayeolsen.com/ac2

Many people relax as soon as their garage door goes up. After all, they are almost in their house, and their day is wrapping up. A possible attack vector is for a criminal to hide by your house and dart into your garage when you pull your car in. The criminal may be able to slide right under your car and avoid being seen. Having a large dog helps prevent this attack as well as clear areas around your house so intruders can't hide as easily. Another tip is to use mirrors on the garage wall that allow you to see the sides of your car. You can angle a couple of mirrors so you can see under your car as well. If you detect this attack, keep your car doors locked and get out of there, calling 911 as you drive away. As long as your entry door to your house is well secured, the intruder isn't going get in anyway. You don't want to be trapped in your garage with an intruder, and you don't want to even the playing field with him by getting out of your vehicle.

The Home Exterior: Windows

Windows around your house are another favorite of criminals. Many people leave them unlocked, partially open, or otherwise insecure. Closing and locking your windows is an excellent first step (duh!). Next, many companies make simple, effective, and inexpensive window locks that prevent the window from opening. These simply tighten up on the window frame and prevent the window from sliding.

You should designate a window in each bedroom for a fire escape— you may want to forgo a window lock on this one. You may be injured, and the window lock may be difficult to remove. These windows should open easily. Lubricate them according to the manufacturer's recommendation. You'll want to test these windows at least once a year. You should have a window breaker close by just in case.

Windows need shades, blinds, or shutters, and they must be closed when you are not home. You don't want people studying what is inside your home while you are not there. You also want these closed when it is dark outside and lights are on in your house—when anyone outside can see you clearly and you cannot see them. Additionally, I would recommend that you frost your all your garage windows so that a person can't look in and see what valuables you have stored in there.

Note that one attack vector is to use a small device that shatters the glass on a window, but the glass stays in place. Surprisingly, this attack can be done without making a lot of noise. The criminal then uses tools such as long needle nose pliers to defeat your locks. Using techniques such as these, an experienced criminal may be able to keep your alarm system window sensor together, remove it, and get in without setting off the alarm. As I will discuss in the alarm system section, don't skimp on sensors such as glass break sensors and motion sensors.

Security Electronics and Their Locations

I recommend you read through the entirety of Part V before deciding where to put things like your camera recorder, doorbell system, alarm panel, etc. Additionally, because we will be using your wireless network extensively, any network routers, modems, and other network devices will need to be in this location or otherwise appropriately protected.

Doorbell Cameras

Video doorbells are helpful. I prefer hardwired systems over wireless ones. Mine is from Comelit[133] and uses the standard doorbell wiring. I mention this because there are many good products to choose from beyond the few that have been promoted.

You may be tempted to purchase a system that bundles an alarm system and a doorbell camera. I would recommend against that for a couple of reasons:

- Many of these systems utilize wireless communication. Unfortunately, this utilization makes your wireless router a single point of failure. Also, since doorbell cameras are outside, they could be stolen and your wireless password obtained, depending on the vendor's security. As such, I recommend a hardwired doorbell camera different from your alarm system vendor.

---

[133] https://clayeolsen.com/comelit

- If all of your security is controlled by a single application, say on your phone, and you have a problem with that application, your home security may be worthless until you have fixed it. Again, this is a single point of failure. While being forced to use a different application for your doorbell camera and a separate application for your alarm system is a bit of a pain, it is more robust against failure.

Be aware that motion detection on a front door camera may give false positives. When your motion detector goes off, you may not pay attention if you get many false positives. For instance, if your homeowner's association has a landscaping crew, a burglar could go up to your door and knock on it after they leave your house. You have likely stopped paying attention to motion alerts or even disabled them while the landscaping crew is there. It is pretty easy to wear a hoodie, sunglasses, and a pandemic face mask to avoid being recognized by people looking at the video. After verifying no one is home, a potential burglar will choose an easier way to get in.

It is usually easy to figure out whether someone is home. Don't be fooled into thinking a burglar has to come up and ring the doorbell. You can usually tell if someone is home by how the window shades are positioned. If a potential burglar has seen the house while it was occupied versus unoccupied, they could pick up on other little things. Some of the more obvious things: if you are going to be gone for a while, you'll want someone to feed and water the dog, mow the grass, trim the shrubs, and pick up the mail and any packages.

Some folks will have timers and even recorded sounds of dogs barking when the doorbell rings so that it appears someone is home. If you have noticed, most law enforcement officers knock on the door rather than ring the doorbell. Many criminals do the same. If you have recorded dogs barking, they will not likely play when someone knocks.

Regardless of what's portrayed in marketing commercials, don't assume that you can utilize your cellphone, talk through your doorbell camera, and your voice will send potential criminals fleeing. If they know you are not home, they may kick down your door anyway. Remember, they can be out of the house long before law enforcement shows up due to response time delays.

Exterior Cameras

Camera systems (not video doorbells) typically come with a network recorder that also powers the cameras via ethernet cables. I've had good luck with Security Camera Warehouse (SCW).[134] They have a wealth of security guidelines and tutorials to go through for free, even if you choose not to purchase through them. Their products are more expensive than what you could get from big-name retailers, but they are of much better quality. This company will also help to design a system for you. You'll want to work with them to determine the hard drive space you need to store your recordings. I would also recommend having a network hard drive backup in a separate location from your video recorder.

Placing cameras high on your house's vertical walls so they can't be tampered with is a good idea. If you go this route, 4K resolution is essential to avoid losing detail when digitally zooming. These cameras have about 100 feet of night vision range, which is excellent. You'll want to ensure your exterior LED lights don't shine into the camera—if it is dark and the lights come on, the camera will be temporarily blinded. The camera's night sensor could suffer damage too.

When placing your cameras, you want to choose locations that give good coverage of your home, including the perimeter, gates, doors, and windows. Typically, these cameras will begin recording when motion or an event is detected. However, you can set the amount of time to save before the activity occurs and after. Let me explain this a bit further. Typically, your camera system is always recording to volatile memory. Let's assume that the default is five seconds' worth of buffer. When the five seconds are up, the camera continuously overwrites the buffer, so the last five seconds are always available. If a motion detection event occurs, the camera can save this to non-volatile memory and save five seconds of footage before the motion detection event. Depending on your device,

---

[134] https://clayeolsen.com/scw

you can set the amount of time to store in volatile memory such that when a motion event occurs, you will be able to go "back in time" before the motion event. In addition, assuming another motion event did not happen, you can also set the amount of time to record after the motion event. For instance, assume that someone triggered the motion detector but was motionless for 10 seconds. If you had five seconds of recording after the event, you would see this someone for five seconds. If they move six seconds later, you will get another motion event and a new recording. This flexibility helps save hard drive space while still giving you what you need.

Some cameras have audio recording capability. But, again, I would highly recommend a consultation with your attorney before setting that up.

For the particular unit I own, I have had a hard drive failure and a power supply failure after several years of use. The hard drive failure wasn't a problem to work around based upon my configuration. However, the power supply failure caused some significant problems. I would certainly look for redundant power supplies or have a spare power supply that you can replace yourself.

The Alarm System

In your house, you will have sensors to detect the opening and closing of exterior doors and windows, an alarm panel, and, usually, a cellular connection to a remote monitoring station. When you leave for work in the morning, you'll set your alarm to "Away." The alarm system allows you a couple of minutes of delay to exit. When you get back home at the end of the day, you open your door, and the alarm system signals an entry delay. You'll have a couple of minutes to enter your PIN. The alarm panel notifies the monitoring station if you don't enter your PIN. A person then calls your phone and asks you for the code word provided when the system was installed. If you don't know the code word, the monitoring station calls the police. If you don't answer the phone, the monitoring station will call another person on your contact list.

The monitoring station will call law enforcement to report the alarm if they cannot contact anyone. Because the monitoring station can call law enforcement on your behalf, you may need a county permit for the alarm system in some US states.

There are reputable alarm system companies as well as do-it-yourself alarms. I have had good luck with Brinks. If I were to do everything again, I would go with SCW's advanced alarms with professional monitoring. Their smart hub has a Z-Wave card that allows advanced customization that may not be available with other alarm systems.

There are a couple of problems with the name-brand alarms. If you live in a rural area, you'll often be hit with an additional remote service charge if repairs need to be done because someone has to drive out to your house. Also, alarm system companies sell coverage to each other from time to time. You might have a given vendor one day, and the next day, your product and coverage will have been sold to another vendor. When they sell coverage, other alarm system vendors know about the sale, and they'll send out sales folks to try and sell you on their system before the switchover. You'll get strangers knocking at your door wanting to see your alarm system and perhaps knowing more about it than you think they should. Real comforting!

You'll want to find an excellent central location for the alarm system panel. This panel will have a speaker, PIN pad, and perhaps a display. It will also need to be by an electrical outlet. If you put the alarm system panel next to a door with glass or within view of a window, bad actors with binoculars could see you enter your PIN.

The alarm system panel will also communicate with the monitoring station, usually by a cellular connection. In some rural areas, the carrier they use may not have reception. In one town I lived in, my coverage was sold to another company that couldn't use the existing cellular connection. I had to switch my alarm system to use the landline.

The alarm system panel communicates with various sensors installed around the house. Don't skimp on sensors. Think of them as "defense in depth." Every outside door and window that opens should have a sensor on it. You'll likely need to specify which doors are entry and exit as well—the front and the garage doors are the most common ones. These doors will provide you with a delay so that you may enter your PIN on the panel. You don't want this option on a sliding glass door. If the alarm is on and the sliding glass door is opened, you want an alarm to go off immediately.

Every room that has a window should have a glass break sensor. You also need a glass break sensor if an entry door has a built-in window (note that an entry door with a window is not recommended).

Your Wireless Network

Your wireless network may be accessible outside your home, especially with an antenna. Hackers have been known to drive their cars into random neighborhoods and use their computers with an antenna booster (like a Pringle's can!). They can then hack into home wireless networks to download child porn and other messed-up things. Sadly, the network owner appears to be doing the downloads, which could result in significant Internet usage charges (depending on your plan). Worse, the material downloaded could get the network owner on the radar of law enforcement. Many of the devices we have discussed use your wireless network to communicate. Unfortunately, most wireless networks are very poorly secured. You'll want to change that and have an extremely hard-to-guess passphrase for your wireless password. You may want to hit the max character limit for your passphrase, complete with numbers, uppercase, lowercase, and special characters. Check out the Diceware[135] page for advice on generating secure passphrases you can remember.

If you are worried about typing in a long passphrase, use the WPS functionality of your wireless router. Having physical access to your router lets you enable WPS on your device (e.g., a laptop) and then press the WPS button on your router. The router then sends the password to the device and no more typing!

---

[135] https://clayeolsen.com/dice

7.7 Better Home Preparation—Inside

If you followed the outside preparation guidelines, your defenses are solid, and there is no easy way around it. But, unfortunately for many homes, if you get through the first line of defense, you'll find there are no other defenses. Not so for the security we are designing. Imagine a determined burglar who finally gets inside only to discover that it doesn't get any easier.

Alarm System

Every room in your house should have a motion sensor connected to your alarm system. If a person can get past the entry and glass break sensors, the motion sensor is the last line of defense to detect them. However, motion sensors are heat sensitive, so you want to ensure they are only deployed in climate-controlled areas. For example, you wouldn't put one in your shed in Arizona because you would get many false positives from heat fluctuations.

When you go to bed at night, place the alarm system in "Stay" mode. This setting disables the motion sensors but keeps the glass break and open/close sensors active. So, if you are sleeping and someone opens or breaks a window, the alarm will go off.

There are particular interior doors or access points you'll want to put open-and-close sensors on. For example, burglars can try to access the main part of your house from the attic, basement, or crawlspace. The burglars will trip the alarm if these access doors have sensors.

If you have a closet or other location where you keep valuables, you may also want to put a door sensor there. Remember, if your alarm is in "stay" mode and you open that door, your alarm will go off. That may not be what you want.

Most alarm system companies offer panic buttons and medical emergency buttons. You'll want to get a few of these. For example, if you believe someone is attempting to get inside your house and your alarm system hasn't triggered yet, you can push the panic button to set it off yourself.

Interior Doors

We will discuss securing our interior doors and selecting a good bedroom as a rudimentary defense room (i.e., a "safe" or "panic" room). A couple of essential things about our interior bedroom doors:

- They are typically 1⅜" thick. Exterior doors are 1¾" thick—be sure any security devices you buy will work with a 1⅜" thick door.
- These doors typically open into the room. If they open outward, you'll need different security measures.
- They are almost always hollow—so a chunky five-year-old with a head of steam could likely run through them.
- The doorknob locks are not secure.
- The fit between the door and the doorjamb is often poor, allowing for tool insertion.

You can start by replacing your hollow bedroom doors with solid core doors, which are much stronger for obvious reasons. You can also look at metal doors. Keep in mind that most interior doorjambs are not machined for deadbolts. If you are less than handy, you may need someone to prepare the door and doorjamb for a deadbolt. Although unsuitable for the elderly and disabled, if you are okay with knobs, you should use them rather than levers. Interior doors typically have wide gaps at the bottom, allowing devices to get through that may be used to move levers and locks.

You may consider an electronic lock on the door handle that you can set to lock automatically after a few seconds. This feature is excellent if you get up for a drink of water in the middle of the night, return to your bedroom, and forget to turn the lock. You can also get an automatic door closer, like a hotel door. This device is also handy in conjunction with electronic locks. But, of course, the best thing is to develop good habits and always lock your bedroom door manually. Also, if your bedroom doors open inward, you'll want door jamb reinforcement just like your entry doors.

As I've stated previously, some items here may be difficult for the elderly or disabled and likely hinder first responders. Other things may prevent or delay you from exiting in an emergency. So be sure you are okay with these compromises you'll have to make to achieve this level of protection.

Defense Room

I don't like the terms "panic room" or "safe room." I use the term "defense room" to refer to a bedroom where we may need to make a stand against a determined foe. This foe wants to hurt you more than they fear getting caught. In short, the consideration for the design of this room is that you are under attack.

For starters, let's consider a childless single person or a married couple with no children. The bedroom that you sleep in should be the defense room. Any windows in this room should have a clear line of sight to your neighbors and the street in front of your house so that if someone is trying to get in, they will be in full view of the neighborhood and law enforcement when they arrive. Our goal for this room is to withstand an attack for at least three times as long as the response time for law enforcement. We want to be in our defense room when law enforcement arrives so we will be safe and law enforcement can do their job with less risk to us.

Ideally, we will only focus our attention on one door in a defense room. We want to make all possible ways of getting in this room just as hard as the primary home entry door. For instance, an on-suite bathroom door must be as secure as your main door to prevent someone from entering that room to attack you. The master bath will usually have a lock to prevent entry from the bedroom. You'll want an additional locking mechanism you can enable to prevent the opposite from happening.

You may want to consider upgrading your defense room door security. However, you don't want to assume that getting through the door is the only way to hurt you. For example, if your defense room shares an interior wall with another accessible room, like a living room, your threat could shoot through that wall. If your defense room shares an interior wall with another room, you may want to investigate Armor-core[136] panels. Consider installing these panels there if bullets can easily breach your exterior walls.

Once a threat realizes they cannot get through your bedroom door, they may go back outside and try to break the windows (or perhaps they will try to break the window first). Therefore, you'll want to investigate measures like polycarbonate windows for your defense room, such as DefenseLite[137] or ArmorPlast.[138] Keep in mind that you may want a different setup for your fire escape window.

911 Options

You'll need to be able to call 911 from your defense room. I would not rely on your cell phone, which you'll likely need to have a hand free to hold. If you have a landline, you should have a 911 pendant that ties in as the first device on the phone network, so if another phone is in use or off the hook, it will cut it off. The landline provides your location to the 911 operator.

Another option is to buy a 911 pendant with a GPS locator that uses the cellular network. You won't need a cellular plan for it to operate, and it can provide the 911 operator with your GPS location. This location signal will only work if your 911 operator has the supporting equipment to receive GPS location information. You'll need to verify that with your 911 system for your area. If you need to provide your location verbally, write it down by the pendant (or put it on the back of your pendant) and your cell phone number. You don't want to waste precious seconds because you temporarily forgot your home address in a stressful situation.

Your alarm system may also offer a pendant. Usually, however, your alarm system will call you to verify the emergency, so it would be better to use the 911 pendant. The alarm system pendant would still help trigger your alarm, though. For instance, if you hear a window break but the alarm

---

[136] https://clayeolsen.com/armorc

[137] https://clayeolsen.com/dl

[138] https://clayeolsen.com/ap

system doesn't go off, you can use the pendant to trigger the alarm. Because most burglars don't want confrontation, they may take off once the alarm goes off. After triggering your alarm, you can use your 911 pendant to call 911. Just ignore the alarm system monitoring call. They will call 911 when they can't get ahold of you. Focus on what the 911 operator is saying.

911 pendants will need to be periodically charged. Keep them on the charger in your defense room, and make sure they are constantly at 100 percent. Then, if a situation develops, you can take the pendant off the charger, place it around your neck, and press the button to reach a 911 operator. 911 calls are public, and the minute you press the button, you should assume what you say will be public information. If your attacker is yelling that he is going to kill and rape you, and the 911 call picks it up, that is good for your legal defense. If you are yelling that to your attacker, that is not good for your legal defense.

Interior Cameras

I would highly recommend putting a couple of tiny cameras outside of your defense room to view the door of your defense room. You need to see who is in front of the door. These cameras should be hidden as much as possible. You don't want your intruder to see them and destroy them.

Using cameras with two-way audio is an excellent choice. If law enforcement shows up, you want to see and communicate with the officer before opening the door. If you are unsure whether you are talking to an actual law enforcement officer for any reason, ask the person for their name and badge number. Next, validate with the 911 operator that this person is a law enforcement officer and is at your location. Then, have the 911 operator call them to verify. Finally, 911 should ask for further information that only the law enforcement officer would know and is not available to someone else at the residence.

Viewing Your Cameras

I use an old iPad to view all my cameras. It is always plugged in. You may want to use one tablet for your exterior cameras and another for your interior cameras. Also, your camera recorder likely has an HDMI output. You can connect that to an HDMI input on your bedroom TV to get live footage. I also have an app on my cellphone to view these cameras.

You may need to change views or change settings on these programs. If you need reading glasses, you should keep a spare next to anything you need to operate.

Weapon

If an intruder gets into your defense room, they have already gone through a great deal of trouble to get to you. You will also be cornered in a closed and confined area. Hence, I do not recommend less-than-lethal weapons such as pepper spray or Tasers in this scenario.

The weapon I keep in my defense room is a suppressed 12-gauge short-barreled shotgun. I recommend suppressed weapons for this situation to reduce the sound and muzzle blast. Ammunition selection is also crucial here—subsonic loads with low flash powder help. This article from Lucky Gunner on muzzle flash[139] will fill you in on the basics.

You should always be concerned about overpenetration. The loads for my shotgun are a subsonic frangible slug and a supersonic number 4 buckshot. This strategy is my attempt to strike a balance between lethality and penetration. My shotgun is stored in a Hornady rapid-access shotgun safe located by my bed. It is imperative to store your defensive weapons safely.

You will also need a backup weapon stored in a second, separate rapid-access safe. You'll also want an entirely different way to access your backup. For instance, I use an RFID wristband for my primary safe and a fingerprint scanner for my backup safe—which a different manufacturer built. I have all ten of my fingerprints stored. Having defensive weapons handy doesn't do you any good if you can't get to them. You may also want to consider adding an alarm system panic button in with your lock boxes.

I've tried to give you an idea of what I do, but you should do what works best for you. What if you don't know what would be best for you?

---

[139] https://clayeolsen.com/lgmf

First, you'll want to find quality self-defense training with *private* lessons. You want private lessons because you have a specific self-defense plan and specific self-defense needs. You don't need general training and you don't require concealed carry training. Instead, you should seek out a quality instructor who will allow you to present your specific situation and tailor any training around that situation. There are many quality self-defense training companies that offer private training. For instance, quality companies like C2 Tactical[140] and Independence Training[141] in Phoenix provide private training. Even if you don't live in Arizona, you can check out their websites and use their classes as a guide to compare to the training offered in your area. I would talk to them about your needs and schedule a private training session. You may be able to try out various weapons and find the one that works best for you. Once you select a weapon, they can develop a training plan for you, a range schedule, and even determine the appropriate ammunition.

For example, your training plan should include drills in darkness, removing your weapon from your rapid-access safe, getting it ready to fire, etc. You'll also want to cover clearing jams and loading the weapon in darkness. It is vitally important that your trainers understand what you are doing and *limit training appropriately*. Find another trainer if your trainer has their own ideas about what you should be doing—like sweeping your house for the intruder. Suggesting ideas within the framework of your defense plan is one thing. It is another to subvert the plan entirely.

7.8 Battery Backup

Once your security system is fully deployed, you'll want to use a product like the Kill A Watt[142] to determine your power usage with all your security devices on and active.

---

[140] https://clayeolsen.com/c2

[141] https://clayeolsen.com/it-pt

[142] https://clayeolsen.com/kaw

Defense Room

Plug all the devices in your defense room—your 911 pendant, tablets, cell phone, and so forth—into a power strip. Make sure nothing is fully charged so you can reach your max power drain. Then use the Kill A Watt between the power strip and your wall outlet to determine the power draw of everything on the power strip. Based on that power draw, you can select an Uninterruptible Power Supply (UPS) that will last at least three times as long as your area's law enforcement response time. If you don't know the response time, assume about 10 minutes in urban areas and 20 minutes in rural areas. Your UPS needs to supply power for at least 30 minutes or an hour, respectively.

Make sure that the UPS in the defense room can be muted. They usually beep when they detect a power loss, which is helpful to warn you when your electricity is off, but it gets annoying. In addition, it may interfere with your ability to hear the 911 operator.

Security and Networking Devices

You'll want to give the same treatment to your security and networking products, especially critical devices such as the modem, Wi-Fi router, driveway sensors, break beam sensors, doorbell cameras, alarm system panel, etc. Put them all on a power strip and use Kill A Watt to determine their power draw.

Cameras and Lights

The most expensive purchase I'll recommend is a battery backup for your exterior lighting and camera systems. These devices will draw a lot more power than the other devices. You may want to get an electrician over and explain to them the following:

- You would like your exterior LED lighting on a GFCI circuit. I would include the exterior LED lighting on a manual switch and any motion-detection lighting.

- You would like your camera recorder on the same circuit, if possible.
- You want the ability to measure the power draw of the circuit.

I would measure the power draw with all the LED lights on and all your cameras active. Next, you want to determine how much power each camera takes, which you can do by disconnecting one camera from the recorder and checking the new power draw. This delta will allow you to calculate the per-camera draw. Finally, if you have available camera ports on your network recorder, plan for all of them to be occupied. That way, you won't have to upgrade your UPS if you add cameras.

You may want to consider a UPS where you can add additional batteries and replace the existing batteries in the unit. UPS batteries have a lifespan, and you'll have to replace them eventually, so look for a UPS device that can tell you when to replace a battery pack.

Protection

Many UPS products do not include power protection; they are just battery backup solutions. Any power fluctuations are passed on to your security devices when the battery is not used in a typical power situation. A simple solution is to use a power strip surge protector on your battery backup and other surge protectors off the battery backup. *I do not recommend this setup.*

Instead, I recommend investing in a power line conditioner, which you can purchase for under $500, to protect your security devices and UPS. This device plugs into the wall, powers your UPS, and protects all the security devices hanging off your UPS while the battery is not in use. Of course, you can use power strips off your UPS to help with your connections, but the power line conditioner will handle any electrical problems.

When electrical power is cut, your power conditioner will not work, but your UPS's battery will take over and power your security devices. UPS battery power is clean power. When electrical power is restored to the house, the power conditioner kicks in and fixes any problems before your devices or UPS get power. Essentially, the power conditioner protects your UPS and the security devices beyond it during bad power situations, like lightning strikes or fluctuating supply from the power company.

You'll need to test your setup. To do so, shut off power to the house at your circuit breaker and ensure every security device and application still works correctly and that your battery life is what you expect.

Backup Generator

I also have a natural gas generator with an automatic transfer switch that handles power outages. An intruder can turn off this generator if they desire because it needs a natural gas shutoff switch in case of emergencies. However, for those intruders who are not that smart or if you have a big mean dog protecting it, the generator can provide power to your security devices for as long as it runs.

7.9 Insurance

Once we introduce a firearm to our home, whether for concealed carry, defense room, or both, we need to factor in theft. One of the harms in our fact box for CCF is arming criminals because we did not secure our firearms, and they were stolen. Additionally, we should secure our firearms to prevent unintentional injury or death (e.g., a child finding an unsecured firearm), another one of our fact box harms.

This section on insurance and the next section on safes provide the necessary information to prevent these harms. I cover insurance here because you should work closely with your insurance company when securing your firearms. They should be on board with what you are doing and your security measures. Involving them will likely mean a lower insurance bill and better coverage!

Most people do not involve their insurance company with firearm security. Instead, they buy homeowner's insurance and feel good about it. Then something happens, like a fire or a burglary. They head down to the insurance office and get a rude awakening—hardly any of their valuables are covered. Let's keep that from happening!

Write down and itemize all your valuables—jewelry, firearms, equipment, etc. Then, I recommend getting them appraised by someone your insurance company will accept (you'll need to ask them). Then, head down to the insurance office and ask them the following questions.

1. What will you pay if I lose these items in a fire? What about smoke damage? What about water damage from an interior sprinkler or firehose used to extinguish the fire?
2. What will you pay if I lose these items due to a burglary or robbery?
3. What will you pay if I lose these items to a water leak? Different scenarios may have different answers: broken water pipe, plugged drainage, groundwater seepage, roof leak due to weather (e.g., a hailstorm damaged the roof), or a roof leak due to an old, degraded roof.
4. How do you handle inflation year-to-year?

You'll probably find firearms are insured a bit differently than other valuables. Usually, there is a small dollar figure cap amount for theft. For example, if you have $10,000 worth of firearms and they are stolen, you may get a *total* of $2,500 to replace all of them. That is a terrible thing to find out after a crime.

The next big problem with homeowner's insurance is their coverage gaps—you will want to check what happens if you get flooded by groundwater, for which you may need flood insurance if you want them to payout.

Firearms and inflation are not covered well either. For example, if you get your firearms appraised and lose them in a fire five years later, the insurance company will pay the appraisal amount. Firearms hold their value pretty well, but you probably won't be able to buy the same firearms for their five-year-old appraisal value due to the impact of inflation.

Unfortunately, appraisals cost money. Have your most expensive firearm appraised every few years to determine whether getting new appraisals is worth it. Assume the percentage difference from the last appraisal to the current appraisal will impact all your firearms. Then you can consider whether it is worth restating their value to your insurance company.

For your valuables, here is a quick summary:

1. Get a list of your valuables and have them appraised by someone your insurance company will accept.
2. Present this list to your insurance agent and get in writing what is covered and what is not based upon the situation (fire, burglary, water leak, etc.) and your policy. Then, adjust your policy based on risk and cost-effectiveness.
3. Determine when you should reappraise based upon inflation and the types of valuables you have.

You could very well find that you have problems with your homeowner's policy that can't be corrected. In that case, you'll need supplemental insurance coverage to protect you. This additional coverage may be something like collectibles insurance. You'll have to evaluate the cost of that insurance against the risk. The most common situation is theft and firearms, which leads us to our next topic.

7.10 Safes

We've discussed keeping two rapid-access safes for your primary and backup defense weapons in your defense room. These safes are usually single-firearm storage units for rapid access in a defense situation. However, they are not resilient against burglary, fire, or theft. To guard against theft, you can add a couple of additional protections.

- Hide a Tile[143] inside in case a burglar grabs the whole unit. *Be sure to test this configuration and ensure the safe doesn't completely*

---

[143] https://clayeolsen.com/tile

block the Bluetooth signal. Even if it does, this may still come in handy if the burglar opens the safe in another location and the Tile remains hidden long enough to be discovered by another person's Tile application.

- Your safes should be secured so that a burglar must physically rip them from the wall or floor. You can use a door alarm system sensor to help with security by placing the first half of the sensor in the wall or in the floor and the other on the safe. You may need to cut out a portion of the floor or wall to make room for the sensor. Then, if a burglar gets into your defense room without sounding the alarm and tries to pull these rapid access safes off their mountings, the alarm will sound.

These are special-purpose safes, but we also need to cover the more general-purpose safes typically bought for theft and fire protection. Here is what most people do: They go to a big brand retailer, see a safe that looks tough and secure, buy it, and then put everything they own of value in it. However, the devil is in the details, so let's examine the details.

1. This safe is likely a Residential Security Container (RSC). It has limited burglary resistance compared to traditional safes.
2. The fire rating is factory tested rather than certified by an independent third party like Underwriter Laboratories (UL).
3. If the homeowner has firearms, they will usually put their ammunition in the RSC too.
4. Homeowners often store their important papers and computer media in the RSC.

All of these things combined are a disaster for keeping valuables safe. Let's examine a hypothetical family and their valuables.

- Three pistols: one primary defensive pistol, one backup defensive pistol, and one concealed-carry pistol. Value: $2500.
- Two rifles: one inherited from a father and one inherited from a grandfather. Irreplaceable.

- Ammunition for the five firearms: $1000.
- All the expensive jewelry the wife inherited from her wealthy family but never wears: $40,000.
- Important papers: wills, financial agreements, and so forth.
- Important Identification: birth certificates, passports, and so forth.
- Several disc drives containing digitized copies of all the family pictures. Irreplaceable.
- Collection of silver coins: $10,000.

Let's focus on burglary first. First, you'll need to figure out the dollar value of your valuables, which you should have already done for your insurance. In our example, we have around $53,500 and several irreplaceable items. Now we can use the Safe and Vault Store's breakdown[144] for burglary ratings and the dollar amount of valuables. In what follows, I've only listed the content value recommendations for a home with an alarm system (edited for readability).

When you're considering purchasing a safe, think about the maximum value and type of the contents you will EVER store inside the safe over the next 10 plus years. Why? As your content value grows over a period of time, the safe you originally purchased some time ago may not be adequate to protect those contents.

Burglary ratings are a mix of manufacturer standards and Underwriters Laboratory burglary ratings. A general guideline for the type of safe versus content value is as follows (you should always ask your Insurance Broker to contact Underwriters Laboratory for additional recommendations on content value storage):

---

[144] https://clayeolsen.com/svs-buy

These ratings and content values are guidelines only:

Burglary Rating	Content Value
B-Rate	Up to $10,000
B/C Rate	Up To $20,000
UL RSC	Up To $30,000
C-Rate	Up To $50,000
UL TL-15	Up To $200,000
UL TL-30	Up To $375,000
UL TL-30X6	Up To $500,000

Right away, we can see a problem. We have a mismatch between the dollar value of our valuables ($53,500) and the protection level of the RSC ($30,000).

We will get into fire ratings later, but most safes are factory tested. The goal is for the internals of the safe not to exceed 350 °F for a given external temperature. Higher-priced safes usually can handle a longer fire exposure time. For instance, different safes could protect the internals for 30 minutes, 60 minutes, or longer. It is crucial to understand how safes keep the internal temperature at a safe level. Here is what the Safe and Vault Store says:[145] "The way that fire material works on all safes with a fire test rating is that they pump moisture into the safe and actually create a 'cloud of steam.'"

This steam should explain why fire-rated safes aren't waterproof. To waterproof something, it needs to be fully sealed. Let's quote more from the Safe and Vault Store: "With nowhere for the steam to go, you are essentially creating a giant bomb by fully sealing your gun safe."[146]

The lack of waterproofing brings us to some critical points for our discussion around safes.

---

[145] https://clayeolsen.com/svs

[146] https://clayeolsen.com/svs

1. In the event of a fire, the items in the safe will be exposed to moisture due to the inherent nature of a safe's fire protection.
2. If the fire department hoses down your safe, additional water could get into the safe because fire-resistant safes cannot be waterproof.
3. If you have an interior sprinkler system in your home, there is even more possibility of water getting into the safe.

We have paper and computer media products in our example, and we don't want them wet. There are other considerations too. Let's look at what the Safe and Vault Store[147] says about documents:

DO NOT store data/media or family photos in a fireproof safe … The word fireproof means "resistant to fire" and some buyers assume that a fireproof safe will protect everything. Unfortunately, data and media (photos, CDs/DVDs and computer disks/tapes, etc.) are very sensitive to heat and humidity/moisture. Your standard fireproof safe is not engineered specifically to protect against these things. Fireproof safes are engineered and designed to protect paper and keep the internal temperature of the safe below 350 degrees, which is the critical temperature where the paper will start to char and burn. Their method of protection is to create steam (moisture) inside the safe. Any sensitive data or media will be badly damaged or destroyed at or above 135 degrees or 85 percent humidity.

Our digital media won't be as well protected as we thought.

Lastly, let's look at our ammunition. There are two things to consider:

1. Ammunition by itself
2. Ammunition chambered in a firearm[148]

---

[147] https://clayeolsen.com/svs-know

[148] The Safe and Vault store also recommends storing your ammunition in another location to reduce the risk to a child or family member.

In the event of a fire hot enough to ignite unchambered ammunition, it won't be like in the movies. Essentially, the brass of unchambered ammunition will expand and pop and will send some debris, but nothing that will endanger firefighters, according to SAAMI.[149] However, chambered rounds could discharge just like you were shooting the gun. This discharge could be hazardous to everyone fighting the fire.

In short, I wouldn't store ammunition in your safe because, if it ignites, it may damage the safe's contents. In addition, when storing a firearm, do not chamber a cartridge; in fact, remove all cartridges from the firearm entirely. I would make an exception for the guns in the rapid access safes, where cartridges are loaded but not chambered. Unfortunately, a revolver always has chambered cartridges, even though only one chamber is in line with the barrel. In the event of a fire, revolvers can be more deadly than a semi-automatic pistol, should they be stored in a rapid access safe.

This safe business is starting to be complex. As the infomercials say, "But wait! There's more!"

You'll be sad to find out that many large UL burglary-rated safes do not carry a UL fire rating.[150] Unfortunately, this mismatch is the problem we have with safes. It is almost impossible to get a safe that is both UL burglary-rated for long items (like rifles) and UL fire-rated. As a result, we have to come up with a new strategy.

One option is to move our valuables that require different protections, such as our digital media, to a bank safety deposit box. However, one major problem is that during the COVID-19 pandemic, many banks did not allow customers to enter their facilities, and these boxes were not accessible. Another consideration is that rental costs do add up. If you had one for 30 years, that is a lot of money you could argue would have been better spent on your safe instead.

Another option is to split up your valuables. For example, you could potentially find a smaller safe that is both UL rated for fire and burglary,

---

[149] https://clayeolsen.com/sammi
[150] UL tests for fire are strict. If you choose to accept a third-party certification from another lab, be sure your insurance company is okay with it. If you are putting irreplaceable items in such a safe, you will want to discuss this with the safe vendor, manufacturer, and third-party certification company.

separate from the safe where you store your guns. This two-safe approach works well in some instances.

There is a third option available that expands on the two-safe approach.

The Russian Nesting Doll Approach

With this approach, we put a safe (or two) inside another safe, just like Russian nesting dolls. Here is the process:

1. Select a safe with the appropriate UL rating for burglary based on your items' dollar value.
2. Based on the number of documents you have, select a UL-rated fire and waterproof container that holds your existing documents and allows room for more to be added in the future.
3. Based upon the number of digital media components you have, select a UL-rated digital media safe that holds your existing digital media and allows room for future growth.
4. Verify that your safes will fit inside your UL-rated burglary safe while still allowing room for your other valuables, like your rifles. If everything doesn't quite fit, one option is to buy two smaller UL-rated burglary safes and split your valuables. In our example, the family could get away with two C-rated safes: one for jewelry, digital media, and papers, the other for firearms.
5. Once you have all your safes set up, you'll need to waterproof the contents with bags that can withstand 350 °F or a water-resistant material that can withstand 350 °F. Safe stores such as the Safe and Vault Store typically sell these bags.
6. Using desiccant packs, you can control the moisture buildup in these waterproof bags. You can get these at the Safe and Vault Store as well.
7. About once a month, air everything out. Make sure your firearms are well oiled and protected.

I have not found any fire- and water-resistant bags that are large enough to contain a rifle. In most circumstances, this isn't a problem. Many modern hunting rifles are designed to handle a few days of moisture. You do not want to put your rifle in a waterproof bag or scabbard and have that material melt at 350 °F. This material would be an absolute mess in the event of a fire. It would be better to have your hunting rifles exposed to moisture than have waterproof material melt all around them.

You'll want your safes to be very well protected, for instance, in a walk-in closet in your defense room. You may also consider beefing up the closet doors in the ways previously described for entry doors. You may need to reinforce the floor to handle the weight depending on where you put the safe. This location may need to be modified so the safe can be fastened to the floor or foundation. Always secure the safe so it can't be hauled away. Another consideration is whether your safes can be hidden behind a false wall or other concealments.

We have protected our papers and digital media with UL fire-rated containers. These containers are in a UL-rated burglary safe. However, our firearms are protected from fire by a factory-tested fire rating. Is there anything we can do to help here?

Absolutely. You may have wondered why I recommended storing your safe contents in waterproof or water-resistant wrappings. One reason is the fire department, which may hose your safe down in the event of a fire. However, there is another reason. Interior sprinkler systems are becoming much more affordable for the home—having one installed with a sprinkler head above your safe is an excellent approach to keep your valuables safe from fire (and protect the people in the house, too!).

The Decoy

One last thing you may want to consider. Many of the big retailer safes are RSCs. You can usually find smaller options at a reasonable cost that you can use to store things like ammunition—but this smaller safe's actual purpose is to be a decoy that a burglar may assume is the only safe in the house. It should be visible, easy to find, and filled with stuff you don't mind losing. We can use all the same tricks for our rapid-access safes on this decoy—like storing a Tile, hidden alarm sensors, and even hidden cameras.

Summary

There is a lot to consider when buying a safe. The last thing you want to do is buy a big, tough-looking safe at a major retailer and throw all your valuables in it. Instead, evaluate your valuables based upon their different protection needs, recognizing that there is a water hazard and planning accordingly.

Do not make this decision in isolation. Be sure to involve your insurance company and ensure they agree with the type of protection and the dollar amount they will cover using that protection. Don't forget to tell them about your alarm system!

7.11 Miscellaneous

The following are some essential items that should be in your home:

- Plenty of lights, flashlights, kerosene lanterns, interior kerosene, etc.
- Fire extinguishers: Make sure they are not too old.
- Interconnected smoke alarms/carbon monoxide alarms. Don't rely on the single smoke detector that came with your alarm system or the old one that came with the house. Instead, get set up with wireless interconnected smoke and carbon monoxide detectors. When one goes off, they all go off.
- Electronic lock on chemicals under the sink. It is best to move these chemicals to a closet/pantry secured by an electronic lock that activates automatically after a few seconds. A device that closes the door automatically is a good idea as well. These devices help to keep your kids and your visitors' kids protected.

- Medical emergency kit. Being unable to breathe or bleeding from an artery will kill you or your loved one before the ambulance arrives. For almost everything else, the EMT can handle it. In Arizona, Independence Training[151] has excellent classes on emergency medical training like this and I'm sure others do in your area as well. You'll learn how to apply tourniquets and many critical practices that can keep yourself or your loved ones alive until EMTs arrive. Be sure to check out their classes to get an idea of the training you'll need.

7.12 Good Habits

Once you have all of this security implemented, you will want to develop good habits around it, so here are some best practices.

- If you hear something outside, go to your cameras first. Don't peek out the window or the peephole, especially when it is dark outside and lights are on inside your house.
- Use your alarm consistently when home and even when you are just going down to the corner market.
- Use your garage consistently. Unless you are cleaning the garage, your cars need to be in there.
- Minimize false positives. If your motion lights are coming on because of natural events, change them to avoid such events in a way that still provides protection. Of course, you never want to ignore security events; the best way to stay on top of them is to prevent false positives from happening without losing true positives.
- Clean your camera lenses. The best way to check them is to look at the night vision pictures. Get into the habit of going through your camera events every morning.

---

[151] https://clayeolsen.com/ifak

- If someone you don't know is at the door, check all your cameras first to ensure there isn't anyone else around. Please don't feel compelled to answer the door or even let them know you are there. If it's important, they can leave a note. You can even provide a pad and a pencil outside.

- If someone is at your door who you don't know, but it seems important, talk to them on your video doorbell. If you need to speak to your visitor in person, open the entry door but not the security door.

- Many people, when they hear a knock at their door (the doorbell was *not* pressed), will instinctively answer the door in person. Get out of this habit. Instead, what you want to do is go check your cameras or your doorbell camera first. Then, if you don't know the individual, use your two-way doorbell camera to start a conversation (if you wish).

Up Next

We've covered quite a bit. Let's assume we have implemented many of the home defense provisions enumerated here. We will now walk through all the examples again and see what happens.

7.13 Opportunistic Threat 2

First, let's look at our opportunistic threats: our neighbor's friend, and the jogger. What happens now?

Well, there is no longer an opportunity available! You've got a fence, a dog, and a sign alerting them to your audio and video recording. Your cars are in the garage, and your tools and other valuables are locked up. These criminals will look elsewhere.

7.14 Home Preparation for Violent Crime: Burglary Threat 2

Let's start with a new burglar in a new Storytime.

Storytime

Our new burglar sees you at a stoplight. You have a nice car, nice clothes, and lovely jewelry. He follows you home and finds out you have a big house too, so he starts casing your home over the next few weeks.

He can see you have a dog. He can also see your security doors, cameras, and possibly an alarm. He decides he will throw some food over the fence, marinated in some tasty doggie knock-out juice. Then he'll try to get through a back window blocked from the view of the neighbors and the back door camera.

He throws the food over the fence in the morning. About an hour later, the dog falls asleep, and he jumps the wall wearing his hoodie, mask, gloves, and sunglasses. Since you don't have any tools lying around, he has to carry some on his person. He checks out the window—he can see a separate window lock and what appears to be a magnetic sensor that he can barely see from an angle. He takes out his small plunger and glass cutters and cuts out a hole big enough for him to get through.

He takes a peek inside and sees a motion sensor. He holds a Mylar blanket in front of him to hide any thermal differences. Taking considerable time, he avoids being detected by the motion sensor.

He reaches the hallway that opens to all the bedrooms. Unfortunately, they all have security on them. He manages to get some tools into the gap between the door and the floor, but he cannot get hold of the door handle lever. Luckily, he has his hole saw. He takes his best guess at which door is the master bedroom and begins drilling a hole in the solid core wood door with his hole saw. Finally, he breaks through. He gets his hand through the hole and turns the doorknob. Unfortunately for him, the motion detector in the bedroom catches the heat signature of his arm and sets the alarm off. He has to haul his butt out of there.

#

We have a formidable burglar in this example. He avoided most of our detection mechanisms and almost got through to one of our bedrooms. Luckily, the motion detector caught him trying to unlock the bedroom door. I wanted to showcase this example where a burglar uses simple tools to avoid a high-dollar system. When law enforcement arrives, all you have is a masked man on camera, a passed-out dog, a cut window, and a door with a hole in it.

Even if he got through, he would still have obstacles before him. We have a decoy safe, hidden high-rated burglary safes, and rapid-access safes—and they are set up to trigger our burglar alarm if he moves them. *However, given enough time and knowledge, all our security mechanisms can be defeated.* Never forget that. If that happens, our insurance plans would have to step in and help us recover.

Bonus: Burglary Threat 2.1

Most self-defense simulations offer the same solution: hear a burglar, arm yourself, and *confront them*. However, I think that this is a bad idea if your home has been appropriately prepared.

Storytime

After a long day, you get off work, and your dog is sick. You take him to the vet, where he needs to stay overnight. When you get back home, you are exhausted from a long workday and from worrying about your dog. You fall right to sleep and start dreaming. In your dream, someone drops a mirror, and it breaks. You wake up wondering if you heard glass breaking in your house. You aren't sure.

#

Sometimes sounds from the outside world are incorporated into our dreams, making it hard to determine what is real. However, given our home defense setup, we have a much better solution than arming ourselves and checking out the house. Remember two things:

1. You are already in your defense room because it is also your bedroom. In addition, your solid-core door is locked, and your alarm is in "Stay" mode, putting you in an excellent defensive position.
2. From your defense room, you can check out your cameras rather than running around the house.

In this story, let's say you don't see anyone outside initially. However, because your cameras are mounted to your house and looking out, you can't check if your windows are secure. Here you find a problem with your home defense setup: your interior cameras only look at your defense room door. In this situation, you discover it would have been way better to have interior cameras throughout your house that are enabled when the alarm is in "Stay" or "Away" mode. These should continue to be active if the alarm is tripped. In addition, these cameras should view the rooms they're in and be positioned to see the windows and doors.

Your defense room is an exception to this rule. You do not want any cameras in there. Let's continue with our Storytime.

You see a man rise from behind a bush as you watch your exterior cameras. He goes to a window where he seems to be knocking jagged pieces of glass out of the frame. You can hear the glass falling inside your home. The glass break sensor must have failed.

#

Our burglar broke the window and then laid low to see if anybody would respond. Fortunately for him, no one seemed to be around, so he decided to try and get in. In a few seconds, the burglar will be in your house and out of view of your cameras. Let's go through your next steps:

1. You arm yourself with your defensive weapon.
2. You press the panic button on your alarm system.
3. You turn on your exterior LED lights and illuminate the outside of your house like a stadium.
4. You use your 911 pendant to call 911.
5. The alarm system company calls your cell phone, but you ignore them because you are already talking to law enforcement.

It turns out that our would-be burglar takes off running as soon as the alarm trips. You explain the situation to the 911 operator while law enforcement is on their way. Once law enforcement gets there, what do they find?

- You are not roaming around your property holding a gun. You are in a safe location in your house.
- The crime scene is pristine.
- Law enforcement can sweep the perimeter knowing that anyone they find will not be someone authorized to be on the property.

Once law enforcement has secured the scene, you can ask the 911 operator to transfer you to an officer or have an officer call your cell phone when they are ready to come inside the house. You will discuss the best way to do this with everyone's safety in mind.

Notice that we are in a much better position than if we had armed ourselves and swept the house. We have avoided a potentially violent situation and enabled law enforcement to succeed in their role. However, we discovered some places where our security could be improved:

- The alarm system panel in your defense room interfered with your ability to communicate with the 911 operator. Moving the speaker to a central location would be great while allowing the alarm system panel to stay in your defense room.
- More interior cameras would have been helpful.
- You have a faulty glass break sensor or one that was not set up correctly.

- If you could light up the inside of your house (except for the defense room) just like the exterior, your interior cameras would be more effective. In addition, if your defense room door or window were breached, the offender would be illuminated while your defense room remained dark. This advantage is good to have.

7.15 Psycho Ex-Boyfriend 2

Storytime

You meet a guy you think is nice, but he gets obsessive about you after a couple of months. After you end the relationship, he is upset and harasses you a lot. Finally, things cool down after a couple more months and you think things are okay. Then, you go out on a date with someone new. It turns out one of your ex-boyfriend's buddies happens to see you. He runs into the ex-boyfriend at a party about a week later and lets him know. The ex-boyfriend freaks out, gets into his car, and heads to your house.

You have just gone to sleep. Your ex pulls up to your place, gets out, and walks to the porch. Your dog attacks him—he shoots the dog. He grabs a metal patio chair on the porch and throws it through your front window. The house alarm goes off, but he doesn't care. He climbs in through the window and marches right to your bedroom.

He begins kicking the door, which doesn't budge. He keeps ramming his shoulder into it, to no avail. Then, he goes outside, picks up the same metal patio chair, and tries to throw it through your bedroom window. It doesn't break. He goes back inside and begins shooting the locks off the door. Finally, he is successful, and he kicks in the door.

#

This terrifying encounter shows how our physical security mechanisms can be overwhelmed. An example like this is why I recommend lethal weapons for your defense room. We had hoped our security would survive long enough for law enforcement to arrive, but it didn't. However, it did give us time to prepare and alert law enforcement. The rest is up to us.

7.16 More Home Preparation

The following are tips for additional protection in your defense room:

- Install a security bar with a latch across your door. (If you are not handy, you can hire a contractor to do this.) This bar is a simple, brute force defensive device that is difficult to disable from the other side of the door (going underneath or above— exploiting the gap between the door and the floor/jamb with tools). With this product, almost half the door has to be defeated before a person can enter your defense room.
- Situate all security electronics and battery backups in your defense room.
- Work with your alarm system company to separate the speaker from the alarm system panel. The alarm system speaker should be centrally located, but the panel should be in your defense room. You do not want the panel to be screeching out an alarm in the room while you are trying to talk to the 911 operator. Alternatively, you could find a simple way to control the speaker volume, but I think it is better when your intruder hears the alarm loud and clear. Along the same lines, do not have pets in your defense room. They will raise hell if you are scared and someone is outside your door or house, and you won't be able to hear the 911 operator or law enforcement.
- An advanced alarm system panel with Z-Wave support will allow you to work with your alarm system company to control external features based on the state of the alarm system. One example is if you have separate security interior lights installed in every room (except your defense room) that are off

by default, your Z-Wave support can trigger the lights to go on if your alarm system is tripped. With your defense room dark and all other rooms lit up, you have an advantage should your door be breached. You may want to activate this measure with a manual override switch; these measures can also be applied to your exterior lighting.

- I would install interior cameras in every unoccupied room except the bathrooms and the defense room.

NOTE: This recommendation has obvious privacy issues. I would not recommend installing cameras in bedrooms that are occupied. The camera should be easily removed if you have an unoccupied bedroom and overnight guests.

One product that I've been evaluating is the Wyze Outdoor Camera v2.[152] Don't let the name fool you, it is a great indoor camera. It works with your wireless network, has a battery, and a magnetic base. This magnetic base allows the camera to be removed and stored away easily. It comes with a base that ties into your existing network and that base has support for up to four Wyze cameras. The base would be stored where connectivity to the cameras would be best.

The Wyze application allows you to turn the cameras on or off. This functionality is extremely useful. For example, you can have your interior cameras off until you go to bed. When you set your alarm to STAY, you can then turn on your interior cameras. The cameras will detect motion, notify you, and begin recording for a certain amount of time.

You can also use this Wyze application on your cell phone when you are away from your house. Suppose you are taking a weekend trip. On the way out, you set your alarm to AWAY. Once you are in the car, you turn on your interior cameras. Let's assume the next night, a burglar gets past your alarm system without it going off. The interior cameras will detect the

---

[152] https://clayeolsen.com/wyze

motion of the burglar, and the Wyze application will notify you via your cell phone. You can even sound a siren on a camera from your cell phone if you want.

The downside to these cameras is there is no continuous recording. It is event based. Another downside is you have to view the cameras one at a time and can't view them all at once. The last downside is that a per camera subscription is needed to get the most out of your cameras. However, given how they are used as interior cameras, in conjunction with event notification, these downsides are not critical. In sum:

Pros

- Battery operated and combined with wireless connectivity means there are no pesky cables.
- The battery can last for up to six months.
- A magnetic base allows for the camera to be easily removed to charge up the battery or for privacy concerns.
- Reasonable cost
- Easy application which runs on your phone or tablet. You can turn cameras off/on, receive notifications, view one camera at a time, initiate a conversation, sound of a siren, schedule recording, and more.
- The application works remotely.

Cons

- A subscription needed per camera to maximize functionality.
- You can't view all the cameras at the same time.
- No continuous recording—event only.
- Only four cameras per base. Multiple bases are supported.

- If your house has gables in the attic, I would use a wire mesh "door" behind them that would need to be moved to get by. This "door" allows an alarm system door sensor to be installed.

- If your home keys are on a ring, you should consider cases for them that would prevent someone from taking a picture of your key and then creating a new key from the image. In case you are wondering, this technique is possible.
- Finally, consider a fire sprinkler system for your home interior, as discussed in the home safe section. These are starting to be much more economical than they used to be.

7.17 Other Threats at Home

We've done our best to prepare our home from opportunistic predators, burglars, and psycho ex-boyfriends, but other threats remain.

Rape

Rape is a horrifying crime. It is terribly underreported and incredibly traumatizing. Most of the time, the offender is someone known by the victim, and it often happens at the victim's home. Let's go through three different scenarios and show how difficult it is to defend against rape.

Storytime

You are starting to like a neighbor of yours who seems cool. You hire a private investigator to do a comprehensive background check on him and nothing out of the ordinary comes up. As you talk to him over the next few weeks, he tells you things that validate what you learned in the background check (he's single, college-educated, etc.).

You are having some problems with your car, and he offers to work on it this Saturday. On that day, you drop your kid off with a babysitter, and he comes over to work on it. You fix a nice lunch.

#

Now you have to ask yourself: how will you protect yourself if things go wrong? Your guard is lowered somewhat, and your burglary defenses aren't going to help you much. After all, you are trying to get to know him better and you've done your work to make sure he is on the up and up.

Storytime Scenario 1

During lunch, you get more tea. He takes the opportunity to put some drugs in your drink. After a bit more conversation, he goes back outside to work on the car; a few minutes later, he finds you passed out on the couch. He starts undressing you.

Storytime Scenario 2

While eating lunch, he grabs you and forces you down to the floor. He recites to you where your daughter goes to school and her schedule. He lets you know that if he doesn't get what he wants, your daughter is the one who will pay. Even if you get him arrested, he knows someone who owes him big time and will hurt your daughter for him.

Storytime Scenario 3

After lunch, he asks if you get high. You say you occasionally do. He says he brought over a couple of small joints. Unbeknownst to you, yours is laced with psychedelics. After getting high, you feel pretty good and a bit out of it. Then, he starts getting sexually aggressive.

\#

All of these scenarios put you at an incredible disadvantage. If law enforcement and the courts get involved, the rapist will claim it was consensual, and you simply changed your mind later. It then becomes a he-said/she-said issue, which is difficult to prosecute. You need two things: proof and protection.

You should manually turn your interior cameras on whenever you have someone you are getting to know in your house or someone you don't know very well. Being able to prove your side of the story in court with audio and video proof is vital—as long as it was legally gathered. Alternatively, you can wear a hidden body camera (discussed in the robbery section), although your rapist could find that and destroy it.

Audio and video recordings don't stop rape; you need to avoid going through that trauma. However, your physical defense skills (or even a weapon) will do you no good if you've been drugged into unconsciousness or become significantly impaired.

One option is to have panic buttons hidden around the house. These buttons will trigger your alarm system and tell the monitoring station to call the police. For example, you can put them on the underside of your couch and in other places where he may be attempting to restrain you. Another option to consider is a highly trained dog, called a protection dog, that will attack on your command. Your protection dog should be there whenever you meet new people in your home. Protection dogs are extremely expensive, but they may be worth the investment depending on your circumstances.

The combination of proof and protection is a good bet for securing your home without ripping meaning out of your life. Meeting new people who are fun and exciting to be with is a good part of life. Most of the time, it works out. We don't want to lose that joy, but we shouldn't be naïve about the threat other people may pose.

Trespassing/Vandalism

The UCR for 2015 to 2019 shows that 28 percent of Aggravated Assault cases were linked to the Destruction, Damage, or Vandalism of Property.[153]

Where we choose to live has a lot of influence on other people's ability to drive up and start tearing our stuff up. The home preparation we've undergone will help minimize these types of escalations. Most people don't want to risk a dog bite or being caught on camera for destruction, damage, or vandalism of property. Let's go through a Storytime to detail how a property crime could escalate to a violent crime.

---

[153] See Appendix A

Storytime

Your dog is at the vet and you are asleep in your rocking chair. You wake up to the sound of a blunt object hitting something. You check your cameras and see that people are trying to break into your storage shed. You decide you should:

Scenario 1. Arm yourself and confront them.

Scenario 2. Yell out to tell them to get off your property.

Scenario 3. Go to your defense room, trigger your alarm, and call 911.

#

In the first scenario, imagine if they pulled out their guns and a shoot-out started. You could go to prison because your threat of force was not appropriate to the situation. Many states do not consider it reasonable to use lethal force to protect property. In the second scenario, they may run away scared because they thought no one was home, or they may say, "What are you going to do about it?" which will probably lead to an escalation. The third scenario is probably your best bet. You've spent time and money securing your home to this level. Why would you abandon your advantage to level the playing field for them? If your security system supports it, you could zoom in on the intruders with your cameras and record audio while waiting for law enforcement. This evidence could help law enforcement if the intruders leave before law enforcement arrives. If they are still there when law enforcement pulls up, you made it easy for law enforcement to know where you are and who the threats are by staying in your defense room.

7.18 Children

Unfortunately, modern home floor plans cause massive headaches for home safety and security. For example, the master bedroom and master bath are usually located far from the other bedrooms, perhaps diagonally across in a single-story floor plan or on separate floors in a two-story plan. When parents are in the master and kids are in the other bedrooms, emergencies gain another layer of complication.

Here are some various scenarios:

- The smoke alarm goes off, you run out of the master bedroom, and a large fire is blocking your path to your kids' bedrooms.
- Your alarm goes off, you arm yourself, and you run out to find an intruder between you and your kids' rooms. You know the dangers of overpenetration and you can't shoot.
- You hear a window break and one of your kids starts screaming.
- Your carbon monoxide alarm goes off and you are dizzy and stumbling as you try to get to your kids.

A further difficulty is that different alarms require different responses:

- Intruder Alarm—kids should stay in their bedrooms with the door locked.
- Smoke Alarm—kids should get out of the house.
- Carbon Monoxide Alarm—kids should get out of the house.
- Mom or Dad Hurt—kids should press the emergency button and leave the house (unless they can render assistance).
- Mom or Dad Under Attack—kids should press the panic button and lock themselves in their bedroom (unless they are older and can render assistance).
- Peeping Tom—kids should press the panic button and go to mom and dad's bedroom.

Think of the challenge your kids would face in these situations—which are confusing enough for adults. They will likely do the wrong thing. If they need to leave the house and the exit doors are blocked, they will need to open the windows. If they are upstairs and successfully open the window, they will need a rope ladder they can deploy.

It should be clear that your kids being upstairs or diagonally across from you is not a good situation when trouble rears its ugly head. You are way better off all sleeping in the same section of the house. It should probably be this way until one of your kids is old enough to make good decisions about their siblings. Then, you'll need to go through all the drills and training with them.

If your kids are too young, you need to stay in the same section of the house as them. However, you can still benefit from a defense room in this situation. For example, if you have a hallway with three bedrooms and one bath, you might want to consider installing a secure door at the beginning of the hallway. This door can be closed to protect you and your kids while you shepherd everyone into your defense room (likely your bedroom). You may even want this door to be fire-rated.

7.19 Conclusion

Many ideas that vary widely in cost have been discussed in this section. The goal is to exhibit a proper mindset about your home defense based on violent crime statistics. We can make our home seem like a very bad target for criminals and sound habits can help keep us safe.

The defense plan outlined here is excellent for an ordinary civilian. It employs a defense-in-depth approach, gives an intruder plenty of reasons to get the heck out of there, and gives law enforcement the best chance of dealing with the situation. If you have to defend yourself, you should be in decent legal standing to do so.

All things considered, you always need to factor in the benefits and harms of every approach. For example, when I stay with my mom, I have much stronger defenses in the house enabled because I am there, and I can help my mom if there are any issues. If I am not there, my mom still enables strong defenses, but not as many as I do. The reason is that she feels it is more likely she will need help from family or first responders than she will need it for protection (she is 90 years old at the time of this writing). The more defenses first responders or family have to get through, the more time goes by and the more deadly it becomes for my mom. I can't argue with her reasoning—it is sound.

PART VI

Interactions with Law Enforcement

In what follows, I will analyze interactions with law enforcement in terms of threats to the law enforcement officer. Because I will be using the words "law enforcement" and "law enforcement officer" quite frequently, I'll abbreviate them in this part to LE and LEO, respectively.

Every interaction an LEO has with a civilian is risky for both parties. For example, an elderly woman who is pulled over for a speeding infraction may think her car is in Park, but it is really in Reverse, and she also left the engine running. All this is going on when the LEO is walking toward the vehicle. One other mistake, such as accidentally pressing the accelerator rather than the brake, could cost an LEO their life. The elderly woman could spend her remaining years behind bars for that mistake.

The following information is not legal advice. As always, you should discuss LE policies and laws with a criminal defense attorney that is an expert in your state.

8.1 Traffic Stops

There are three things to keep in mind about traffic stops:

1. Threat Mismatch—A traffic stop is an irritating inconvenience for many drivers. However, for an LEO, it could be a life-ending event. This section will detail how small changes by the driver can significantly reduce the danger of a traffic stop.

2.   Technology—Assuming it is legal in your state, body cameras, audio recorders, and dashcams with GPS and speedometer recording can all be used to help you with any legal issues should you need them. Again, unless required by law, there is no reason to inform the LEO of this technology. In fact, to do so could make the LEO defensive and cause problems. The point of this technology is to help you later in court, not during the traffic stop. You want the traffic stop to go smoothly and without issue.

3.   Recognition—You may have done nothing wrong. Unfortunately for you, your car may have matched a description for an amber alert, silver alert, or even a bank robbery getaway vehicle. Regardless of whether you did something wrong or whether you matched a description, the LEO has what is called Reasonable Articulate Suspicion (RAS) or Articulate Suspicion. I'll use the RAS acronym. What this means is the LEO can conduct a short investigation.

As discussed in Part I, when LEOs are killed, it is often during vehicle patrol by people who are on an active justice status, such as parole, out on bail, or probation. Many of these offenders have been previously arrested for violent crimes and often use handguns to kill. When you have a handgun in your vehicle or on your person, you are checking off one of these boxes. This reason is why there is considerable debate in the concealed carry community about whether to tell an LEO *proactively* that you have a weapon, either on your person or in the vehicle. You can see why by doing a threat analysis. Let's go through an example traffic stop and showcase how dangerous they can be for an LEO.

Attitude

When you are driving, and an LEO flips on their lights to pull you over, remember four things:

1.   You are responsible and accountable for obeying the rules of the road.

2. You are responsible and accountable for keeping proper maintenance on your vehicle.
3. You are responsible and accountable for having proper identification and paperwork.
4. You are responsible and accountable for having your identification and paperwork in an easy-to-access nonthreatening location. This location is *not* the glovebox or console box.

Guess what the good news is? All of these things are entirely in your control. So plan and prepare *before* being stopped.

If any of these things make you mad, you had better be mad at yourself. You are to blame for being in this situation probably around 99 times out of 100. Recognize that and control your emotions. Always think to yourself: If the audio conversation I'm about to have with the LEO is made public, the people who hear it should think, "that driver was the most polite and courteous driver I have ever heard."

The Next Few Seconds

The next few seconds after the LEO's lights and siren come on are critical. That is where the LEO will get their initial determination as to what type of person you are. I recommend turning your hazard lights on and slowing down to a speed that allows you to pull off the main road when a safe location appears. Slowing down tells the LEO you are not running and putting your hazard lights on lets the LEO know that you are aware that you are being pulled over.

Once you have slowed down and have your hazard lights on, if you have inconspicuous dedicated recording equipment and it is legal in your state, you should switch them on, provided you can safely do so. This equipment should not require you to lean over or look like you are trying to find a weapon. A simple push of a button on the dash should be all that is required. You *never* want to appear like you are searching for anything because the LEO will think you are trying to find a weapon.

Safe Location

In this age of distracted driving, finding a safe place off the main road to pull over is imperative. If you are on a road that isn't very busy, then the shoulder may suffice if you can't find anything safer. However, on an Interstate, State Highway, or any moderately busy road, you should attempt to get several yards away from the road if possible.

Coming to a Stop

When I get pulled over (yes, it happens even in my dorky electric car), here is what I do:

1. Keep my seatbelt on.
2. Turn off my hazard lights.
3. Put the car in park (for automatic transmissions or electrics).
4. Take my foot off the brake.
5. If I have electric windows, roll all of them down.
6. If it is dark outside, turn on the interior lights.
7. Turn off the car (for a manual transmission, put the car in gear if it needs to be and set the parking brake). If I have keys in the ignition, I set the keys on the dashboard. However, if they are in my pocket (i.e., an RFID Key Fob), I don't dig for them. I just keep them in my pocket.
8. If I have sunglasses on, take them off.
9. I keep a small packet with my IDs and paperwork beside me. I place that on the dashboard as it is usually on my arm.
10. Sit there with my hands on the steering wheel.

While you can never take the danger out of a traffic stop, by following these steps, you help reduce it. Here are the threats:

- Your vehicle is a threat. The vehicle in park, the engine off, and the keys on the dashboard are good signs for the LEO. The LEO knows that to use your vehicle as a weapon, you have to perform some actions—it cannot be done instantaneously. These actions would give the LEO time to respond.

- You can be a threat in many ways and this procedure helped reduce your threat to the LEO. First, you stayed in the car with your seatbelt fastened. Second, the windows are down and the LEO can see inside. Third, you have your hands on the steering wheel.

Interaction

Remember: If the audio conversation you are about to have with the LEO is made public, the people who hear it should think, "that driver was the most polite and courteous driver I have ever heard."

Here are some tips:

- If you are at fault, be honest and admit it.
- If the LEO says you have a taillight out, accept it as gospel. You have a taillight out. There is no need for you to verify it during the traffic stop.
- Be sincere.
- Be respectful.
- Be professional.
- Be brief.

An LEO will often approach the vehicle from the passenger side so he can easily see your body and is not on the side of traffic (if you are not pulled over in a safe area). The LEO will often have their hand on their weapon.

What the LEO does next will likely depend on why they pulled you over. The bottom line is they will want to see your driver's license, registration, and proof of insurance. Chances are, they've already run your car plate. By running your driver's license, they will have much better information about who you are and the type of threat you may be.

I have that information in a small packet on the dash. I chose to include my concealed carry permit in that packet as well. Keeping *both* hands on the steering wheel, I tell the LEO that I have my information in the packet on the dash and ask the LEO if it is okay to hand them the packet. If the LEO says it is okay, I keep one hand on the steering wheel and use one hand to give the LEO the packet. I move at about the speed I would hand a child a pair of scissors to cut out paper dolls. Once the LEO takes it, return your hand to the steering wheel.

When the LEO sees the concealed carry permit, what happens next is up to the LEO. They will probably ask me if I have a weapon on my person or in the car. This question is why I do not carry a firearm on my person while driving. I'm far more likely to get pulled over by LE than need a firearm while driving. A firearm on your person is a significant threat to the LEO if you are a criminal. Depending on skill level, whether someone is right or left-handed, the location of the firearm, the location of the LEO, and the tiny distance away the LEO is from a driver, it is possible for a driver to operate their firearm and shoot accurately in under a second. That is a substantial threat to an LEO. Someone may respond that the fact that a concealed carry permit should indicate that the driver is not a threat to the LEO. On the contrary, I know many people with no criminal record that I wouldn't allow in my house. A concealed carry permit is evidence for the LEO that you are not a threat, but it is not conclusive.

This reasoning is why it is controversial in the concealed carry community to proactively notify an LEO of a firearm. For me, I prefer full voluntary disclosure. The permit lets the LEO know in advance that I'm likely not a felon, a wife beater, or a druggie. Let's assume the LEO asks me if I have any weapons on my person or in the car. I state the following (*I do not point or remove my hands from the steering wheel.* This restriction is hard for me because I talk with my hands!):

"Yes, Officer. I have an unloaded 1911 in my console lock box, and it is locked. In a separate lockbox, I have the 1911 magazines. That lockbox is also locked. I have no weapons on my person and no other weapons in the vehicle."

The LEO may be satisfied with this explanation, or maybe not. The LEO doesn't have to believe me. What happens next is again up to the LEO. They may ask their partner to come over, call for backup if they are alone, or simply run my driver's license. My worst situation is if the LEO asks me to hand my firearm to them. This situation is my worst one for the following reason: *I will not touch my firearm in the presence of LE*. It is simply too dangerous. I will let the LEO take possession of my firearm as long as I do not have to physically handle it. If this comes up for you, the important thing is to be honest with the LEO on why and make sure they understand you are willing to surrender your firearm, but you simply want the LEO to physically handle it rather than yourself. Make sure the LEO understands that you will cooperate in whatever way makes them feel safe during the process where *they* take possession of your firearm.

At this point, we have two possibilities:

1. The LEO did not take possession of your weapon, wrote you out a ticket/warning, and then you signed it.
2. The LEO did take possession of your weapon, wrote you out a ticket/warning, and then you signed it. Then, it comes time to return your weapon. This situation is where a lockbox comes in handy. You can instruct the LEO to return it there, and they can lock it.

Ultimately, we all want the traffic stop to be safe and as pleasant as possible. If the LEO did a great job making sure the traffic stop was safe, make sure you let them know, even if you got a ticket. If you plan on fighting the ticket or taking some type of legal action, no one needs to know except you and your attorney.

Leaving

After the traffic stop is over, the LEO will wait for you to leave unless they have been called to another location. You'll want to observe all traffic safety rules. If you have to get back on a busier road, it is best to do that with your hazard lights on until you can get back up to a safe speed. At this time, you may want to disable any recording you have going to make sure you don't overwrite the previous interaction.

Other Advice

- Never forget your driver's license. That is the magic key that is going to help the LEO understand what kind of a threat you are. Guess who also doesn't have a driver's license on them? Felons who are illegally possessing firearms. You know, the ones that are an existential threat to LEOs. They won't have a license, will often give a fake name, and hope that they don't get searched. An ordinary civilian forgetting their license is placed by the LEO in the "this person could be a felon" category. That is not a category you want to be placed in.

- Get a US Passport Card and use that for all your non-driving identification. The only people that need to see your driver's license are LEOs. The only people that need to see your concealed carry permit are LEOs. This separation may allow you to organize more effectively.

- Create a small packet with copies of *all* your vehicle registrations, vehicle insurance cards, driver's license, and concealed carry permit. *You always carry this with you even when you are not driving.* Some insurance companies make this easier by having one insurance card with all your vehicles on it. As a bonus tip: Have a copy of the bill of sale of your concealed carry firearm. This bill of sale needs to have your name listed as well as the serial number of the firearm. You'll need it if your weapon is confiscated and you want it back (e.g., you were in an accident and woke up in the hospital).

8.2 Personal Interaction (No Vehicle Involved)

Imagine you are looking for your spouse at one of those sprawling outdoor outlet malls. You have been searching for a while, and you are getting a bit frustrated. Then, out of the blue, an LEO appears and starts asking you questions.

With a vehicle, things are a bit different. The LEO usually is a witness to something you did, like speeding or a broken taillight, and can pull you over. If you are walking around the street and getting questioned, the LEO needs to have RAS. *In this section, I'm going to assume that you are not a criminal and have no idea why you are being questioned.*

What is likely going on is you fit the description of a suspect. For example, someone who recently shoplifted, was speeding in a parking lot, or was yelling and putting a person in fear. Worse, you could fit the description of a bank robber. However, you simply do not know. A potentially criminal event happened; you are under RAS and don't know anything about it. This situation is the primary reason (among others) that I do not open carry a firearm. I may fit the description of a deadly criminal, but the LEO has RAS, and now I am in an incredibly stressful situation without a clue as to why.

This situation can also become fatal if you carry your weapon next to your wallet. As I've stressed in this book, please keep your identification separate from your wallet. I usually have mine on my arm via a band (in the summer) or in my front shirt pocket (in the winter). If an LEO asks me for my identification and I CCF, there is no risk of reaching for my wallet and the LEO catching sight of a weapon. I have more than my identification in this packet. I have my driver's license, concealed carry permit, vehicle registrations, and insurance card.

If the LEO asks for your identification, you can hand them your small packet. This packet is the same packet you'll hand over at a traffic stop. The LEO can do a lot of things with this packet. The goal is for the LEO to have the critical information to find the actual suspect and eliminate you as a suspect. I find this trade-off appropriate. If you live in a community and care about crime, you often want to support LE as much as possible. However, there is a critical limit. It is fine to help LE when they investigate crimes that don't involve you, but you may have witnessed (e.g., you were crossing the street and saw a hit-and-run). *However, if you are the subject of the investigation, you never want to talk to LE without your lawyer present.*

Unfortunately, too often, what people know about crime and their rights comes from television shows. For dramatic effect, these shows depict situations you should never be in as a suspect. Here are some necessary clarifications:

- LE does not have to read you your Miranda rights (e.g., the right to remain silent) until you are arrested AND you are going to be interrogated.
- Everything you say to LE before being arrested AND interrogated does NOT fall under Miranda. If you are arrested and continue to blab to LE, that does not fall under Miranda. LE is free to take notes and present them at your trial.
- LE cannot negotiate deals. If you hear something like, "If you cooperate, things will go a lot easier in court for you." LE does not have the authority to do that.
- LE can lie to you, make misleading statements, and promise you the world and not deliver. Not only that but they will also not be held liable for it. This flexibility may seem unfair, but it is what it is. Keep in mind that most of the time, LEOs are not interacting with humanity's best representatives.

To make an arrest, an LEO needs Probable Cause (PC). If all an LEO has is RAS, they will attempt to talk to you in order to get enough information for PC. This behavior is great if the suspect is guilty of the crime. It allows LE the opportunity for the suspect to mess things up and get them out of the community. *Unfortunately, if you are innocent (which is the assumption in this section), you may accidentally incriminate yourself in a crime you did not commit.*

As far as you know, the LEO may already have PC. They are keeping that information from you until the last possible moment. This moment is when you ask if you are free to leave, and then they place you under arrest. As I said in this section, I'm assuming you are innocent of the crime the LEO is asking about.

What does this mean? Well, if the LEO asks you something other than what is in your packet, then alarm bells should go off in your ears

(NOTE: This is also true of a traffic stop for things that the LEO didn't witness). For example, if the LEO says: "Where were you last night at about 11:30 pm?" Upon hearing that, you need to stop the conversation immediately. Indicate that you are invoking your constitutional rights to remain silent, that you do not consent to any searches anywhere, and will not answer any more questions without your lawyer present. *The LEO will know your rights better than you.* The LEO may say something like, "Well, if you were innocent, you wouldn't have a problem talking to me," in an attempt to get you to say more. The appropriate response in that situation is to ask, "Am I free to go?" The answer will tell you if you are being arrested or detained. If you can go, do so quietly. If not, answer all future questions by invoking your constitutional rights and that you want to speak with your lawyer immediately.

Note that there may be an occasion that LE shows up at your house. I recommend keeping them outside the house and following the same advice as if you had met them in the street. LE may be there to serve a search warrant or arrest warrant. They would let you know and provide the warrant. Always call the LE agency they are from using a telephone number you get from a valid source (other than the people at your door) and validate they are supposed to be there.

I'm not a criminal and do not behave like one. I enjoy helping LE when I can and hope we can make our community safer. However, if I am the subject of an investigation, I invoke my constitutional rights and demand to speak with my attorney. I do not want to be convicted of a crime I did not commit. When you are innocent and under investigation, talking to LE without a lawyer is one of the worst possible things you can do. LE will try to convince you otherwise simply because they usually deal with criminals. You are innocent, so don't believe them.

8.3 Before, During, and After Violence

These situations are when LE shows up unexpectedly and are extremely dangerous for an armed civilian. Unfortunately, many firearm classes showcase the following situation:

You hear something. You arm yourself. You go investigate. The bad guy gets shot. You call 911. You wait for LE to show up.

It is no wonder this situation is described as there are no complications at all. However, LE may show up because someone else called 911 and they may arrive at an inopportune time (to put it mildly). Their arrival could complicate an already dangerous situation. Let's go through some examples.

Early Arrival

You hear something outside your home. You arm yourself and go investigate. Without your knowledge, your neighbor saw something suspicious and called LE. You don't know that LE is coming. LE could arrive with lights and sirens, or they may arrive quietly, hoping to catch someone in the act. Here is what they would find: a man (you) with a firearm walking around.

When it comes to LE, many people are guilty of projection. They think LE knows what they know. They assume LE knows they are the homeowner and that they pose no threat to LE. Unfortunately, LE knows nothing about you until they investigate. They most certainly aren't going to simply believe what you say. You are a guy with a firearm and likely the guy they got summoned to handle.

In this situation, you need to do whatever LE says for you to do and you need to do it slowly. Make sure LE knows you are going to cooperate, that you are the homeowner *and that you believe there is a trespasser on the property.*

Arrival During Violence

This circumstance is challenging to generalize as it can take many forms. Let's work through an example. You are at a convenience store, and the guy in front of you decides to rob the place. He pulls a gun and points it at the cashier. You pull your CCF and shoot and miss. He shoots the clerk and jumps behind the counter. You retreat to the back of the store. You exchange more shots. LE arrives.

Quick question: In the initial determination by the LEO, who is the good guy and who is the bad guy here? You may have been initially implicated as the bad guy because the real bad guy is behind the counter, where the good guy usually is.

When violence is ongoing, and LE arrives, you should keep in mind that you will be put in the category of "active threat" and not in the category of "good guy." You could easily be in no man's land if an LEO wants you to drop your weapon and surrender while another active threat targets you.

Something to consider: If you are in an active violent situation and see LE arriving, unarmed (or weapon concealed) retreat may be your best option to survive. Once you are at a safe location, you can call 911 and turn yourself in under better circumstances.

After Violence

Many people that are gunshot do not die. Data from 2003 through 2012 show a case fatality rate of 22 percent.[154] Usually, they go into shock. If an LEO shoots a suspect and the suspect goes into shock, the LEO will remove any weapons from the suspect's possession and likely handcuff the suspect while waiting for the ambulance. The LEO may provide medical care depending upon the injury (e.g., tourniquet application). If you CCF and had training derived from LE curriculum, you might want to do the same thing. However, I'm here to argue that you should not.

Let's assume you put down an active shooter, and there were no other threats. You may want to go over and pick up the shooter's weapon and get it away from him. Now, LEOs arrive on the scene of what they believe is a live incident with an active shooter. The 911 calls have described the weapon. There are people down and shot. The LEOs arrive on the scene to see you holding that same weapon. Is this a good situation for you?

---

[154] Cook, et al.(2017)

Rather than disarming the shooter, my (perhaps controversial) recommendation is to holster your weapon if you CCF (again, assuming there are no other threats). Leave the *immediate* area in case the active shooter comes out of shock, so he won't be able to shoot you in the back. When LE arrives, surrender and explain that the active shooter is down but is still armed.

There are many problems with this approach. For one, the active shooter could come out of shock and start shooting again. As an ordinary civilian, you must weigh this risk versus the risk of being gunned down by LE. Whatever you decide to do, understand that an army of LEOs is coming, and a big question relevant to your survival is: What are you doing when they arrive?

Incomplete Information

So far, what we've been covering is incomplete information regarding LE. LE must investigate to determine who are the good and bad actors in a situation. Sometimes, the situation is dynamic, and LE must make a split second decision because there is no time to investigate.

However, incomplete information happens anytime a good actor is a witness to a violent crime incident and doesn't have enough information to determine the other good and bad actors. In particular, I'm talking about a violent incident and multiple people who CCF.

One phenomenon that obscures the incomplete information problem is the active shooter. Two characteristics of active shootings that make it easy to identify the bad guy are:

- When they occur in a gun-free zone, the guy with the gun is the bad guy.
- Active shooters are usually loaded for bear. They may carry multiple handguns, multiple magazines, body armor, and so forth. As a result, they stick out like a sore thumb even when they are not shooting people in the back.

In other violent crimes, it is also easy to figure out who is the bad guy— for instance, a convenience store robbery. In a small store, you can see everyone, and the guy with the mask pointing the gun at the clerk is the bad guy.

However, all is not well for people who CCF in cases of incomplete information. For example, take a look at a situation where there is gunfire and multiple CCF people are there. Imagine if each concealed carrier is not sure who the bad actor is. For example, there are shots, people are hit, and people are running around with pistols, but no one knows who the good and bad guys are. In this situation, making a mistake with a firearm can land an ordinary civilian in prison. Worse, it could lead to multiple mistakes being made. LE compensates for these situations via radio communication, clearly identified uniforms, and consistent training. However, even if an LEO makes a mistake, they are tasked with protecting the public and could be exonerated due to a challenging situation involving incomplete information. This exoneration will not be available to an ordinary civilian.

The point isn't to change your mind about CCF. Each person should make that decision on their own. The point is to show an underappreciated issue about training derived from law enforcement or the military. That training often assumes that teammates recognize each other and communicate with each other. Also, teammates already know they've gone through similar training—they rely on it.

Open carriers and concealed carriers do not know each other, haven't trained together, and don't wear unique clothing or have communication equipment. As such, violent situations involving incomplete information between people who CCF are incredibly dangerous.

Surrendering Yourself and Your Weapon to Law Enforcement

What we still need to cover is if you are in a public place, used your weapon defensively to stop a personal threat, and that threat is down. There are a wide variety of situations here and many variations in each situation, so I'll just cover the basics.

I'll assume that an altercation happened, and you used your weapon in self-defense. You are now standing there with your weapon still in hand. You are probably extremely nervous, your hands are shaking, and perhaps you've even thrown up. These are natural reactions to the chemical cocktail that your body released due to the stressful incident. I'm also going to assume you are in a decent public area, not a crime-ridden area full of hostile witnesses or people looking to take advantage of you.

1. Recognize that you are the immediate threat to everyone because you are standing there holding a weapon. Bystanders (including others who have weapons) may have incomplete information and not know who the good and bad guys are. In other words, they may treat you as a threat. LE unexpectedly arriving will consider you a threat, the criminal on the ground certainly considers you a threat, and any of the criminal accomplices that ran away will also consider you a threat.

2. If the weapon you used was a less-than-lethal weapon, you are on the clock. Civilian Tasers are active for about 30 seconds. With pepper spray, you may have minutes. With a firearm, as we discussed previously, 78 percent of the people who are shot do not die. This fact means that the person on the ground probably isn't dead and can still be a life-threatening danger for you and your family.

3. If other offenders ran away upon your using your weapon, they are unaccounted for offenders. They may never come back, or they may come back with weapons. You do not know.

4. If you were accompanied by friends, relatives, your spouse, your kids, or some combination of all these, you have their safety to think about as well as your own.

An important point here is that if law enforcement were in the same situation as you, they would handle it differently. The reason is that they can. They are clearly identified as LEOs, can call for backup, and can alter the crime scene to make it safer (e.g., pick up a weapon, cuff the suspect). As an ordinary civilian, weapon in hand, performing these tasks could get you killed or sent to prison. For ordinary civilians, I recommend these steps:

1. You must determine if there are any imminent threats to you or your family. If there are threats and you can safely retreat to avoid further violence, you should.

2. If there are no imminent threats, you should holster your weapon. In the case of a civilian one-shot Taser, you will just leave the weapon.

3. You must determine whether you or your loved ones are in any danger remaining on the scene. In the case of less-than-lethal weapons, you probably are in danger because you have no idea of the law enforcement response time.

4. If you feel you must leave the scene for safety, ask someone to call 911 if there are witnesses and tell them you are leaving the scene for the safety of yourself and your family and that you are going to turn yourself in. You must call 911 immediately once you have arrived at a safe location and ask to turn yourself in. If you are driving away, call 911 and ask for directions to the nearest police station so you may turn yourself in.

5. If you remain at the scene, ask someone to call 911. If no one is there to call 911, you'll need to.

6. If you have kids with you, you will need to call a family member who can take custody of your children should you be arrested.

7. When surrendering to law enforcement, you should have your hands in the air and your weapon unavailable (on the ground, in the car, or whatever). You should never yell "gun" or anything like that, such as "my GUN is on the ground" or "my GUN is in the car." Everyone will be on edge here and the word "GUN" is not a word you should be using in these circumstances.

At this point, many criminal defense attorneys will scream not to leave the scene. They interpret it like you were leaving the scene of a fatal traffic accident. However, that is not what is going on here. You can't stand trial if you are dead. Importantly though, going to prison is a failed mission. Therefore, with the safety of yourself and your family as top priority (as per our mission), if you need to leave the scene, you need to notify law enforcement and turn yourself in as soon as it is safe to do so.

Important Points

- If you have a family, memorize every phone number of someone that can take custody of your kids. I know you have your kids memorize your cell phone number; you must do it too (just for different people).
- These situations should clearly show how wearing a body camera can help your defense.

PART VII

Legal Implications

Using a holistic self-defense strategy, ordinary civilians can legally put themselves in a strong position should they be forced to defend themselves. However, there are some things you can do that will significantly hurt your legal standing in a self-defense case. Let's break them down into two different categories:

Prior to Violence

1. You don't need to worry about legal standing if you are dead. This entire book has been about putting an ordinary civilian in the best situation possible to survive a wide variety of violent crime threats. Keep in mind that injuries and the psychological trauma of violence can be debilitating and lead to depression and possible suicide. So always strive to put yourself in the best position to avoid these horrible things.
2. There have been many ordinary civilians that have been criminally charged after they successfully defended themselves. Sadly, the thought of being forever in debt, legally defending themselves, and possibly spending the rest of their life in prison prompted some of them to commit suicide. Therefore, it is vitally important to have an attorney on retainer for significantly reduced costs in legal defense and consultations on your holistic defenses. Please seek help if you are depressed or have suicidal thoughts.

3. You can't defend yourself if you've been stripped of your weapons. If you live in a state with red flag laws, ask your attorney if they are prepared to defend you from red flag law abuses and get your weapons back. Red flag laws are usually set up a bit differently than standard criminal cases and be sure your attorney knows this fact. Even better, tell your attorney you want a complete walkthrough of what will happen if you are falsely accused and how to respond. Get another attorney if your attorney cannot help you with red flag laws.

4. If you have alcohol or drugs in your system when you defend yourself, you've significantly compromised your legal position. There are cases where this cannot be helped. For instance, not much can be done if you are relaxing in your home having a glass of wine and an ex-boyfriend decides to attack you. In most cases though, people are out drinking or doing drugs (or both) at a party, and then a violent situation erupts. They are forced to use lethal means to defend themselves. If this is the case, recognize that you've put yourself in a bad legal situation. If you are out and about, don't drink or do drugs if you have firearms in your vehicle or firearms on your person.

5. Do not leave a party or gathering due to "violence drama" and return with a firearm. Should the situation further escalate and you have to defend yourself, the fact that you returned with a firearm will be used against you. If you are in fear for your life or the lives of others and can leave, stay gone. If other people are in danger, this is a situation for law enforcement.

6. You should have either no social media accounts, or they should be very clean of rhetoric around violence or self-defense. If you are being prosecuted, your posts can be used against you.

7. If you take self-defense classes or firearms training, keep track of your training records. They show yourself to be a responsible firearm owner.

8. While I already went over the considerations for home defense ammunition, for outside the home, you should consider carrying the same type of ammunition that your local law enforce-

ment carries, provided it is accurate and functions well in your firearm. Some self-defense ammunition is branded or marketed in ways that may undermine your legal defense if you use it. When asked about your ammunition, you can simply say you carry what local law enforcement carries.

Immediate Aftermath of Violence

1. If you defend yourself and your victim is wounded and incapacitated, do not give medical treatment. This act can be used against you to say you felt remorse for an accident or felt guilty for acting inappropriately. Leave that to the EMTs.

2. If you defended yourself and you don't know if law enforcement is on the way, ask someone to call 911 for you. If no one is around, then call 911 yourself. State your name and the address where you are currently located. If someone needs medical attention (including yourself), state that fact. Then, simply indicate you were a victim of a violent crime. If, for example, three people tried to rob you and you shot one of them, and the other two ran off, state that there are violent offenders unaccounted for in the area. Be sure to state what you look like and what you are wearing.

3. If you feel you have time, call your attorney for advice on the situation so they can prepare you for what is coming.

4. As soon as the law enforcement officer asks you about something other than getting custody of your firearm, unaccounted violent offenders, custody of children (if your family was present for the incident), or medical issues (if you are wounded), invoke your constitutional rights. State specifically that you do not consent to any searches anywhere, that you are invoking your right to remain silent, and that you want to talk to your lawyer before making any statements to law enforcement. Repeat that continuously in response to any question by law enforcement.

PART VIII

Conclusion

In this book, I tried to do several things:

- Separate perceptions from reality regarding violent crime threats to ordinary civilians.
- Focus on the circumstances of injurious and non-injurious violent crime.
- Develop a methodology to evaluate self-defense solutions.
- Develop self-defense solutions based on likely civilian violent crime threats.
- Detail law enforcement and legal interactions for everyday situations and situations involving violence.

We first looked at how the news misleads civilians about violent crime. News programming is such that it emphasizes murder and firearms. Repeated exposure to this emphasis by news programming puts many civilians in fear of violent crime, particularly murder and firearms, which has been extensively researched and documented. We then looked at the influence of self-defense instructors, most of them being former military and law enforcement. We saw how they are training civilians to respond to the most dangerous threats to law enforcement officers —strangers who are armed and violent criminals. Unfortunately, it isn't clear that civilians usually face this same threat. In addition, this training doesn't cover interfacing with law enforcement very well because it assumes the audience is law enforcement.

Next, we took a deep dive into violent crime statistics. The threats to civilians are not like those of law enforcement officers. When civilians are injured in violent crime, the offenders are more likely to be people the victim knows, and the location is more likely to be a place where the victim feels comfortable. Additionally, firearms are not used often when the victim is injured. These facts are in stark contrast to news programming, the CDC, and the curriculum developed by many self-defense instructors.

We then discussed the benefits and harms of CCF. Given the civilian threat model, CCF may have too many harms for most civilians. In addition, early research has shown civilian DGUs to be much different than what is taught in firearms training. Therefore, additional research is needed to adequately address the benefits and harms of CCF. However, we did utilize the fact box to express the benefits and harms of a given self-defense solution, which comes in handy as a template for individuals evaluating their self-defense options.

In Parts II through VII, we discussed self-defense solutions designed to deal with the violent crime threats civilians most often face. In addition, civilian escalations and consent issues were discussed as well as these can lead to violent crime charges. However, for civilians and injurious violent crime, the primary threats are "people you know," and the primary location is "your home." I have never seen these topics discussed in self-defense classes. We extensively covered them and how to detect and avoid problems in these areas. Finally, we covered a subject also missing from most self-defense classes—how to interface with law enforcement and legal implications.

In researching this book, I was somewhat taken aback by what I found. I made many small changes in my life to help avoid becoming a violent crime victim when traveling. Although firearms are a part of my self-defense plan, I no longer carry them on my person very often, opting for a JPX6 instead. My firearms are typically locked in rapid access security boxes in the home and in my vehicle. Perhaps one day, we can get a concealable-friendly JPX6 with some of the improvements I've suggested in Appendix D (fingers crossed!).

Of course, no self-defense plan is perfect, nor is the data we use to derive it perfect. We certainly have problems with the following:

- The inability to account for criminal violence. America is currently experiencing Prohibition-era criminal violence due to the buying, selling, and distribution of illegal drugs. Sometimes this violence spills over and innocent people are injured or killed. America needs to be able to take the money out of this illegal trade and provide for the treatment rather than imprisonment of non-violent drug addicts. Sadly, a street-smart 12-year-old in a moderately sized city can point you to a person or location where you can buy any drug in the world. Clearly, the drug "war" has failed.

- Firearm violence is shown in the media disproportionately to other injurious violent crime circumstances. When it is shown in this way, it puts political pressure to deprive some of the rights of all firearm owners in America.

- Mass shootings are challenging to defend against. While people who CCF provide some defense to certain mass shooting situations, a better defensive system must be thought through. In gun-free zones, for instance, a heavily armed guard can provide a murderer with all the weapons needed if they can take that guard out without using a firearm. On the other hand, snipers with a lot of rifles and ammo can kill over extended periods, and people who CCF are still defenseless against them. Also, if our mass murder defenses are successful, mass murderers may utilize or invent other more deadly methods than the typical firearm. We must plan for that too.

- Mass shootings typically drive red flag laws. These laws circumvent due process, follow civil rather than criminal courts, which means high court costs for the defendants. Unfortunately, they will probably be misused like Amber Alerts; where most of these alerts come from divorces, relationship issues, or custody battles. We must do better here: Mass murderers tend to bring attention to themselves before committing murder, and given those hard-to-miss clues, we should act. However, we need to do so in a way that protects due process and the natural rights of the American people.

In short, responsible firearms owners, natural rights advocates, and effective self-defense advocates all have their work cut out for them. However, I feel it is a winnable fight if we work together.

I am very critical of advertising revenue and other ways undue influences can corrupt the truth. Here are the steps I've taken to make sure that you can rely on my content:

- I independently financed this book.
- No products were given to me for free or at a discount to evaluate. Any product recommendations I make were products purchased with my own money.
- I do not accept advertising on my website.
- I do not allow for comments, shares, likes, or anything of the form on my website. I have a contact form if you want to discuss a post or issue. If I feel others can benefit from your points or issues, I'll update my posts, provide new ones, or post corrections to the text. I will happily give credit to those individuals who find problems or point out great solutions I had not considered.
- The only way I break even is through book sales. So if you liked the book, please recommend it to your friends, relatives, and your local public library.

Thank you for your purchase and your time! I hope this book contributed positively to your life and the protection of your loved ones (and in addition, that it positively contributed to accomplishing your mission).

APPENDICES

APPENDIX A

Uniform Crime Reports

A.1 General Uniform Crime Reports Information[155]

The Uniform Crime Reporting (UCR) Program generates reliable statistics for use in law enforcement. It also provides information for students of criminal justice, researchers, the media, and the public. The program has been providing crime statistics since 1930.

The UCR Program includes data from more than 18,000 city, university and college, county, state, tribal, and federal law enforcement agencies. Agencies participate voluntarily and submit their crime data either through a state UCR program or directly to the FBI's UCR Program.

There is also A Guide to Understanding NIBRS.[156] Also, there is a lot of good information available on the Additional Resources[157] page.

UCR Totals

Table 1 shows the violent crime numbers reported by the UCR In the period from 2015 to 2019.

---

[155] https://clayeolsen.com/ucr-services
[156] https://clayeolsen.com/ucr-nibrs
[157] https://clayeolsen.com/ucr-res

Table A1. UCR Violent Crime 2015-2019

Violent Crime	Count
Aggravated Assault	4,006,873
Robbery	1,528,977
Rape	600,865
Murder	82,869
Total	6,219,584

Table 2 shows these numbers as a percentage of total crime.

Table A2. UCR Percentages 2015-2019

Violent Crime	Percent of Total
Aggravated Assault	64.4
Robbery	24.6
Rape	9.7
Murder	1.3

Significantly, the UCR reports that 89 percent of all violent crime in the United States from 2015 to 2019 was aggravated assault or robbery.

To get the totals for the UCR, you'll need to go to each violent crime category and pull the numbers from the overview section. Click on "Aggravated Assault," then "Robbery," then "Rape," and finally "Murder" to see the totals for each category. The links and the totals are as follows:

2015[158]

- Aggravated Assault: 764,449
- Robbery: 327,374
- Rape: 90,185 rapes (legacy definition)
- Murder: 15,696

---

[158] https://clayeolsen.com/ucr-vc-2015

2016[159]

- Aggravated Assault: 803,007
- Robbery: 332,198
- Rape: 95,730 rapes (legacy definition)
- Murder: 17,250

2017[160]

- Aggravated Assault: 810,825
- Robbery: 319,356
- Rape: 135,755
- Murder: 17,284

2018[161]

- Aggravated Assault: 807,410
- Robbery: 282,061
- Rape: 139,380
- Murder: 16,214

2019[162]

- Aggravated Assault: 821,182
- Robbery: 267,988
- Rape: 139,815
- Murder: 16,425

---

[159] https://clayeolsen.com/ucr-vc-2016

[160] https://clayeolsen.com/ucr-vc-2017

[161] https://clayeolsen.com/ucr-vc-2018

[162] https://clayeolsen.com/ucr-vc-2019

UCR Rates

Rates are used to account for population differences and to prevent misleading information. For instance, if I only compared the raw number of violent crimes in Place X to Place Y, and that number was 50 in both places, you may conclude that they were equally safe. However, if Place Y has one billion people and Place X has one million, that would not be a correct determination. So, rates are used to account for population differences.

The FBI Crime Data Explorer[163] is an excellent user interface for UCR data and captures rates quite easily. To see the same information as I am reporting here, select the United States and 2019. Then scroll down to "Trend" and under "Crime Select," choose "Aggravated Assault." Here you can also select the time period; choose the years 2009 to 2019.

Aggravated Assault Rate per 100,000 People

From 2015 to 2019, we had a decent rate of stability with Aggravated Assault, especially over the period of 2016-2019.

- 2015: 238.1
- 2016: 248.3
- 2017: 249.2
- 2018: 248.2
- 2019: 250.2

Essentially, from 2015 to 2019, there were around 246.8 aggravated assaults per 100,000 people in the United States.

Robbery Rate per 100,000 People

To see the same information as I am reporting here, select "United States" and "2019." Then scroll down to "Trend" and select "Robbery" for "Crime Select" and the years 2009 to 2019.

---

[163] https://clayeolsen.com/crime-explorer

From the years 2016 to 2019, we had a downward trend of robberies.

- 2015: 102.2
- 2016: 102.9
- 2017: 98.6
- 2018: 86.1
- 2019: 81.6

From 2015 to 2019, there were an average of 94.3 robberies per 100,000 people in the United States.

Rape Rate per 100,000 People

To see the same information as I am reporting here, select the United States and 2019. Then scroll down to "Trend" and select "Rape" for "Crime Select" and the years 2009 to 2019.

We will use the new definition of rape (i.e., lack of consent versus forcible only) for these rates.

Rapes per 100,000 people:

- 2015: 39.3
- 2016: 40.9
- 2017: 41.7
- 2018: 44
- 2019: 42.6

For these five years, rapes averaged 41.7 per 100,000 people.

Homicide Rate per 100,000 People

To see the same information as I am reporting here, select the United States and 2019. Then scroll down to "Trend" and select "Homicide" for "Crime Select" and the years 2009 to 2019.

The rates of Homicide from 2015 to 2019:

- 2015: 4.9
- 2016: 5.4
- 2017: 5.3
- 2018: 5
- 2019: 5

For five years, Homicide was at an average of 5.12 per 100,000 people.

US State Specific Rates

To get the information from your state, select your state and 2019. Go through the same steps listed previously for each violent crime.

A.2 National Incident-Based Reporting System

The UCR has extra details on violent crime captured in the National Incident-Based Reporting System (NIBRS). However, not all violent crimes processed by the UCR are part of NIBRS because not all law enforcement agencies can provide the extra data. I believe this changed starting in 2021 (I'm not 100 percent sure of the status because of the impacts of COVID on a variety of programs), and the NIBRS will be used exclusively.

In what follows, I will be pulling statistics pertaining to the United States. You can go through each of these same steps to get the information for your particular US state if you wish. Just select the US state rather than the United States. The rest of the steps are the same.

A.2.1 Aggravated Assault

Here is the UCR's definition from 2019[164] (my emphasis is in italics):

> The FBI's Uniform Crime Reporting (UCR) Program defines aggravated assault as an unlawful attack by one person upon another for the purpose

---

[164] https://clayeolsen.com/ucr-vc-2019-aa

of inflicting severe or aggravated bodily injury. The UCR Program further specifies that this type of assault is usually accompanied by the use of a weapon or by other means likely to produce death or great bodily harm. *Attempted aggravated assault that involves the display of—or threat to use—a gun, knife, or other weapon is included in this crime category because serious personal injury would likely result if the assault were completed.* When aggravated assault and larceny-theft occur together, the offense falls under the category of robbery.

[...]

Assaults that do not involve the use of a firearm, knife or cutting instrument, or other dangerous weapon and in which the victim did not sustain serious or aggravated injuries are reported as other assaults—simple, not aggravated. These data are not included in the aggravated assault statistics.

Going to the FBI crime data explorer,[165] you'll want to find the NIBRS section. Select "Aggravated Assault" for "Crime Select." Select "2019" for "Year Select," then for "Include Previous Years," choose "Last Five Years." Click the "percent" button to see the values in percentages.

Age

- Offender's age range under 40: 67 percent
- Victim's age range under 40: 65 percent

Sex

- Offenders Men: 73 percent
- Victims Women: 45 percent

Victim Demographics: Location

- Location Residence Home: 56 percent
- Location Public Area: 27 percent

---

[165] https://clayeolsen.com/crime-explorer

- Public Area: Highway/Alley/Street/Sidewalk: 21 percent
- Public Area: Garage/Parking Lot: 6 percent

Victim Demographics: Relationship

- Offender Stranger: 16 percent
- Offender Relationship Unknown: 22 percent

Offense Characteristics: Weapon

- Weapon Firearm: 25 percent
- Weapon Personal: 26 percent (e.g., fists). I'm assuming these represent cases where the victim was severely injured.
- Weapon Knife or Blunt Object: 32 percent

Offense Characteristics: Linked

- Linked Damage of Property: 28 percent
- Weapon Law Violations: 17 percent.

A.2.2 Robbery

The UCR definition of robbery[166] is as follows (my emphasis in italics):

The FBI's Uniform Crime Reporting (UCR) Program defines Robbery as the taking or attempting to take anything of value from the care, custody, or control of a person or persons *by force or threat of force or violence and/ or by putting the victim in fear.*

Going to the FBI crime data explorer[167], you'll want to find the NIBRS section. Select "Robbery" for "Crime Select." Select 2019 for "Year

---

[166] https://clayeolsen.com/ucr-vc-2019-ro
[167] https://clayeolsen.com/crime-explorer

Select," then for "Include Previous Years," choose "Last Five Years." Click the "%" button to see the values in percentages.

Age

Offender's Age

- 20–29: 32%
- Unknown: 25% (likely disguised or at night).
- 10–19: 22%
- 30–39: 13%

Victim's Age

- 20–29: 32%
- 30–39: 20%
- 10–19: 15%
- 40–49: 13%
- Offenders 10–39 age range: 67%.
- Victims 10–39 age range: 67%.

Sex

- Male Offenders: 83%
- Male Victims: 65%

Victim Demographics: Location

- Public Area: 77%
- Residence Home: 19%

Victim Demographics: Relationship

- Offender Stranger: 42%
- Offender Unknown: 41%
- Acquaintance/Other: 13%

Offense Characteristics: Weapon

- Weapon Firearm: 39%
- Weapon Personal: 29% (e.g., fists)
- Weapon None: 10%
- Weapon Knife/Cutting Instrument: 8%

Offense Characteristics: Linked

- These are all over the place and don't do much for our analysis. Aggravated Assault was at 7%, and Simple Assault was at 5%, suggesting Robberies that escalated from Assault total around 12%. Burglary/Breaking-in was linked at 10%.

A.2.3 Rape

Here is the UCR definition of rape is as follows, with my emphasis in italics:[168]

> The carnal knowledge of a female forcibly and against her will. Beginning with the 2013 data year, the term "forcible" was removed from the offense title, and the definition was changed. The revised UCR definition of rape is: penetration, no matter how slight, of the vagina or anus with any body part or object, or oral penetration by a sex organ of another person, *without the consent of the victim.* Attempts or assaults to commit rape are also included in the statistics presented here; *however, statutory rape and incest are excluded.*

Going to the FBI crime data explorer,[169] you'll want to find the NIBRS section. Select "Rape" for "Crime Select." Select "2019" for "Year Select,"

---

[168] https://clayeolsen.com/ucr-vc-2019-ra

[169] https://clayeolsen.com/crime-explorer

then for "Include Previous Years," choose "Last Five Years." Click the "%" button to see the values in percentages.

Age

- Offender Male under 50: 77%
- Offender Male under 40: 66%
- Victim Female under 30: 76%

Sex

- Offender Male: 93%
- Victim Female: 89%

Victim Demographics: Location

- Residence Home: 71%

Victim Demographics: Relationship

- People You Know: 76%
- Relationship Unknown: 16%
- Stranger: 8%

Offense Characteristics: Weapon

- Personal Weapons (e.g., fists): 54%
- None: 31%

Offense Characteristics: Linked

- Kidnapping/Abduction: 24%

A.2.4 Homicide

Here is the UCR definition of homicide[170], my emphasis in italics:

> The FBI's Uniform Crime Reporting (UCR) Program *defines murder and nonnegligent manslaughter as the willful (nonnegligent) killing of one human being by another.*
>
> *"The classification of this offense is based solely on police investigation* as opposed to the determination of a court, medical examiner, coroner, jury, or other judicial body.

The demographics of homicide can be found by going to the FBI crime data explorer[171]; you'll want to find the NIBRS section. Select "Homicide" for "Crime Select." Select "2019" for "Year Select," then for "Include Previous Years," choose "Last Five Years." Click the "%" button to see the values in percentages.

Offender Age

- 20-29   35%
- 30-39   19%
- 10-19   16%
- Offender age range under 40 is 70%

Victim Age

- 20-29   31%
- 30-39   21%
- 40-49   13%
- 10-19   10%
- Victim age range under 50 is 75%

---

[170] https://clayeolsen.com/ucr-vc-2019-m

[171] https://clayeolsen.com/crime-explorer

The UCR has an expanded homicide table overview that is easier to go through. I've included them here by year. You'll find a similar pattern for each year.

Please remember that homicides accounted for only 1.3 percent of violent crimes from 2015 to 2019.

UCR 2019 Expanded Homicide Table Overview[172]

(My emphasis is in *italics*.)

- *78.3% of murder victims were male*
- 50.6% were single offender/single victim
- *88% of offenders were male*
- *73.7% used firearms (62.1% handguns)*

Victim-Offender Relationship

- 28.3% were killed by someone they knew
- 13% were killed by a family member
- *9.9% by a stranger*
- *48.9% Relationship Unknown*
- 58.8% of the murders have known circumstances
- 43.2% happened during arguments
- 24.6% happened during the commission of another felony

UCR 2018 Expanded Homicide Table Overview[173]

- 77.3% of murder victims were male
- 49.2% were single offender/single victim
- 87.7% of offenders were male
- 72.7% used firearms (64.3% handguns)

---

[172] https://clayeolsen.com/ucr-eh-2019
[173] https://clayeolsen.com/ucr-eh-2018

Victim-Offender Relationship

- 27.8% were killed by someone they knew
- 12.8% were killed by a family member
- 9.9% by a stranger
- 49.5% Relationship Unknown
- 61% of the murders have known circumstances
- 39.4% happened during arguments
- 24.5% happened during the commission of another felony

UCR 2017 Expanded Homicide Table Overview[174]

- 78.4% of murder victims were male
- 45.6% were single offender/single victim
- 88.1% of offenders were male
- 72.6% used firearms (64% handguns)

Victim-Offender Relationship

- 28% were killed by someone they knew
- 12.3% were killed by a family member
- 9.7% by a stranger
- 50% Relationship Unknown
- 59.8% of the murders have known circumstances
- 39% happened during arguments
- 24.7% happened during the commission of another felony

UCR 2016 Expanded Homicide Table Overview[175]

- 78.4% of murder victims were male
- 88.8% of offenders were male
- 73% used firearms (64.6% handguns)

---

[174] https://clayeolsen.com/ucr-eh-2017
[175] https://clayeolsen.com/ucr-eh-2016

UCR 2015 Expanded Homicide Table Overview[176]

- 78.8% of murder victims were male
- 45.6% were single offender/single victim
- 89% of offenders were male
- 71.5% used firearms (67% handguns)

Victim-Offender Relationship

- 29.2% were killed by someone they knew
- 12.8% were killed by a family member
- 10.2% by a stranger
- 47.8% Relationship Unknown
- 60.1% of the murders have known circumstances
- 39.9% happened during arguments
- 24.9% happened during the commission of another felony

Justified Homicide

Justifiable Homicide by Weapon, Private Citizen 2015-2019[177]

- 2015: Total: 333; Handguns: 216
- 2016: Total: 334; Handguns: 201
- 2017: Total: 368; Handguns: 238
- 2018: Total: 375; Handguns: 229
- 2019: Total: 386; Handguns: 237
- Average of Total: 360
- Average for Handguns: 225

Justifiable Homicide by Weapon, Law Enforcement 2015-2019[178]

- 2015: Total: 457; Handguns: 316
- 2016: Total: 440; Handguns: 313

---

[176] https://clayeolsen.com/ucr-eh-2015

[177] https://clayeolsen.com/ucr-jh-pc

[178] https://clayeolsen.com/ucr-jh-le

- 2017: Total: 444; Handguns: 284
- 2018: Total: 435; Handguns: 292
- 2019: Total: 340; Handguns: 248
- Average of Total: 424
- Average for Handguns: 291

A.3 Persons Arrested

Here are the statistics from 2015 to 2019. All the years are very close. I've taken the 2019 Overview directly from the webpage. Because the data is so similar from year to year, for the sake of space, I only show 2019. The URLs are listed after 2019 from 2015 to 2018.

2019[179]

- "Nationwide, law enforcement made an estimated 10,085,207 arrests in 2019. Of these arrests, 495,871 were for violent crimes, and 1,074,367 were for property crimes …
- The highest number of arrests were for drug abuse violations (estimated at 1,558,862 arrests), driving under the influence (estimated at 1,024,508), and larceny-theft (estimated at 813,073)."
- The Overview section reports 495,871 arrests for violent crime out of a total of 10,085,207 arrests, or 4.9 percent. In other words, *95 percent of arrests made in 2019 had nothing to do with violent crime.*
- By way of comparison, drug abuse (1,558,862) and driving under the influence (1,024,508) accounted for 25.6 percent of arrests.

---

[179] https://clayeolsen.com/ucr-pa-2019

Persons arrested from 2015 to 2018:

2018[180]
2017[181]
2016[182]
2015[183]

Other Arrest Details: 2015 to 2019

If you dive into the details of the arrest tables, you can do the math and find out some surprising information.

If you calculate the top 13 arrest categories responsible for 95 percent of the total arrests, Aggravated Assault is the only violent crime to make the list—typically under 4 percent. Alcohol and drug arrests were around 30 percent, where 86 percent of that 30 percent were for possession.

A.4 Violence Against Women

There are two ways to approach the answer to this question: the simple and the complex. Unfortunately, these differing ways give two different answers.

The Simple Way

Let's go to the FBI Crime Data Explorer, NIBRS section, and select the following:

1. Crime Select: All Violent crime
2. Year Select: 2019

---

[180] https://clayeolsen.com/ucr-pa-2018
[181] https://clayeolsen.com/ucr-pa-2017
[182] https://clayeolsen.com/ucr-pa-2016
[183] https://clayeolsen.com/ucr-pa-2015

3. Include Previous Years: Past 5 Years

We can then select "Sex" and look at "Victim" (the right side). Unfortunately, even if you hit the percentage button, I was not able to get the percentages calculated for me (at the time of this writing). Here is the percentage calculation based on the numbers provided:

- Men: 1,061,043
- Women: 1,009,990
- Unknown: 8,694
- Total: 2,079,727
- Men: 1,061,043/2,079,727 = 51%
- Women: 1,009,990/2,079,727 = 48.56%
- Unknown: 8,694/2,079,727 = 0.42%

The percentages are pretty close to adding up to 100 percent. It looks like men edge out women as being victims of violent crime. Most people would likely conclude that violent crime equally victimizes the sexes.

But, there is a more complex way that gives us a different answer.

The Complex Way

Once you understand how the various ways violent crime statistics are gathered, you may want to supplement "The Simple Way" via these four ways in combination:

1. Was the Victim Injured?
2. Reporting Bias
3. Victim Injury Circumstances
4. Percentage Relations

Was the Victim Injured?

As we have seen, the violent crimes of aggravated assault and robbery have much wider victimization ranges than rape and homicide. Most importantly, though, rape and homicide do not have a non-injurious form. The victim is always considered injured in rape, and the victim dies in a homicide. Aggravated assault and robbery include cases *where the victim is not injured.* Unfortunately, the UCR does not keep track of victim injury for these two violent crimes. Thus, only injurious violent crimes are mixed with violent crimes that can be either injurious or non-injurious.

Logically, this fact may not seem critical. After all, one may think that the only difference between non-injurious violent crime and injurious violent crime is the escalation to brutality. Therefore, the circumstances between the two would remain the same. However, as we investigated previously, that is not the case. The demographics and circumstances are usually different between the two cases. As we will see in this section, the inclusion of non-injurious aggravated assault and non-injurious robbery skew the circumstances and demographics of violent crime in the UCR.

Reporting Bias

The NCVS allows us to see whether the crime was "reported to the police." We will take these percentage values from the NCVS and apply them to the numbers of the UCR. First, let's get the total number of crimes from 2015 to 2019 using the FBI Crime Data Explorer from Appendix A. Here are the totals:

- Aggravated Assault (AA): 1,079,864
- Robbery (RO): 390,538
- Rape (RP): 267,064
- Homicide (HD): 24,441

The NCVS shows that 40 percent of AA, 40 percent of RO, and 76 percent of Injurious Rape/Sexual Assault are not reported to the police. Keep in mind because the NCVS is a sample, there is a confidence interval range. For this section, the mean (average) will be used. Also, let's assume that all homicides are reported to the UCR, so there is no unreported rate for homicide. Finally, let's calculate our best guess as to what the UCR would have reported if the reporting rate to law enforcement was 100 percent:

- AA: X(.60) = 1,079,864; X = 1,079,864/.60; X = 1,799,774
- RO: Y(.60) = 390,538; Y = 390,538/.60; Y = 650,897
- RP: Z(.76) = 267,064; Z = 267,064/.76; Z = 351,400
- HD: 24,441

All these new values dramatically increased, except for HD, due to our assumption.

Victim Injury Circumstances

The NCVS can determine when the victim is injured versus when the victim is not injured. For AA and RO, the victim is not injured about 66 percent of the time. Again, this is a mean sample within a confidence interval. I'm simply going to use the mean. Let's revisit the math and calculate the totals where the victim is injured. Note that IAA is injurious aggravated assault, and IRO is injurious robbery.

- IAA = 1,799,774 * 0.33 = 593,926
- IRO = 650,897 * 0.33 = 214,797

We've looked specifically at UCR violent crime and corrected for victim injury and the reporting bias, which came from the NCVS. In short, we are looking at injurious violent crime at a 100 percent reporting rate. Here are the new numbers:

- IAA: 593,926
- IRO: 214,797
- RP: 351,400
- HO: 24,441

Percentage Relations

Let's look at what the victim's sex breakdown is when the victim is injured. Based on the NCVS, men and women are very close to 50 percent for IAA and IRO, so I'm just going to say 50/50. For rape and homicide, I used the Victim Sex percentage breakdown in the UCR. I'll ignore any situation where the victim's sex was "unknown," as it didn't seem significant when I calculated the simple way (less than half a percentage point).

- IAA: 50% male
- IRO: 50% male
- RP: 10% male
- HO: 75% male

Now, let's determine the male/female split:

- $IAA\_S = 593{,}926 * 0.5 = 296{,}964$ M, $296{,}964$ F
- $IRO\_S = 214{,}797 * 0.5 = 107{,}398$ M, $107{,}398$ F
- $RP\_M = 351{,}400 * 0.1 = 35{,}140$
- $RP\_F = 351{,}400 * 0.9 = 316{,}260$
- $HO\_M = 24{,}441 * 0.75 = 18{,}331$
- $HO\_F = 24{,}441 * 0.25 = 6{,}111$

Let's add them up:

- Men: $296{,}964 + 107{,}398 + 35{,}140 + 18{,}331 = 457{,}833$
- Women: $296{,}964 + 107{,}398 + 316{,}260 + 6{,}111 = 726{,}733$

Now, let's calculate the percentages:

- Men = $457{,}833 / (457{,}833+762{,}733) = 457{,}833/1{,}220{,}566 = 37.5\%$
- Women = $762{,}733 / (457{,}833+762{,}733) = 762{,}733/1{,}220{,}566 = 62.5\%$

APPENDIX B

National Crime Victimization Survey

B.1 National Crime Victimization Survey Background[184]

The BJS National Crime Victimization Survey (NCVS) is the nation's primary source of information on criminal victimization. Each year, data are obtained from a nationally representative sample of about 240,000 persons in about 150,000 households. Persons are interviewed on the frequency, characteristics, and consequences of criminal victimization in the United States. [...]

The NCVS[185] has many supporting documents. Simply click on the tab "Supporting Documents" to review. You can also look at the NCVS Wikipedia page.[186]

Here is a helpful image that shows the differences between the UCR and NCVS from the UCR Wikipedia entry:[187]

---

[184] https://clayeolsen.com/ncvs

[185] https://clayeolsen.com/ncvs-sd

[186] https://clayeolsen.com/ncvs-wiki

[187] https://clayeolsen.com/ucr-wiki

Violent Crime Arrests, Reports, and Unknown

UCR Arrests

UCR Reported Crimes

NCVS Reported Crimes

Unknown Crimes

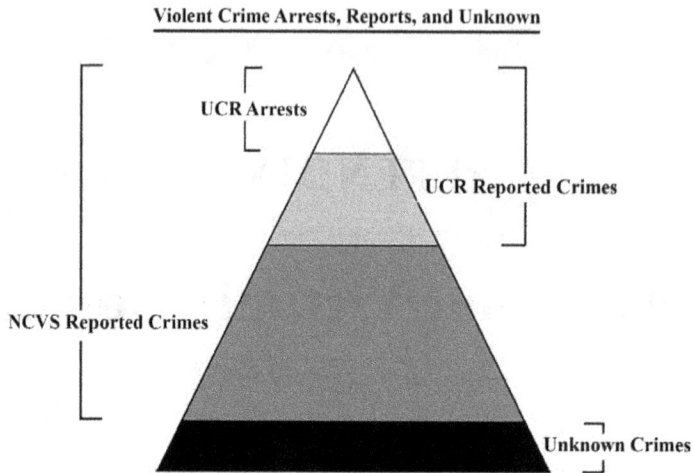

I feel this diagram is a bit misleading for "Unknown Crime." Based upon what we've discussed in this book, I wouldn't be surprised if the black base representing "Unknown Crime" was larger than the totals of all the other crimes. Of course, there is no way to prove that.

N-DASH, NVAT, and My Approach

The main user interface to the NCVS database is a tool called N-DASH. From a self-defense perspective, N-DASH has two significant limitations:

- Rather than have two categories of "Not Injured" and "Injured," N-DASH provides three categories of "Not Injured," "Injured—Not Treated," and "Injured—Treated," which refers to whether the physical injuries of the victim were medically treated. There is a tendency to assume that the severity of the injury has a lot to do with whether medical treatment is given to the victim. In reality, there are a lot of additional factors such as insurance coverage, physical location of the medical facility, and others. Unfortunately, N-DASH does not allow for simply using "Injured," thus needlessly complicating the analysis.
- N-DASH did not fully implement all the functionality of the previous NCVS user-interface tool, which was called NVAT. Essential to my analysis was the category "Location of Incident," which was not available via N-DASH at the time of this writing.

To compensate for these issues, I contracted with a statistics company to examine the NCVS data and report on both "Injured" and "Location of Incident," as well as using advanced statistical functions to help narrow the confidence intervals appropriately. However, I am also very keen on data transparency, so I went ahead and did the statistical analysis using N-DASH and Microsoft Excel™ for all parameters except "Location of Incident," which is not implemented by N-DASH. This separate analysis approximates the results reported here very closely.

NCVS Totals

To calculate the totals for the NCVS, you'll need to generate a table for each violent crime. If you download my Excel spreadsheet, I've already done that for you, with everything broken down.[188] However, you can duplicate what I did by performing the following steps:

1. Go to N-DASH, the front-end tool to access NCVS data.[189]
2. Select "Custom Graphics," then "Multi-Year Trends," then "Characteristic."
3. Select "Person" for Crime Category.
4. Select "On" for Confidence Interval.
5. Select "Medical Treatment for Physical Injuries" for Comparison Characteristic.
6. Select "Aggravated Assault" for Crime Type.

You can go through the graphs at the bottom. There is also a selection for "Download Table" or "Show Table." If you are following along with the Excel spreadsheet, the tab AA corresponds to Aggravated Assault, Ro for Robbery, and RA for Injurious Sexual Assault (rape). To select the different violent crimes, simply change the value for Crime Type.

---

[188] Unfortunately, N-DASH totals for violent crime differ from their totals based upon the violent crime versus for violent crime broken down by Medical Treatment for Physical Injuries. N-DASH does not show you the category of "Unknown" when you break down the data by Medical Treatment for Physical Injuries. As a result, these values are slightly less than what you would get via other means.

[189] http://clayeolsen.com/n-dash

For Injurious Rape/Sexual Assault, you'll only be looking at "Treated" and "Not Treated" in the data. The NCVS combines sexual assault and rape into one statistic, so I used Injurious Rape/Sexual Assault for a better comparison to the UCR data. Here are the totals I come up with in Table 3:

Table 3. NCVS Violent Crime 2015-2019

Violent Crime	Total
Aggravated Assault	4,912,863
Robbery	2,752,001
Injury Rape/Sexual Assault	991,968
Total	8,656,832

Table 4 shows these data as percentages so we can compare them with the UCR.

Table 4. NCVS Percentages 2015-2019

Violent Crime	Percent of Total
Aggravated Assault	56.8
Robbery	31.8
Injury Rape/Sexual Assault	11.46

According to the NCVS, aggravated assault and robbery total about 88.6 percent, in line with the UCR's 89 percent. However, the NCVS shows higher rates of robbery (31.8 percent) and lower rates of aggravated assault (56.8 percent) than the UCR.

NCVS Selected Variables

Here is a list[190] of all the variables considered. I have marked the variables I decided to use for my research in *italics*.

---

[190] http://clayeolsen.com/n-dash

Victim sex
Victim race/Hispanic ethnicity
Victim age
Victim household income
Victim population size
Victim region
Victim marital status
Reporting to the police
Medical treatment for physical injuries
Victim services use
Victim-offender relationship
Weapon category

B.2 Aggravated Assault

The NCVS definition[191] (my emphasis is in italics):

> "An attack or attempted attack with a weapon, *regardless of whether the victim is injured, or an attack without a weapon when serious injury results.*"

To view the data that appears here, follow the procedure outlined below. If you do not want to do this procedure, I've gathered the data into an Excel spreadsheet which you can download here.[192]

1. Go to N-DASH, the front-end tool to access NCVS data.[193]
2. Select "Custom Graphics," then "Multi-Year Trends," then "Characteristic."
3. Select "Person" for Crime Category.
4. Select "On" for Confidence Interval.

---

[191] https://clayeolsen.com/ncvs-terms

[192] https://clayeolsen.com/excel

[193] http://clayeolsen.com/n-dash

5. Select "Medical Treatment for Physical Injuries" for Comparison Characteristic.
6. Select "Aggravated Assault" for Crime Type.
7. Select "All" for Filter Characteristic.

The resulting data will be shown on the Excel spreadsheet for AA in tabs "AA – Not Injured," "AA – Not Treated," and "AA – Treated."
To go through other Filter Characteristics, simply select one. To match the Excel spreadsheet, follow these steps:

8. Select "Reporting to the police" for Filter Characteristic.
9. Select "No" for Filter Characteristic Value.

The graphs are automatically updated. The resulting data will be shown on the Excel spreadsheet on tabs "AA – Police | *" and "AA – No Police | *."

10. Select "Weapon Category" for Filter Characteristic.
11. Select "Firearm" for Filter Characteristic Value.

The graphs are automatically updated. The resulting data will be shown on the Excel spreadsheet on tabs "AA – Weapon *."

12. Select "Victim-offender relationship" for Filter Characteristic.
13. Select "Strangers" for Filter Characteristic Value.

The graphs are automatically updated. The resulting data will be shown on the Excel spreadsheet on tabs "AA – Rel *."

14. Select "Victim sex" for Filter Characteristic.
15. Select "Male" for Filter Characteristic Value.

The graphs are automatically updated. The resulting data will be shown on the Excel spreadsheet on tabs "AA – Victim *."

16. Select "Victim marital status" for Filter Characteristic.
17. Select "Never Married" for Filter Characteristic Value.

The graphs are automatically updated. The resulting data will be shown on the Excel spreadsheet on tabs "AA – Marital *."

Location of Incident

The following location codes were used in the NCVS database and mapped to these labels:

- At or Near Victim's Home (Codes 01, 02, 03, 05, 07)
- At or Near Friend/Neighbor/Relative Home (Codes 08, 09, 11)
- Public Areas (Codes 15, 16, 21, 22)
- Hotel/Motel Room (Code 04)
- Apartment Complex Shared Area (Codes 06, 10, 17, 20)
- Commercial Places (Codes 12, 13, 14, 24, 25, 26, 27)
- School (Codes 18, 19)

B.3 Robbery

The NCVS definition,[194] my emphasis in italics:

"The unlawful taking or attempted taking of property that is in the immediate possession of another, *by force or threat of force, with or without a weapon, and with or without injury.*"

To view the data that appears here, follow the procedure outlined below. If you do not want to do this procedure, I've gathered the data into an Excel spreadsheet which you can download here.[195]

---

[194] https://clayeolsen.com/ncvs-terms
[195] https://clayeolsen.com/excel

1. Go to N-DASH, the front-end tool to access NCVS data.[196]
2. Select "Custom Graphics," then "Multi-Year Trends," then "Characteristic."
3. Select "Person" for Crime Category.
4. Select "On" for Confidence Interval.
5. Select "Medical Treatment for Physical Injuries" for Comparison Characteristic.
6. Select "Robbery" for Crime Type.
7. Select "All" for Filter Characteristic.

The resulting data will be shown on the Excel spreadsheet for RO in tabs "RO – Not Injured," "RO – Not Treated," and "RO – Treated."

To go through other Filter Characteristics, simply select one. To match the Excel spreadsheet, follow these steps:

8. Select "Reporting to the police" for Filter Characteristic.
9. Select "No" for Filter Characteristic Value

The graphs are automatically updated. The resulting data will be shown on the Excel spreadsheet on tabs "RO – Police | *" and "RO – No Police | *."

10. Select "Weapon Category" for Filter Characteristic.
11. Select "Firearm" for Filter Characteristic Value.

The graphs are automatically updated. The resulting data will be shown on the Excel spreadsheet on tabs "RO – Weapon *."

12. Select "Victim-offender relationship" for Filter Characteristic.
13. Select "Strangers" for Filter Characteristic Value.

The graphs are automatically updated. The resulting data will be shown on the Excel spreadsheet on tabs "RO – Rel *."

---

[196] http://clayeolsen.com/n-dash

14. Select "Victim sex" for Filter Characteristic.
15. Select "Male" for Filter Characteristic Value.

The graphs are automatically updated. The resulting data will be shown on the Excel spreadsheet on tabs "RO – Victim *."

16. Select "Victim marital status" for Filter Characteristic.
17. Select "Never Married" for Filter Characteristic Value.

The graphs are automatically updated. The resulting data will be shown on the Excel spreadsheet on tabs "RO – Marital *."

B.4 Rape

The NCVS definition,[197] my emphasis in italics:

> Unlawful penetration of a person against the will of the victim, *with use or threatened use of force,* or attempting such an act. Includes psychological coercion and physical force. Forced sexual intercourse means vaginal, anal, or oral penetration by the offender. Also includes incidents where penetration is from a foreign object, such as a bottle. Includes male and female victims, and heterosexual and same-sex rape. *Attempted rape includes verbal threats of rape. (Rape and sexual assault are combined into one victimization measure.)*
>
> *Sexual assault—A wide range of victimizations, separate from rape or attempted rape.* Includes attacks or attempted attacks generally involving unwanted sexual contact between victim and offender, with or without force. Includes grabbing or fondling *and verbal threats....*
>
> Injury—A measure of whether bodily hurt or damage was sustained by a victim as a result of criminal victimization. This applies only to personal victimization where there was contact between the victim and the offender. The types of injuries suffered are used to distinguish between

---

[197] https://clayeolsen.com/ncvs-terms

serious and minor assaults. Serious injuries include knife or gunshot wounds, broken bones, loss of teeth, and loss of consciousness. *A completed rape is classified as a serious injury.* Minor injuries include bruises, black eyes, cuts, scratches, and swelling. Other injuries that can't be identified as serious or minor are distinguished by the amount of hospitalization required. Injuries suffered from an attack during a crime incident include any and all physical (bodily) damage experienced by the victim (e.g., broken bones, bruises, cuts, and internal injuries). *Emotional and psychological trauma are not included.*

Unfortunately, the NCVS combines Sexual Assault and Rape into one metric. To separate them, I focus only on Injurious Rape/Sexual Assault.

To view the data that appears here, follow the procedure outlined below. If you do not want to do this procedure, I've gathered the data into an Excel spreadsheet which you can download here.[198]

1. Go to N-DASH, the front-end tool to access NCVS data.[199]
2. Select "Custom Graphics," then "Multi-Year Trends," then "Characteristic."
3. Select "Person" for Crime Category.
4. Select "On" for Confidence Interval.
5. Select "Medical Treatment for Physical Injuries" for Comparison Characteristic.
6. Select "Rape/Sexual Assault" for Crime Type.
7. Select "All" for Filter Characteristic.

The resulting data will be shown on the Excel spreadsheet for RA in tabs "RA – Not Treated," and "RA – Treated."

To go through other Filter Characteristics, simply select one. To match the Excel spreadsheet, follow these steps:

8. Select "Reporting to the police" for Filter Characteristic.
9. Select "No" for Filter Characteristic Value.

---

[198] https://clayeolsen.com/excel
[199] http://clayeolsen.com/n-dash

The graphs are automatically updated. The resulting data will be shown on the Excel spreadsheet on tabs "RA – Police | *" and "RA – No Police | *."

10. Select "Weapon Category" for Filter Characteristic.
11. Select "Firearm" for Filter Characteristic Value.

The graphs are automatically updated. The resulting data will be shown on the Excel spreadsheet on tabs "RA – Weapon *."

12. Select "Victim-offender relationship" for Filter Characteristic.
13. Select "Strangers" for Filter Characteristic Value.

The graphs are automatically updated. The resulting data will be shown on the Excel spreadsheet on tabs "RA – Rel *."

14. Select "Victim sex" for Filter Characteristic.
15. Select "Male" for Filter Characteristic Value.

The graphs are automatically updated. The resulting data will be shown on the Excel spreadsheet on tabs "RA – Victim *."

16. Select "Victim marital status" for Filter Characteristic.
17. Select "Never Married" for Filter Characteristic Value.

The graphs are automatically updated. The resulting data will be shown on the Excel spreadsheet on tabs "RA – Marital *."

Potential Improvements to the NCVS

NCVS

- N-DASH is an excellent tool, but they retired NVAT before N-DASH had implemented all the functionality of NVAT. Hopefully, this will change soon.

- It is tedious to perform a meta-analysis using downloaded tables. I used multi-year characteristic with "Medical treatment for physical injuries" as a filter. If I want to download rather than graph, I have to download 3 separate tables (Not Injured, Treated, Not Treated) rather than just one.

- I would like to see N-DASH give the user more control of aggregation. For instance, I was only interested in Injured/Not Injured for "Medical treatment for physical injuries." However, N-DASH forces you to deal with two separate injury categories "Not Treated" and "Treated." Being able to choose what gets aggregated and what gets separated out would be helpful.

- It would be nice for N-DASH to calculate relative percentages. For example, you could select something like "Medical treatment for physical injuries" and be able to calculate relative percentages based upon Injured or Not Injured.

- I would also like to see N-DASH overlay the 67% CI inside the 95% CI. The reason is that the range given in the 95% CI gives the impression that all values within that range are equally likely. This is not true. By overlaying or shading the 67% CI in the graph, a person without a statistics background could better see the bell curve around the mean. The 67% CI should also be available via download.

- An understanding if whether a firearm was used as a blunt instrument or discharged to inflict a victim injury.

APPENDIX C

Statistical Issues

Statistical Significance

The NCVS indicates that they do not test for statistical significance. This stance makes sense because statistical significance is based upon hypothesis testing. You must have a hypothesis to determine whether the results of the hypothesis are statistically significant. This point is best explained by several examples:

- Hypothesis 1: If you are a victim of an aggravated assault, you are more likely to be injured than not injured.
- Hypothesis 2: If you are a victim of a robbery, you are more likely to be injured than not injured.
- Hypothesis 3: If you are a victim of an aggravated assault, you are more likely to be injured by a stranger than by someone you know.
- Hypothesis 4: If you are a victim of a robbery, you are more likely to be injured by a stranger than by someone you know.
- Hypothesis 5: If you are a victim of rape, you are more likely to be raped by a stranger than by someone you know. NOTE: In this formulation, a victim of rape is always injured due to the nature of this violent crime.
- Hypothesis 6: If you are a victim of an aggravated assault, you are more likely to be injured in a public place than in a familiar private place.

- Hypothesis 7: If you are a victim of a robbery, you are more likely to be injured in a public place than in a familiar private place.
- Hypothesis 8: If you are a victim of rape, you are more likely to be raped in a public place than in a familiar place.
- Hypothesis 9: If you are injured in an aggravated assault, the offender likely used a firearm as a weapon.
- Hypothesis 10: If you are injured in a robbery, the offender likely used a firearm as a weapon.
- Hypothesis 11: If you are raped, the offender likely used a firearm to threaten and intimidate you into being raped.

Ultimately, it would lead to the following hypothesis:

- Hypothesis X: If you are injured in one of the violent crimes of aggravated assault, robbery, or rape, you are more likely to have been injured by a stranger using a firearm at a public location.

The above hypothesis I would call the standard view of violent crime.

In statistics, what is tested is the null hypothesis. A null hypothesis is not quite the same as the negative of the hypothesis you want to test. As an example, let's look at Hypothesis 1 and reformulate it as a null hypothesis:

- Null Hypothesis 1: If you are a victim of an aggravated assault, you are just as likely not to be injured as you are to be injured.

Basically, the null hypothesis is a statement that nothing interesting is happening. You would then pull the data from the NCVS involving aggravated assaults and victim injury, and non-injury. Let's say you pull this data from the NCVS using N-DASH (described in Appendix B). I use the multi-year characteristic for personal crime and turn confidence intervals on. I select "Medical treatment for physical injuries" as the characteristic and the Crime Type to "Aggravated Assault." At this point, you can look at the various graphs on N-DASH.

N-DASH uses absolute numbers and graphs each year separately. This behavior is great when there are big differences, like between injured versus not injured for aggravated assault. However, if you want to know the difference in circumstances when a victim is injured compared to when the victim is not injured, it becomes hard to do because the absolute percentages of these circumstances are small and hard to read when the victim is injured. Also, we don't necessarily want a year-by-year analysis. A year-by-year analysis is great when you are looking for abnormalities, but it would be nice to summarize the various years into one figure. When using samples like the NCVS uses, you have to use what is called a meta-analysis to get accurate summaries.[200]

After filtering those years, I used a relatively simple rule you can get from these values: If the mean is above 50% and the 95% Confidence Intervale (CI) lower bound is above 50%, then that is a majority. In this example, it was 67% (59%–75%). The mean is above 50%, and the lower bound 95% confidence interval is also above 50%, actually close to 60%. This data tells me that the null hypothesis must be rejected. It is not equally likely for a victim to be injured or not injured in an aggravated assault. In other words, without requiring my readers to use statistical software, I can use N-DASH, Microsoft Excel™, and show the reader how the result is statistically significant. A similar process is used when the mean and the upper 95% CI is below 50%. For example, my null hypothesis may say that firearms are used in injurious robberies just as often as any other weapon. However, if I am unable to find statistically significant firearm use for injurious robberies and other weapons have statistical significance, I can reject the null hypothesis.

At this point, I have a separation between non-injurious and injurious violent crimes. This separation allows me to ask the question: When the victim is injured, what are the characteristics of the violent crime? This question is important because predominately violent crime is non-injurious and can dilute the circumstances of injurious violent crime if those circumstances happen to be different. In my research, the circumstances are different.

---

[200] Neyeloff, Fuchs, Moreira (2012)

However, to understand the characteristics of the crime within the context of victim injury, relative percentages would need to be used. For example, when the victim is injured, how often are firearms used compared to other weapons? That value would be a relative percentage rather than an absolute percentage.

When we dive into these different circumstances, we have to be careful because sample sizes can be small and lead to large confidence intervals. However, large confidence intervals aren't necessarily due to small sample sizes. For example, if we randomly ask hundreds of thousands of people to roll a 100-sided die, our mean value may be 50, but our confidence interval will be wide—from 1 to 100. That doesn't mean our sample size was small. However, if we are asking whether firearms were used as a weapon against victims of rape who were medically treated for their injuries, I could see a wide confidence interface simply because the sample size is not very large. N-DASH flags data that it believes needs to be treated with caution, such as the previous example. For the most part, I'll restrict my meta-analysis to those variables that are significantly more than other variables.

APPENDIX D

JPX6 Review

This appendix is my informal review of the JPX6. I use it for my own protection, and I am a big fan. However, there are some things I feel can be greatly improved.

In any case, personal protection is, well, personal. Therefore, I would encourage you to evaluate any weapon based on your mission as well as your abilities.

Advantages

- Not classified as a firearm by the ATF.
- The JPX series doesn't require the pinpoint accuracy of a firearm. The OC discharge from the JPX6 is like a shotgun birdshot pattern: very tight initially and gradually expanding.
- The JPX series performs well at typical attack distances. However, I felt 18 feet was the limit in my testing, where the pattern started to get a bit too wide. The user manual indicates an effective range of up to 23 feet.
- It can be reloaded easily (JPX6).
- Four OC cartridges can be fired without reloading.
- Practice cartridges are available.
- It can be dry-fired for practice.
- Not subject to temperature variations like aerosol pepper spray.

Disadvantages

- It is almost twice as thick as my concealed carry 1911 especially around the barrel. This product is difficult to conceal. I have found concealed-carry breakaway[201] pants to be adequate for concealing the JPX series.

- Each cartridge pack is around $65, even for the inert practice rounds. Incredibly expensive. Luckily, it can be dry-fired.

- I dislike a laser on this product. Lasers will showcase nervousness as they bounce around all over the place if the user isn't steady.

- If you come from a semiauto pistol background, you may use the "two thumbs forward" method of holding a pistol with your off-hand in a moment of stress. Unfortunately, you will likely depress the cartridge release if you do that. Someone with a revolver background shouldn't have a problem.

- I haven't tested this, but it appears that you may be susceptible to a negligent discharge while reloading. If you are reloading the cartridge pack in a stressful situation and you miss the bottom guide that aligns the cartridge pack, the cartridge pack could slam the back of the weapon and be misaligned. A rod secures the cartridge pack at the back of the weapon, and it seems small enough to hit the "primer" and discharge an OC cartridge. The firing pins recede on pressure, so only the rod that slides into the cartridge pack is a concern.

- The trigger pull is not the best for quality shooting.

- If you are shooting outside and in high wind, you'll need to compensate for the drift.

- In close-quarters combat, you'll need to shoot for the head. You may not get another shot. Aiming for the chest, as the manual recommends, is more hopeful than practical. If you shoot your attacker in the chest, you could end up wrestling with him, and what you thought would disable your attacker could impact you.

---

[201] https://clayeolsen.com/ccb

- From an OC perspective, the range is incredible. However, compared to a handgun, the range is limited.

Improvements

- I would prefer something much more formal and legal from the ATF regarding the JPX classification. Something like a Form 4 for a suppressor. Of course, I don't want the wait time nor the tax for that! But having an official ATF document referencing your serial number and stating clearly that it is not a firearm would be preferred in a legal self-defense situation.
- I'm not sure why the company doesn't do something more in line with the derringer style of two vertical barrels. A cartridge pack of two reloadable vertical barrels would solve the concealment problem. A product called the Kimber Pepper Blaster II is concealable, seems to use the same technology, and uses two vertical barrels. However, the range suffers dramatically compared to the JPX series.
- Both the JPX4 Compact and the JPX6 need better cartridge release mechanisms. The JPX4's release mechanism can get caught on a rivet in your Levis. Also, those with a semiauto pistol background could unintentionally disengage the cartridge pack in a stressful situation with the JPX6. On the other hand, double-action revolvers have a suitable mechanism that has been in use for over 100 years. They might as well use that mechanism. Just make it ambidextrous.
- A heavy trigger is fine as long as it is smooth and predictable instead of mechanical and stacking. Much improvement is needed here.
- A rail to attach a light rather than a built-in laser would be preferable, or a built-in light rather than a laser.
- Would like to see additives to the OC cartridges to help law enforcement identify people hit by the spray. For example, the OC spray should stain, like the dye they use in bank money

bags. Also, a stain that glows in the dark, like a fluorescent pink, would be preferable.

- The most challenging part with this technology is that it needs to hit the face to be most effective. Aiming for the head can be problematic compared to aiming for the chest, especially with a laser. Luckily, if you aim for the higher part of the chest, you should be fine at most distances due to how the OC spreads. I believe this product could benefit from a more advanced aiming sight—something like a holographic circle you could center on the offender's head. The company would need to change the reloading mechanism to support such a sight, but I believe such a change would be beneficial. Alternatively, the laser sight could be sighted in a foot low from the actual discharge path, allowing a laser aimed at the chest to hit the head. In general, though, lasers tend to bounce around and exacerbate nervousness, especially with a challenging trigger.

- There may be a need for different OC cartridges. A wide dispersal cartridge, good to about eight feet, and the longer-range cartridge. Much like an over/under shotgun or some derringers, the ability to select which cartridge fires first would be needed. For instance, you could have a wide/wide/distance/distance set of cartridges in a JPX6 and select the first cartridge fired to be the first wide cartridge. Thus, on each pull of the trigger, the firing order would be wide, wide, distance, distance.

Bibliography

Beatty, Lauren G, and Tracy L Snell. 2021. *Profile of Prison Inmates, 2016.* December. https://bjs.ojp.gov/content/pub/pdf/ppi16.pdf.

Chiricos, T, K Padgett, and M Gertz. 2000. "Fear, TV News, and the Reality of Crime." *Criminology* 38: 755-786. doi:https://doi.org/10.1111/j.1745-9125.2000. tb00905.x.

Christensen, Loren W. 1996. *How to Live Safely in a Dangerous World.* El Dorado: Desert Publications.

Cook, Phillip J, Ariadne E Rivera-Aguirre, Magdalena Cerdá, and Garen Wintemute. 2017. "Constant Lethality of Gunshot Injuries From Firearm Assault: United States, 2003–2012." *American Journal of Public Health* 107: 1324_1328. doi: https://doi.org/10.2105/AJPH.2017.303837.

English, William. 2021. *National Firearms Survey: Updated Analysis Including Types of Firearms Owned (May 13, 2022).* Georgetown McDonough School of Business Research Paper No. 4109494. doi:http://dx.doi.org/10.2139/ssrn.4109494 .

Freeborn, Varg. 2018. *Violence of Mind: Training and Preparation for Extreme Violence.* One Life Defense Publishing.

Gigerenzer, Gerd. 2002. *Calculated Risks.* Simon & Schuster.

—. 2014. *Risk Savvy: How to Make Good Decisions.* Penguin Books.

Gilliam Jr, Franklin D, and Shanto Iyengar. 2000. "Prime Suspects: The Influence of Local Television News on the Viewing Public." *American Journal of Political Science* (Midwest Political Science Association) 44 (3): 560-573. doi:https:// doi.org/10.2307/2669264.

Gonzales, Laurence. 2017. *Deep Survival: Who Lives, Who Dies, and Why .* W. W. Norton & Company; Reprint edition.

Greenberg, M.S. 2015. "Crime Victims' Decision to Report Crime." Edited by A. Jamieson and A. Moenssens. *Wiley Encyclopedia of Forensic Scence.* doi:https:// doi.org/10.1002/9780470061589.fsa472.pub2.

Holiday, Ryan. 2012. *Trust Me, I'm Lying: Confessions of a Media Manipulator.* Portfolio.

Horne, Patrick Van, and Jason Riley. 2014. *Left of Bang: How the Marine Corps' Combat Hunter Program Can Save Your Life.* Black Irish Entertainment LLC.

Hughes, Nick. 2017. *How To Be Your Own Bodyguard: Self Defense for men & women from a lifetime of protecting clients in hostile environments.* Nick Hughes.

James, Doris J. 2004. *Profile of Jail Inmates, 2002.* July. https://bjs.ojp.gov/press-release/profile-jail-inmates-2002.

Kane, Lawrence A. 2006. *Surviving Armed Assaults - A Martial Artist's Guide to Weapons, Street Violence, & Countervailing Force.* Boston: YMAA Publication Center.

Kerbel, Matthew R. 2000. *If it BLEEDS, it Leads.* Westview Press.

2004. *The Missing LInk - Self-Protection Through Awareness, Avoidance, and De-Escalation.* Performed by Bill Kipp.

Langton, Lynn, and Jennifer Truman. 2014. *Socio-emotional Impact of Violent Crime.* September. https://bjs.ojp.gov/content/pub/pdf/sivc.pdf.

Lowry, Dennis T, Tarn Ching Josephine Nio, and Dennis W Leitner. 2003. "Setting the Public Fear Agenda: A Longitudinal Analysis of Network TV Crime Reporting, Public Perceptions of Crime, and FBI Crime Statistics." *Journal of Communication* 53 (1): 61-73. doi:https://doi.org/10.1111/j.1460-2466.2003.tb03005.x.

MacYoung, Marc "Animal". 1993. *A Professional's Guide to Ending Violence Quickly - How Bouncers, Bodyguards, and Other Security Professionals Handle Ugly Situations.* Boulder : Paladin Press.

2012. *Facing Violence: 7 Thing Every Martial Artist Must Know.* Directed by David Silver. Performed by Rory Miller.

2016. *Training for Sudden Violence - Drills.* Directed by David Silver. Performed by Rory Miller.

2015. *Scaling Force - dynamic decision-making under threat of violen ce.* Directed by David Silver. Performed by Rory Miller and Lawrence A Kane.

Mosher , Clayton, Timothy C Hart, and Terance D Miethe. 2010. *The Mismeasure of Crime.* 2nd. Sage Publications.

Mukherjee, Siddhartha. 2010. *The Emperor of all Maladies.* Simon & Schuster.

Nance, Richard. 2016. *gunFIGHT! - An Integrated Approach to Shooting and Fighting in Close Quarters.* Flushing: Looseleaf Law Publications.

Neyeloff, J.L., Fuchs, S.C. & Moreira, L.B. n.d. "Meta-analyses and Forest plots using a microsoft excel spreadsheet: step-by-step guide focusing on descriptive data analysis." *BMC Research Notes* 5,52 (2012). https://doi.org/10.1186/1756-0500-5-52.

O'Brien, Robert M. 1985. *Crime and Victimization Data.* Sage Publications.

Plantinga , Adam. 2014. *400 Things Cops Know: Street-Smart Lessons from a Veteran Patrolman.* Quill Driver Books.

Rader, Nicole E, David C May, and Sarah Goodrum. 2007. "AN EMPIRICAL ASSESSMENT OF THE "THREAT OF VICTIMIZATION:" CONSIDERING FEAR OF CRIME, PERCEIVED RISK, AVOIDANCE, AND DEFENSIVE BEHAVIORS." *Sociological Spectrum* 27 (5): 475-505. doi:10.1080/02732170701434591.

Reaves, Brian A. 2006. *Violent Felons in Large Urban Counties.* July. https://bjs.ojp.gov/content/pub/pdf/vfluc.pdf.

Romer, D, K.H. Jamieson, and S. Aday. 2003. "Television News and the Cultivation of Fear of Crime." *Journal of Communication* 53: 88-104. doi:https://doi.org/10.1111/j.1460-2466.2003.tb03007.x.

Schmuller, Joseph. 2022. *Statistical Analysis with Excel for dummies 5th edition.* Hoboken: John Wiley & Sons, Inc.

Silva, Jason R. 2019. "A Media Distortion Analysis of Mass Shootings." PhD dissertation, Criminal Justice, The Graduate Center, City University of New York. Accessed July 27, 2022. https://academicworks.cuny.edu/gc_etds/3275/.

SIlva, Jason R. 2019. "PhD Dissertation, The Graduate Center, City University of New York." *A Media Distortion Analysis of Mass Shootings.* May. Accessed July 27, 2022. https://academicworks.cuny.edu/gc_etds/3275/.

Strong, Sanford. 1996. *Strong on Defense.* New York: Pocket Books.

Thompson, George J, and Jerry B Jenkins. 2013. *Verbal Judo - The Gentle Art of Persuasion.* New York: HarperCollins.

Vickers, Andrew. 2010. *What is a p-value anyway?* Boston: Pearson Education, Inc.

Weitzer, Ronald, and Charis E Kubrin. 2004. "Breaking news: How local TV news and real-world conditions affect fear of crime." *Justice Quarterly* 21 (3): 497-520. doi:10.1080/07418820400095881.

Yanich, Danilo. 2004. "Crime Creep: Urban and Suburban Crime on Local Tv." *Journal of Urban Affairs* 26 (5): 535-563. doi:10.1111/j.0735-2166.2004.00214.x.

Index

About the Author

Clay grew up in rural Arizona. He worked on his father's and uncle's farms, which grew cotton, grains, and hay. His grandfather ran a small cattle ranch, and Clay and his dad helped there too. Later, he worked in California for Amdahl and Hewlett-Packard in a variety of engineering positions. He returned to rural Arizona in 2015 to assist his mom.

Clay studies philosophy with a particular focus on Nietzsche, Schopenhauer, Hume, and the latter Wittgenstein. He also spends time on home remodeling, landscaping, full-spectrum and monochrome photography, music theory, and is just learning the piano. He is a lifelong shooter and handloader who works with various cartridges from the .22LR to the .50 BMG.

www.ingramcontent.com/pod-product-compliance
Lightning Source LLC
Chambersburg PA
CBHW080416030426

42335CB00020B/2469